THE TWENTIES

Also by John Montgomery

HISTORY

The Fifties

1900: The End of an Era

Toll for the Brave

Abodes of Love

NOVELS

Mr. Sparrow

Village Green

The Christmas Cat

ANIMAL BOOKS

Two Men and a Dog

Your Dog

Looking After Your Cat

Royal Dogs

The World of Cats

CHILDREN'S BOOKS

Foxy

My Friend Foxy

Foxy and the Badgers

THE CINEMA

Comedy Films 1894–1954

I. *The Prince of Wales lights the Lamp of Remembrance at the* Toc H *Birthday Festival, London, December 1924.*

THE TWENTIES

by

John Montgomery

LONDON

George Allen & Unwin Ltd

RUSKIN HOUSE MUSEUM STREET

FIRST PUBLISHED IN 1957

REVISED EDITION 1970

SBN 04 900020 9

PRINTED IN GREAT BRITAIN
BY PHOTOLITHOGRAPHY
BY COMPTON PRINTING LTD
LONDON AND AYLESBURY

To Collie Knox

FOREWORD

MOST OF US are remarkably ignorant of the history of our own times; we soon forget what happened yesterday.

It was H. G. Wells who said, 'What man has done, the little triumphs of his present state, and all this history we have told, form but the prelude to the things that man has yet to do.'

This book offers a quick backward glance at some of the events which occurred in Britain between the years 1918 and 1930. It is intended to appeal both to readers who do not remember the period and to those who seek a nostalgic reminder.

Some people call them the *roaring twenties*, others the *gay twenties*. It is a mistake, however, to think of this period only in terms of short skirts, Eton crops, jazz music, backless dresses, Oxford 'bags' and bizarre colours. There is much more to it than that. In 1936 Winston Churchill said, 'The use of recriminating about the past is to enforce effective action at the present.' History sometimes repeats itself, but it is now clear that Britain has emerged from the 1939–45 war more favourably than she did from the 1914–18 conflict. The eleven post-war years between 1945 and 1956 did not contain the changes—or the drama—that were the features of the period 1918 to 1929. But there are lessons to be learned from looking at the past.

There have been several books about the nineteen-twenties. In 1932, John Collier and Iain Lang wrote an excellent informal history entitled *Just the Other Day;* in 1940 came *The Long Week-end* by Robert Graves and Alan Hodge, a comprehensive social history of the years 1918–39, with an authors' note which included the statement, 'A score of books could be written on the same general lines as ours, each completely different from the rest.'

Believing this, I have attempted wherever possible to avoid covering the same ground as the two earlier books. But there are many gaps still to be filled, and it is impossible in a small space to deal adequately with the whole history of the country during the period, or to do justice to all the events and names which should be mentioned. I have therefore concentrated on giving a general picture of the times, assisted by a selection of photographs.

The book was first published in 1957, when it was received with gratifying interest. I have revised this new edition only slightly, making some corrections in the text.

My principal sources of information, in addition to the newspapers and periodicals of the times, are listed in a bibliography at the end of the book. I trust that other benefactors and copyright owners whom I have failed to acknowledge or thank will accept my gratitude and forgive my shortcomings.

J. M.

CONTENTS

ILLUSTRATIONS

Those treacherous, deceiving years that had glittered so bravely on the horizon, that had looked so warm and hospitable, that had promised so much and had brought so little.

ALEC WAUGH *Myself When Young*

ACKNOWLEDGMENT

The author wishes to thank Mr. J. B. Priestley, Mr. Alec Waugh, Mr. John Gloag, and the executors of the late Mr. Arnold Bennett, for generously allowing him to quote long extracts from their work. He also thanks the Editor and Librarian of the *News Chronicle* for kindly giving him research facilities.

Photographs and other material were supplied by the late Mrs. Kate Terry Gielgud, the *Daily Mail*, *Daily Mirror*, *Illustrated London News*, *Punch*, the *Architectural Review*, the *Dancing Times*, London Transport Executive, the Automobile Association, the Nuffield Organization, J. Lyons & Co., the Cunard Steam-Ship Company, Selfridges, Harrods, Gamages, and the leading photographic agencies.

The chapter *A Day in 1925* includes material kindly provided by Mr. R. S. Thompson of the *Wimbledon Boro' News*.

CHAPTER ONE

The End of the War

I

'IT IS AN hour for thanks,' announced the Prime Minister, David Lloyd George, on July 19, 1919, when some eighteen thousand troops of fourteen victorious nations marched through London. Near Albert Gate young women ran into the road to throw roses in the path of Marshal Foch and Sir Douglas Haig.

The greatest war the world had ever known had ended eight months before, at the eleventh hour of the eleventh day of the eleventh month of 1918. When they heard that Foch and the German leaders had signed an armistice, the people of London, Paris, New York, and the other capitals of the world, became delirious with joy.

On Armistice Day the London traffic outside the Bank of England was stopped by a solid wall of humanity. New York's Broadway was ankle deep in torn paper. In Toronto the pavements were white with flour and rice powder. From the balcony of Buckingham Palace, King George the Fifth and Queen Mary acknowledged the cheers of their people, as they had done four years earlier on the outbreak of war. Omnibuses, commandeered by yelling mobs, were driven at random through crowded streets, where ribald caricatures of the Kaiser and the Crown Prince were carried shoulder high. Complete strangers met in the street and kissed. That night at the Alhambra Theatre, Leicester Square, the audience joined George Robey, Violet Lorraine and Lorna and Toots Pounds, and danced excitedly on the stage. Outside in the square the crowds joined hands to sing *Let the Great Big World Keep Turning*, *Roses of Picardy*, *Keep the Home Fires Burning*, and *Tipperary*.

That morning the newspaper headlines had announced GERMANY SURRENDERS! The Allies were to occupy the Rhineland; the German fleet was to be surrendered, together with all U-boats, 200 aeroplanes, 5,000 guns, 5,000 locomotives, and 150,000 railway trucks. All allied prisoners were to be immediately repatriated. The question of reparations was to be settled later.

The King toured London, addressing the crowds. Parliament, after acclaiming Mr. Lloyd George, went to St. Margaret's, Westminster, to give thanks. The King attended a service at St. Paul's. The *Daily Mail* reported that the scenes of rejoicing were 'beyond credence.' In Trafalgar Square, Australian troops lit a huge bonfire and damaged Nelson's column. In Oxford a woman danced up and down the street with her skirts over her head. On the third and final night of the celebrations many thousands of people danced in the Strand and in the side turnings, whistling popular melodies and singing songs where music was not available. Drunken men staggered around the streets.

Most of the troops were still at the front. Many of them hardly realized that the war to end wars, which had killed over seven million men and altered the whole world, was at last over. A new era had begun, and although it would take several years before she could be regarded as an equal, Germany was no longer the foe. President Wilson had already said, 'We are not enemies of the German people, and they are not our enemies. They did not originate or desire this hideous war, and we are vaguely conscious that we are fighting their cause, as they will some day see it themselves.' He believed in the inherent equality and goodness of every nation and all peoples, and he shared Germany's conviction that the war had been started by autocrats against the wishes of the people.

Everybody was tired of war, and wanted only peace. In Britain the password was reconstruction, but there was a tendency to look back to the golden era of pre-war prosperity, rather than into the future. People wanted the 'good old days' to return; there was a general feeling of moral and mental fatigue, a confusion of thought and a listlessness which Mr. Lloyd George called 'a fever of anaemia.' There was apathy about the comparatively dull business of peace-making, which could no doubt be safely left to the politicians. There was little doubt that—somehow or other—Britain would return to her old glory. Had not she won the war? Men who had narrowly missed death in the trenches, who had buried their comrades in Flanders, now returning to their homes and families, were anxious to enjoy life to the full, to turn back the clock and recapture the youth which they had lost on the Marne and the Somme and at Mons. It was good to be alive, so many were dead. But the vast victory could not easily be digested. Waving his arms eloquently, the Prime Minister pointed the rosy way to a consolidation of the moment of triumph, which sounded only too easy:

> 'Let us make victory the motive power to link the old land up in such measure that it will be nearer the sunshine than ever before, and that at any rate it will lift those who have been living in dark places to a plateau where they will get the rays of the sun.'

The task, he said, was to make Britain 'a fit country for heroes to live in.' It was a phrase which was to be remembered, a companion for his other memorable slogans, to 'make Germany pay' and to 'hang the Kaiser.'

The German Emperor, the scapegoat of the war, had appeared on November 10, 1918, at the Belgian frontier. After waiting anxiously in the fog, he and his small group of faithful followers were allowed to enter Holland. Newspapers in Britain then discussed how the war criminal should be tried when he was brought to London and lodged in the White Tower. A formal demand for his surrender was made, but as late as November 20, 1920, the Prime Minister informed the House of Commons that it was, after all, impossible to secure his extradition. Most Englishmen were relieved.

The problem of making Germany pay for the war was even more difficult. The Governor of the Bank of England, Mr. Montagu Norman, boldly announced that Germany was capable of paying nearly £24,000,000,000, regardless of the fact that the end of the war had brought starvation to central Europe. In the victorious countries people rejoiced, imagining that President Wilson's famous fourteen points, which had been accepted by the defeated powers, would somehow, without much effort, set the pattern for a brave new world.

2

After the Armistice two months passed before the first meeting of the victors. Thirty-two delegates had to make arrangements to meet in Paris, where the treaty was to be discussed, and this took time. In Britain, Mr. Lloyd George appealed to the people for a vote of confidence and called a General Election for December 14th. He was returned as the leader of a Coalition Government with an overwhelming majority.

Early in 1919 the victorious delegates arrived in France, the most distinguished gathering of statesmen ever assembled. For France there were the aged Clemenceau, Pichon, Tardieu and Cambon; for the United States there were President Woodrow Wilson, Lansing, and Colonel House; for Great Britain there were Lloyd George, Arthur Balfour, and Bonar Law; for Italy, Orlando, and Sonnino. The South African delegation was headed by Generals Botha and Smuts. All the politicians were anxious to be in at the kill, to divide the spoils. Only the defeated powers were not represented, for this was to be a dictated peace, and the losers were required only to accept and sign the completed treaty. Theirs was perhaps the easier task.

On the motion of Wilson, Clemenceau was elected President of the conference. The 'big four,' the most important delegates, were Clemenceau, the tired but still capable old 'tiger'; Lloyd George, the shrewd, alert, demonstrative, dynamic politician, suspicious of everyone but inclined to be increasingly lenient with Germany; Wilson, the idealist, behaving like a gentle church minister but with no positive plan and very little knowledge of European conditions; and Orlando, eloquent, learned, but playing only a minor role, and often ignored by the others.

Their aims were opposed, and could not be reconciled. Orlando knew no English, and Lloyd George and Wilson no French. Only Clemenceau spoke both languages.

Arriving in Paris, Wilson declared his hopes and faith in the future of the civilized world. But almost immediately he received a long memorandum from Marshal Foch, who severely criticized and mistrusted the new German Republic, and did not share Wilson's innocent trust in his fellow men. The note included the sentence:

> A German republic based on the same principles of centralization and militarism as the old Empire will still present great dangers and will still be a redoubtable menace to peace.

Foch thought that the new German regime, hastily contrived to persuade the Allies that the country had put her house in order, could not cloak the true temperament and traditions of Prussia. Prophetically, he suggested that one day a new and even more dangerous enemy might arise out of the ashes.

From the first day of the conference there was disagreement among the victors. Two months later Wilson wearily addressed the delegates, pleading, 'Gentlemen, I am in trouble, and I have sent for you to help me out. I do not know whether I shall see Monsieur Clemenceau again. I do not know whether he will return to the meeting this afternoon. In fact, I do not know whether the peace conference will continue. Monsieur Clemenceau called me *pro-German* and abruptly left the room.'

When someone suggested that Clemenceau should return and talk to the American President, the old man laughed. 'Talk to Wilson!' he said. 'How can I talk to a fellow who thinks himself the first man in two thousand years to know anything about peace on earth?'

Eventually Clemenceau gave way, in spite of his firm conviction that only misfortune could follow over-generous treatment of Germany. He did not believe that the peace was permanent or that it would last for long. Ten, twenty years, he said, and Germany would be at France's throat again.

> 'It's easy to foresee what will happen one of these days. They will kill one another to the last man. At most a dozen will escape, some negroes in the Congo. Then they'll begin the whole story again. The same old story.'

Human beings, said Clemenceau, were like apes who had stolen Jupiter's thunder. To him the Germans remained the one nation which would never change. He therefore stood out for a League of Nations which would be backed by a strong international army to be provided by France, America and Britain. This, he said, was the only way to keep Germany in order.

Wilson, sure that the world had now learned its lesson and that all men genuinely desired peace, opposed the scheme. 'We must distinguish between what is possible and what is not,' he announced. Discord at the conference continued. When he asked the delegates, 'If France does not get what she wishes, will she refuse to act with us? In that event, do you want me to go home?' Wilson looked straight at Clemenceau.

'I do not wish you to go home,' replied the old man, 'but I intend to do so myself.' And he walked out again.

Ironically, the name given to him by his countrymen, *Père la Victoire*, was turned by a Parisian wit into *Perd la Victoire*. Each country now blamed its own delegates for the apparent failure of the conference. In Britain there was a strong suspicion that Germany was already winning the peace. Every day, at the top of its leader column, Lord Northcliffe's *Daily Mail* published a solemn warning to its million readers:

> They will cheat you yet, those Junkers! Having won half the world by bloody murder they are going to win the other half with tears in their eyes, crying for mercy.

The *Daily Mail's* savage attacks on Lloyd George reflected Lord Northcliffe's personal grievance, that he had not been allowed to become a member of the British delegation. Northcliffe, who considered that he could solve many of the problems of the world, never forgave Lloyd George. The battle between them revived a joke from an earlier period. People now asked, 'Have you heard? The Prime Minister has resigned, and Northcliffe has sent for the King.'

In April the violent press campaign had led 370 Conservative Members of Parliament to send Lloyd George a telegram expressing anxiety at the progress of the conference. The Prime Minister immediately returned to London to defend himself and to attack Northcliffe and his newspapers in the House. He returned to Paris with the thunderous applause of the Commons ringing in his ears.

Less happily, Wilson had returned to Washington in February, to deal with urgent matters of state. When he came back he obviously possessed less power than he had previously held. In April, when it was made clear that the Allies would not give Fiume to Italy, Signor Orlando walked out of the conference, leaving the remaining 'big three' to draft the treaty without him.

3

Clemenceau tried to ensure that France would be protected from the military jackboot of Germany. When the conditions were being finally settled, someone asked, 'Well now, have we forgotten anything?' Clemenceau at once replied, 'Yes! We have forgotten something very important. We have omitted to ask for the Kaiser's breeches!'

Very little else was left out. The treaty provided for the restoration of Alsace and Lorraine to France, and for a small extension of the boundaries of Belgium. It gave the people of Slesvig the right to choose between German and Danish territory. It also compelled Germany to surrender her Polish territory, which was formed into a republic, and all her colonies, which were entrusted under mandate of the League of Nations to one or other of the Allies. Further, it severely restricted German arms, and authorized the occupation of the Rhineland.

Article 231 stated:

> The Allied and Associated Governments affirm and Germany accepts the responsibility of Germany and her allies for causing all the loss and damage to which the Allied and Associated Governments and their nationals have been subjected as a consequence of the war imposed upon them by the aggression of Germany and her allies.

On May 7, 1919, the completed treaty was presented to a German delegation, under guard, at the Trianon Hotel in Paris. Six days later their leader, Count Brockdorff-Rantzau, rejected the treaty.

'We have no intention of absolving Germany from all responsibility for the war,' he protested, 'but we expressly intend that Germany, whose people were convinced that they were fighting a defensive war, should not be saddled with the whole responsibility. Those who sign this treaty will sign the death sentence of many millions of German men, women and children.'

The German nation supported this view and acquitted its former leaders of any guilt in the crime of causing the war. Some Germans alleged that it had been planned and staged by the Allies, who had been jealous of German superiority. Others said that no one was responsible, but that the war had 'arisen' or 'broken out' as a result of an oppressive capitalist system. The Germans were guiltless, and had been engaged in honourably defending their fatherland. And even as President Wilson was travelling to Paris for the conference the German Guards regiment was returning to Berlin, where Friedrich Ebert, one of the leaders of the new democratic republic, made a speech welcoming the return of 'our undefeated army.' War 'guilt' meant not the responsibility for having started the war, but of having failed to win it. As for the treaty, this had in German eyes been drafted at a 'meeting not of sane and earnest experts but by the inhabitants of a lunatic asylum.'

Even while the peace conference was in session, people in Germany were dying of undernourishment. The blockade was still in existence, and the army of occupation found itself living among starving people. The British Commander-in-Chief sent a telegram to the conference urging that food should be supplied to the civilian population. Sickness was spreading, and the Germans were beginning to despair.

When Count Brockdorff-Rantzau protested at the terms of the treaty, a London newspaper complained that he had made his speech while *sitting down* in front of the victors. Should he not have been forced to stand?

David Lloyd George complained, 'Those insolent Germans made me very angry . . . their conduct showed that the old Germany is still there. But the strange thing is that the Americans and ourselves felt more angry than the French and Italians. I asked old Clemenceau why. He said, "Because we are accustomed to their insolence. We have had to bear it for fifty years. It is new to you and therefore it makes you angry." '

Although the mass of the German people felt no more responsibility for the war than their children did twenty-seven years later after the Second World War, public opinion in Britain could hardly be absolved from having welcomed the war. Tens of thousands of Londoners had cheered and rejoiced when war was declared, dancing with joy. The identification of the Germans with the devil was sanctioned by the churches; 'Hun' atrocity stories were widely spread. When dedicating a motor ambulance at Ilford the Bishop of Chelmsford predicted not only that the conflict would be long, but he also thanked God that the war was going on, for it would be a folly and a crime to put aside the sword until the purposes for which it had been drawn were achieved. Clergymen did not hesitate to instruct their flocks to kill Germans and to 'give their sons' in this holy cause. 'Every man who kills a German is performing a Christian act,' declared one patriotic bishop. God was on the side of the Allies, and had decided to approve the murder if the victim was a German.

In Britain the 'Hate the Huns' campaign continued after the Armistice. During the war it had become almost a mania. In 1917, when Lord Charles Beresford was dining at the Savoy Hotel in London a number of guests had suddenly hurled their plates on the floor. 'We have actually been dining off German plates!' protested Lord Charles. The hotel manager later told the *Daily News*, 'I at once gave instructions to the staff to search among the plates, but only one has been found bearing the German stamp.'

Count Brockdorff-Rantzau's counter-proposals to the treaty were immediately rejected, Wilson stubbornly refusing to alter a word of the draft. Germany was told to sign by 7 p.m. on June 23rd, and at 5.20 p.m. on that afternoon, having no alternative, her delegates agreed. In the great Hall of Mirrors, where Bismarck had founded the German Empire, the treaty was at last signed. When the Allies were seated the Germans were admitted, being led in silence to their seats opposite a table of rose and sandalwood on which the book of the treaty, a bulky three hundred pages, had been placed. Clemenceau then invited them to sign, which they did. The other delegates added their signatures in alphabetical order of countries, while guns boomed outside.

The *Frankfurter Zeitung* summed up the feelings of the

German people: 'Never has a murder been committed with more courteous form in more cynical equanimity.'

President Wilson went home to face the Senate. Lloyd George returned to London to find King George and the Prince of Wales waiting at Victoria Station to greet him and take him in a carriage to Buckingham Palace. He had come back with trophies which even Chatham might have envied; the enemy fleet out of action, their mercantile marine decimated, new British interests in Mesopotamia, Palestine, Africa, a share of the German reparation payments, and recognition of the Dominions as worthy of separate representation in the League. It was his hour of triumph.

On July 10, 1919, President Wilson presented the treaty to the American Senate with the words, 'The stage is set, the destiny disclosed. It has come about by no plan of our conceiving, but by the hand of God who led us into the way. We cannot turn back. We can only go forward, with lifted eyes and freshened spirit, to follow the vision. It was of this that we dreamed at our birth. America shall in truth show the way. The light streams upon the path ahead and nowhere else.'

Unfortunately, America did not choose to follow Wilson's path. He had fought stubbornly at Versailles for what he believed to be right, he had persuaded Clemenceau to modify his demands, and the other delegates had accepted his mandate principle. Yet the result was a compromise, and America rejected it. Vote after vote turned against Wilson and the treaty. And although he lived on in Washington for over three years after his crushing defeat, he never recovered from the shock. His countrymen, having reversed the judgment of their accredited representative, now decided to stay out of the League of Nations for which he had been largely responsible. The League therefore became mainly the responsibility of Britain and France, the United States having virtually withdrawn from European affairs. With the admission in later years of Germany and Italy to its council, it in time became unworkable, with no strength or power. Had America become a member, and supported the League, it is possible that the Second World War might have been averted. Clemenceau's original proposal, that the League should be backed by a strong army, was ignored by the United States.

According to H. G. Wells, 'Wilson exaggerated in his person our common human tragedy, he was so very great in his dreams and so incapable in his performance.' The constitution of the League, said Wells, was 'unpractical.' But among his countrymen Wilson was almost alone in recognizing the responsibility of every nation to support the League and what it stood for.

4

Meanwhile the English remembered their dead. In churchyards and on village greens, in school chapels and town and city squares, the memorials were erected, crosses and stones of granite and sandstone and Portland stone inscribed LEST WE FORGET. Prince Henry went to Winchester to unveil a memorial to 12,825 men of the King's Royal Rifle Corps; the Earl of Lonsdale unveiled the Northern Cenotaph in Rickerby Park, Carlisle, dedicated to the memory of ten thousand Cumberland and Westmorland men who lay in Flanders, Mesopotamia, Italy, and beneath the sea. Lord Byng unveiled the Canadian Pacific Railway memorial in Montreal, to eleven hundred railwaymen. Every hamlet in Britain, each ranch in Canada and Australia, every fruit farm in South Africa, each sheep station in the great fertile plains of New Zealand, all had contributed someone or made some sacrifice in the cause of Empire. The young Prince of Wales, who had soldiered in the trenches and was regarded by ex-servicemen as their champion, supported Earl Haig's British Legion and Toc H, and unveiled hundreds of memorials to his fallen comrades.

The British Legion fought for ex-servicemen, and looked

after their interests. Like Toc H, it embodied a mood, the feeling that the fellowship of the trenches was the sole survivor of the disenchantment and the slaughter and the betrayals by the politicians. In 1922, when Toc H was well under way, its founder, the Rev. Philip Thomas Clayton, M.C., became vicar of All Hallows on Tower Hill, one of the ugliest parishes in London. Between the wars he devoted himself to his parish and the movement, so that soon there were twenty thousand members in Britain, many of them in the House of Commons, and the Prince of Wales was Patron. One of the achievements of Toc H was its blood transfusion service for hospitals, and later its support of leprosy villages in Nigeria.

On November 11, 1920, the permanent stone Cenotaph in Whitehall, designed by Edwin Lutyens, was unveiled by the King. On the same day a British soldier was buried with great pomp in Westminster Abbey 'in proud memory of those warriors who died unknown in the Great War,' to quote the inscription on the King's wreath.

On February 21, 1921, the Prince of Wales unveiled a memorial on the South Downs near Brighton to Indian soldiers who had died in the war. At Chester a beautiful Gothic cross, 35 feet high, standing on the green outside the cathedral, was unveiled by two mothers who had between them lost seven sons. It commemorated 769 men of the city.

Later, in May 1922, the King and Queen visited the war graves in Belgium and France. When Marshal Foch and Earl Haig shook hands the King placed his hand over theirs. On the third day of their tour they went to the cemetery at Etaples, and then to the great cemetery above Boulogne where 3,200 British soldiers are buried. At the stone of remembrance, draped in the Union Jack, the Queen laid a wreath of carnations and rosemary, and the King spoke to the great crowds gathered in the spring sunshine:

'In this fair land of France, which sustained the utmost fury of the long strife, our brothers are numbered, alas! by hundreds and thousands.

They lie in the keeping of a tried and generous friend, a resolute and chivalrous comrade-in-arms, who with ready and quick sympathy has set aside for ever the soil in which they sleep, so that we ourselves and our descendants may for all time reverently tend and preserve their resting-places. I have many times asked myself whether there can be more potent advocates of peace upon earth through the years to come than this massed multitude of silent witnesses to the desolation of war.'

When Marshal Foch went to the unveiling of a war memorial at Abbeville, and met Lord Cavan, the British Chief of the Imperial General Staff, he took him by the arm and, pointing to the monument, said, 'Let us show our dead that we are united.' But in the years to come the spirit of the Entente was largely ignored by the leaders of both Britain and France. In the age of conferences, of slow and clumsy efforts to readjust their internal affairs, both nations neglected the strength of the comradeship which had saved them from their common enemy. Divided, they became weak. And with time, the Germans were regarded as a people who, after all, could hardly be expected to continue to suffer for a war which had not really been of their choosing. Should not Germany be encouraged to grow strong and prosperous again? Thus the European balance of power was upset.

Although she had lost the war, Germany had retained her honour. Her armies were undefeated in the field, and only two days after the signing of the peace treaty her navy had scuttled its surrendered fleet at Scapa Flow. The ships had been manned only by watchmen, who had escaped in boats before the men-of-war were sunk by opening the sea-cocks. Five battle cruisers, ten battleships, five light cruisers and twenty-eight destroyers went to the bottom. Only two destroyers and the *Emden* remained afloat. The loss to the Allies and the damage to their prestige was considerable. In Germany it was felt that the honour of the Imperial Navy was saved. Perhaps the Allies would yet lose the peace?

5

In October 1919 the motion, 'That the League of Nations is worthless as a guarantee of international peace and is a radically unsound and dangerous project,' was defeated at Cambridge Union by 723 votes to 280. But people were already beginning to fear the next war. And in 1921, completely disregarding the League, Greece went to war with Turkey.

During the twenties and thirties the major topic of conversation was the possibility, almost the certainty, of another war. Young men, familiar with tales of the frightful slaughter of the 1914 war, wondered what would happen next time. Their only hope appeared for a while to lie in the magic of the League.

The work of the League was many-sided, and did not aim only to prevent war. It sought to create positive reconstruction, as in the case of the financial restoration of Austria and Hungary, improvements in international traffic and health, and progress in the control of the traffic in women, children, and drugs. Article XXIII of the Covenant provided for securing fair and humane conditions of labour, and for the just treatment of natives; the suppression of the 'white slave' traffic; the supervision of dangerous drugs and arms and ammunition; the freedom of communications and trade between member states, and the prevention and control of disease.

In May 1923 it had a membership of fifty-two countries, and its budget during the previous year had been £822,730, recovered from members. It had inherited a Europe with many millions of starving people, ten million dead, twenty million wounded, and revolution in Russia. In spite of apathy among many members, it at first gained influence. Until 1929 it looked as if it might succeed. But unfortunately the looseness of its charter and the fact that each member put individual sovereignty before its duty to the League, gave it no power as an active body. During the first ten years France and Britain controlled it with a policy of compromise. The French wished to develop the League as a military machine to hold down Germany, but Britain wanted to ensure that it never grew too powerful to threaten her Empire.

At the second and third assemblies in 1922 and 1923 the dreadful conditions in Russia, which had followed the war and the revolution were discussed; millions of Russians were dying. But the members of the League, being afraid of the Communist regime, decided to offer no help. The Yugoslav delegate stated frankly that his country would prefer to see Russians starve. Many countries expressed sympathy, but most of them regretted they were unable to help. Finally, some money was raised by private charities, and the United States sent a large amount of wheat that was unsaleable.

Sir Arthur Salter, the director of the League's economic and financial section, thought that the system failed because it was too weak to resist and control the new and greater forces that had developed within the economic and political systems. But in spite of this he felt that the member states need not be ashamed of their achievement, the constructive intelligence of mankind being faced with a more stupendous task than ever before.

The members claimed that social justice was the foundation of world peace; what was needed was a real, practical and effective system of world government. Only when it became clear that to achieve this they must interfere with private enterprise, colonial imperialism, and national sovereignty, was the League abandoned in favour of anarchy, power politics, a new arms race, Fascist aggression, and appeasement.

In his short play *The Instrument*, Laurence Housman imagined President Wilson protesting, 'Yes, I *was* tempted to cry it aloud—to make a clean breast of it, to say, "We, the Governments of the People, the Democracies, the Free Nations of the World, have failed—have lost the peace which we could have won, because we would not give up the things which we loved so much better—profit, revenge, our own too good opinion of ourselves, our own self-righteous judgment of others'' . . . I was tempted to it; and yet it has been charged against me that I would not admit failure because I wanted to save my face.'

The four months from the end of March to the beginning of August 1945 might be considered the most fateful period in Britain's modern history. The months which resulted in the signing of the treaty of Versailles similarly affected the future of Europe. But while during the twenties and thirties Germany was concerned with what she considered the terrible injustice of Versailles, the people of Britain looked hopefully and longingly back to the golden pre-war days, never forward. They did not doubt that soon things would be as before, with Britain reclaiming her position as the greatest and richest nation in the world. The 'good old days' would undoubtedly return, without too much effort.

CHAPTER TWO

Peace

I

THE IMMEDIATE TROUBLES of the post-war world included quarrels among the victors, housing problems, disillusionment about the League, unemployment, and strikes.

Very few houses had been built during the war, but demobilization brought thousands of new families seeking homes. At the same time the cost of building soared. Between the wars, from 1919 to 1939, over four and a half million houses were built, but few were completed until 1924. The first figures were:

1920–24	369,446
1925–29	1,009,903
1930–34	1,147,297

In most of the new houses only minimum standards of space and comfort were provided. The old Victorian spaciousness was missing, even in houses designed by architects for private individuals. Rooms were small and ceilings were low; furniture became smaller, grand pianos gave way to 'midget' or 'baby' models, the solid mahogany and oak and marble of earlier days was sent to sale-rooms or was stored in attics, to make way for tubular metal chairs and tables, for plywood, laminated wood, rubber and plastics, light wood bedsteads and divans. Mass production had replaced craftsmanship, floral wallpaper was out of favour, giving way to paint and distemper. Millions of people were soon living in small semi-detached houses built in rows, each with a strip of garden and some with a garage. These were the homes built to suit the pockets of the new lower-middle class.

Because there were at first few houses, many ex-servicemen returned to find themselves homeless. In March 1922 the *Daily News* reported that an ex-soldier of the Royal Field Artillery was living with his wife and four children in London under a patchwork shack of tarpaulins, old army groundsheets and bits of tin and canvas.

'If they'd told me in France,' said the ex-soldier, 'that I should come back to this I wouldn't have believed it. Sometimes I wish to God the Germans had knocked me out.'

He had been living there for nine months, surrounded by the respectability of Chadwick-Road, Camberwell, with all the family sleeping in a space measuring 10 feet by 6 feet. He was unemployed, on the dole, and unable to find anywhere else to live.

The experience of the soldiers in the trenches could never be shared by the people at home, and there was at first a breach between the returning fighting men and the civilian population. Many of the men who came back were changed and shocked, and had left their youth in Flanders.

By August 1921 there were nearly two million unemployed, half being ex-servicemen. Seven million workers had received wage cuts. Ex-soldiers paraded London streets carrying posters inscribed,

THE LAND FIT FOR HEROES
Over 3,000
Ex-Service Civil Servants
have been sacked
by the Government
and
over 26,000
non-Servicemen
are retained

In 1919 Mr. Lloyd George had tried to invite Mr. J. H.

Thomas, the General Secretary of the National Union of Railwaymen, to dine with him. He wanted to find out what the working classes really wanted, and told his friend Lord Riddell, 'We meet people who tell us what they *think* the working classes want, but the information is usually unreliable and tinged deeply with the personal views of the narrator.' Lord Riddell replied, 'Apart from the general issue, these are the things they want: (1) more wages to compensate for changed money values, (2) lower prices of essentials, and (3) houses. Employers will not recognize that one pound today will purchase only as much as 9s. 6d. before the war.'

Throughout the twenties and thirties the threat of unemployment constantly hung over the heads of tens of thousands of workers Yet these were the men on whom Britain relied for her exports, and therefore for her prosperity. The war had completely altered the nation's position in economic affairs. In the nineteenth century her coal and iron deposits and the making of heavy industrial machinery had formed the backbone of her vast wealth. When the war ended she did not doubt that she would reclaim this position, recapture her export trade, and pay off her immense war debts to the United States.

The first step was to create confidence in the pound by settling debts in notes backed by gold. For a time this policy succeeded, and in 1924 the gold standard was officially restored. A Bank of England pound note was still worth a golden sovereign. But by then Britain was no longer the world's leading factory and the other countries of Europe, hard hit by the war, could not afford to buy British goods. British employees demanded higher wages to meet the increasing cost of living. But the Government assured the workers that even if they were unemployed they would still be paid a minimum wage, a 'dole.' Further, a tax was put on many luxury imports, and despite a general distrust of the 'Bolsheviks,' trading was started with the Soviet Union.

II. *Armistice Day in London, outside the Royal Exchange on November 11, 1918.*

The Victory Parade marching up Whitehall, June 19, 1919.

III. (Above) *Beach fashions of 1920: a bevy of Mack Sennett's Bathing Beauties, daring and provocative, setting the standard for Brighton and Bognor.*

(Below) *Leather motoring coats at $5\frac{1}{2}$ or 10 gns., beige kasha trimmed with opossum fur, and silk knitted suits were worn by fashionable women in 1922.*

Unemployment and the trade depression led in February 1922 to the 'Geddes Axe,' a report by the Geddes Economy Committee which recommended cuts of over £75,000,000 in national expenditure. The Air Force estimates were to be cut by £5,500,000 and the Army by £20,000,000. The Navy protested at their proposed cut of £21,000,000, education costs were to be reduced by £18,000,000, war pensions by £3,500,000, but the working classes remained unimpressed by the plan, in spite of Lord Inchcape's declaration that the country was facing bankruptcy. Eventually the government accepted cuts of £64,000,000, the proposed naval reductions were halved, and the saving on education was reduced to £6,500,000.

2

Britain emerged from the war with a Coalition Government. In 1916 Mr. Lloyd George had forced Mr. Asquith out of office and had taken over the leadership of the country. In November 1918, when the Armistice was signed, eight years had passed since the last election. In December 1918, just before going to France to join in the Versailles peace conference, Lloyd George was returned to power. He had appealed for a continuation of the wartime Coalition Government, for the punishment of German war criminals, the prevention of dumping cheap foreign goods in Britain, and a speedy settlement of the Irish question. It was then that he made use of his famous election-winning slogans.

The Coalition returned to power with 484 members, of whom 338 were Unionists or Conservatives, 136 Liberals, and 10 were Labour or other Coalition supporters. The Labour Party itself returned 59 members, and the Asquith Liberals 26 Mr. Lloyd George went to France confident that he enjoyed the support of the country, but by 1921 his Conservative supporters had become restless and the new

Tory leaders, Bonar Law and Stanley Baldwin, plotted to overthrow the Government. It was time, they said, for a return to power of the party which was the main strength of the Coalition. In 1922 Lloyd George was therefore forced out of office and Bonar Law became Prime Minister.

David Lloyd George had enjoyed none of the advantages of a public school or university education, but had shown remarkable powers as a young lawyer. When he was twenty-six he was a county council alderman, and a year later Member of Parliament. His first office, in 1906, was President of the Board of Trade. Two years later he was a stormy Chancellor of the Exchequer, launching the Liberal Party on a programme of social reform which anticipated many of the points of the modern welfare state.

During the war he had been a tireless Minister of Munitions and after 1916, as Prime Minister, he infused great personal energy into the war machine. On October 23, 1922, he paid his last official visit to the King, as Prime Minister. At four o'clock that afternoon he walked out of 10 Downing Street alone, with his collar turned up, swinging a golf club presented to him by a janitor, confident that he would soon return. The King himself shared this view, but it was not to be.

'His life had been full of surprises,' says Ivor Brown, 'and this was the greatest. In the same week the Fascists marched on Rome and the King of Italy made way for Mussolini.' New leaders were rising to power in Europe.

In failing to return Lloyd George, the nation had endorsed Bonar Law's remark that the drummer boy was an asset in battle but that he and his drum were a nuisance among the casualties in hospital.

Bonar Law had very little time in which to achieve anything spectacular. In May 1923 he resigned owing to ill health, and by the end of the year he was dead. Quiet, unobtrusive, he had succeeded in making both the Asquith and Lloyd George Coalitions work smoothly. A talented parliamentary debater, he had little personal magnetism. He had been Colonial Secretary in Asquith's Government, and then deputy Prime Minister under Lloyd George. As Prime Minister he increased his reputation for honesty and integrity, but made no claim to greatness. 'If I am a great man, then a good many great men have been frauds,' he said. If he was ever ambitious, he ceased to have ambitions when his wife died and his two sons were killed in the war. He never recovered from this tragedy. But if he did not appear to enjoy his duties as Prime Minister as obviously as his successors, he carried them out in an exemplary manner. When his health failed, and it was discovered that he had cancer of the throat, he was replaced by his deputy, Stanley Baldwin.

Baldwin had been born in 1867, in the middle of Queen Victoria's reign, and it has been said that he always remained a Victorian.

'I am a provincial, heart and soul,' he once said, thus identifying himself with the majority of English men and women. Later he announced that he wanted 'to read, to live a decent life, and to keep pigs.'

After Harrow and Cambridge he had become an iron-master in the family business. His father was a wealthy Member of Parliament for West Worcestershire, and by 1908 the son was also in the House. In 1916 he became Parliamentary Secretary to Bonar Law, and when Lloyd George succeeded Asquith and Bonar Law become deputy Prime Minister, Baldwin was made Financial Secretary to the Treasury. In 1921 he became President of the Board of Trade and entered the Cabinet.

On Lloyd George's resignation Bonar Law chose Baldwin as his Chancellor of the Exchequer. One of Baldwin's first duties was to go to the United States with Montagu Norman, the Governor of the Bank of England, to endeavour to arrange a cancellation or settlement of war debts. Britain had already wiped out many millions of pounds owing to her, declaring that the Allies had all made sacrifices in the common cause.

The famous 'Balfour note,' sent in August 1922 to the French and Italian Governments, expressed Britain's feelings:

> The food, the materials, the munitions, required for the immense naval and military efforts of Great Britain, and half the £2,000,000,000 advanced to the Allies, were provided by internal borrowing and taxation. Unfortunately, a similar policy was beyond the power of any other European nation. Appeal was therefore made to the United States; but it was only on our security that they were prepared to lend it.

There was a strong feeling that the American contribution to the war effort had been comparatively slight, and that she should not claim war debts. Further, she had refused to ratify the peace treaty, on which the future of Europe to some extent depended. Was it right that she should now bleed the nations with whom she was unwilling to co-operate?

Baldwin's task was not easy. America looked with suspicion on European affairs, and considered that she had already saved the old world from destruction. She mistrusted British Imperialism, partly as a matter of habit. But whatever Baldwin told the United States Treasury officials, or intended to tell them, he was politely but firmly informed that the British taxpayer must pay £1,000,000,000 in interest on the debt of £900,000,000, a rate twice as high as that later demanded from France and eight times higher than was claimed from Italy. When Baldwin returned home and announced that he had agreed to the American terms and that Britain was pledged to pay up, Lloyd George cynically remarked that the visit had been 'in the nature of a negotiation between a weasel and its quarry.'

A well-known American politician, who had been engaged in the negotiations, is said to have remarked, 'You should never have sent Baldwin. I almost died of shock when he offered five per cent. We expected two, at most.' According to President Roosevelt, the Americans put forward their full terms, and Baldwin accepted them without bargaining.

In spite of this apparent failure, Baldwin became Prime

Minister in May 1923. The public knew very little about him. Bonar Law, ill and soon to die, is said to have remarked, 'If I were asked to name my successor I am afraid it would have to be Baldwin.' Max Beerbohm drew a cartoon in his series *The Old and the Young Self* in which Baldwin as a schoolboy looked at Baldwin the man and said, 'Prime Minister? *You?* Good Lord!'

Critics later saw the Ramsay MacDonald and Baldwin ascendancy as both shameful and harmful to Britain. Yet it was to last until 1937, when he finally resigned his seals of office and was created Earl Baldwin of Bewdley. By that time Hitler had set up his monstrous tyranny in Germany and had transformed his country into a gigantic arsenal. All over Europe, during the post-war years, the governments were addressing themselves to the people, asking them to choose their leaders. But the people could see no more clearly in the twilight of the war than their rulers. And so the rulers whom they selected were often the wrong ones.

Was Stanley Baldwin the right man to be Prime Minister? In the Conservative ranks there was very little choice. Lloyd George had once said of Bonar Law that he was 'honest to the verge of simplicity,' a statement which is said to have won Bonar Law the 1922 election. The British public liked a politician who, as far as could be seen, was honest. And Stanley Baldwin filled this role perfectly, without being simple. He appeared to be a thoroughly reliable, pipe-smoking, shrewd English gentleman. Inviting the Old Berkeley hunt to meet at Chequers, he was photographed patting one of the hounds on the head. If he betrayed signs of laziness, this was a national characteristic. To millions of people he was John Bull come to life, and although described by an M.P. as 'a man who sits in the smoking room of the House reading the *Strand Magazine*,' he appeared to offer stability and sound common sense. In 1925 he was able to say, in a speech which won him national acclaim, that his party had 'rightly or wrongly succeeded in creating the impression that we stood for stable government and for peace in the country between all classes of the community.' Baldwin's success was due to the fact that he consistently 'succeeded in creating an impression,' and one which the British public respected. He ended his speech with the words

> 'Although I know that there are those who work for different ends from most of us in this House, yet there are many in all ranks and all parties who will re-echo my prayer: "Give peace in our time, O Lord." '

This was the nation's prayer of the twenties and thirties, an oft-repeated plea for peace, but with no definite indication that anyone was prepared to work hard for it, or make any real effort to ensure it. Peace and a quiet life were what the average Englishman wanted, summed up in Baldwin's ambition, 'to read, to live a decent life, and to keep pigs.' Only towards the end of his life, when large sections of the public actively disliked him because they thought he had failed to ensure that the prayer was answered, did he reveal himself to be a broken man.

Lord Curzon, who had been Viceroy of India, was one of the few men who might have been Prime Minister instead of Baldwin. He was the wealthy and influential son of Lord Scarsdale, and had been educated at Eton and Balliol. In 1886 he was Conservative Member for Southport, and in 1895 he became Viceroy. In India he carried out far-reaching reforms, and was led by mistrust of Russia to form the North-West Frontier Province and to send an armed expedition into Tibet. In 1906, after a dispute with Lord Kitchener over the control of the Indian army, he resigned and returned home to take a leading part in parliamentary affairs.

Curzon was spending the Whitsun recess at Montacute House in Somerset when he received a letter from Bonar Law announcing his resignation as Prime Minister. The house was not on the telephone, and a whole day was spent in an agony of suspense, wondering whether he would succeed to the office, when he received a telegram from the King's private secretary asking him to go to London, he not unnaturally thought that his moment had come. In the train he and his wife discussed their future; at Paddington they posed for photographers, whose presence no doubt heightened their ambitions. But on arriving at Buckingham Palace, Curzon was told that the Prime Minister must be in the Commons. Bitterly disappointed, Curzon wept. But later, when he had overcome his resentment, he loyally supported Baldwin.

One of the new Prime Minister's first acts was to announce that he would fight the rising figures of unemployment by abandoning free trade in favour of tariff reform. This change in policy demanded an appeal to the people, and the Government at once went to the country. From America, Lloyd George sent a cable criticizing the move as 'an insult to the intelligence of the nation.' He returned at once, with his cloak slung over his shoulder and his long grey hair, turning white now, blowing in the wind. To his delight, Asquith announced his intention of rejoining him, which led Lloyd George to laughingly declare that the re-uniting of the Liberal party had been the sole achievement of Baldwin's short term of office.

Like the Liberals, the Labour Party, led by James Ramsay MacDonald, also rejected tariff reform, saying that it would raise the cost of living. In addition, Labour wanted a capital levy on all personal fortunes of £5,000 and over, the nationalization of mines and railways, increased pensions, and a revision of the Treaty of Versailles.

'There will be no peace,' announced MacDonald at Leicester, 'so long as the Versailles Treaty is in existence.'

Most Britons had already forgotten about Versailles. As Lord Carson said, 'There is nothing that England likes better than forgetting. It is easy to forget, particularly if it costs nothing.'

Meanwhile Baldwin stuck to his tariff policy. Free trade, he said, would still exist within the Empire, but Britain must be protected from cheap foreign goods.

The result of the election showed that the country

rejected protection. Baldwin was returned to power, but with an unworkable majority. Labour had added forty-eight new seats to its total, and the Conservatives were outnumbered in the House by the combined Labour and Liberal opposition. Asquith held that the Labour Party, as the largest group in opposition, had a right to office. Baldwin was therefore forced to resign in favour of Labour, who had the support of the Liberals. But Baldwin knew that Labour was unprepared to govern the country, and he was ready to sit back and profit from the mistakes which were obviously going to be made. Like most Conservatives at that time, he did not think the new Government would last long. When it failed, the Conservatives would return, stronger than ever.

CHAPTER THREE

The Changing Scene

I

THE END of the war was the end of a generation and a way of life. There was no sudden revolution, but the spirit of change pervaded everything, the old traditions were quickly wilting, people talked of 'pre-war' prices and customs as if they were part of another world. And indeed they were.

High prices and inflation were now the great enemies of the middle classes. Everyone was affected by the rise in the cost of living. The farmers, who had enjoyed several years of prosperity, were hard hit by the repeal of the Corn Production Act in 1921; the governing classes were gradually being deprived of political power, their estates were dwindling. Only a few wartime 'profiteers' prospered. Throughout the country there was a slow, gradual levelling out of social relationships, landowners were moving out of their big estates, people who had faithfully employed coachmen and butlers and footmen and stablemen and several maids now found themselves looking for somewhere less expensive to live, unable to afford more than one servant. It was not until 1934 that film producer John Baxter made *Lest We Forget*, but the story was typical of the post-war era; the reunion of four men who had arranged, in a shell-hole, to meet again in Britain. Three came to the officer's house, one having died. Their host seemed ill at ease. Only at the end of the film was it revealed that he was now the butler, and had borrowed the house from his employer, to keep up appearances.

Times had altered, and in few periods of English history

have there been such social upheavals. Letters to the correspondence columns of newspapers reflected the changes which were taking place in England:

The Editor, *The Sunday Times*.

Sir—Cannot you say a few words for poor householders who cannot get servants? The Labour Bureau is perfectly useless, and employs thousands of girls who ought to be in domestic service and training for the future. In my own experience, one girl asked for £55 a year, and had never been out before. It is monstrous that girls are paid for jobs while men are paid for doing nothing.

A Londoner.

Worse was to come. While for some the nineteen-twenties are in retrospect to be connected with the 'bright young things,' short-skirted flappers who wanted the vote (and got it) and young men with Valentino haircuts and Oxford 'bags' playing noisy ukuleles in the dickey seats of open touring cars, for many more it was a period of unemployment, strikes, extreme poverty, and misery.

Unemployment, the great feature of English life in the twenties and thirties, was not new to Britain. In 1879 it had amounted to 11 per cent of the industrial workers, and in 1886 to 10 per cent. After 1874 it was never less than 2 per cent. The highest peak was reached in July 1921 when the figure rose to 2,508,000. Six months later it was 2,003,000. Then the figures remained fairly constant, around the 1,200,000 mark, until July 1930, when they rose to 2,070,000. But the real problem was the permanent million unemployed from 1921 onwards.

In August 1930, when the figures again passed the two million mark, half of the unemployed came from Lancashire, Yorkshire, Staffordshire and Durham. People in the south of England still do not appreciate what conditions were like at that time in the north. In Blackburn 52·7 of the population were unemployed, in Accrington 44·3, in Burnley 42·1. Many thousands of young men went into the Army because there was no other way of living. But many more managed to live on the dole. Ex-public schoolboys were now only too glad to take jobs as commercial travellers, selling motor-cars, vacuum cleaners, silk stockings and electric lamp bulbs.

Unemployment did not arise from any 'unemployability' on the part of the workers. Work could have been found for more people if the general scale of wages had been lowered. But the public preferred high wages with unemployment to lower wages with the unemployed reabsorbed. Lower wages would mean a reduction in the general standard of living, and this was unacceptable.

In 1920, unemployment insurance—as the dole was politely called—was extended by law to include all workers except domestic servants and agricultural labourers, and in 1921 a special allowance for dependants was added. With the passing of the years unemployment became a tradition, to be accepted. Originally, in order to receive the dole, a worker had to prove that he had been 'genuinely seeking work but unable to obtain suitable employment.' By 1930 he was no longer expected to seek work for himself, and the dole was his right, even if he never worked again.

In April 1925 *Punch* referred to a strike in Lancashire, joking that it was now settled, but that 'hundreds of men were thrown into work.'

The most dangerous and demoralizing aspect of the dole was the slow breaking down of the will to work. Sometimes an unemployed man was better off when not working; in November 1927 *The Times* quoted the case of an engineer-fitter from Southwark, aged 36 years, married and the father of five children, who had been unemployed almost continuously since 1925. He received 43s. a week unemployment benefit, and since the birth of his last child, 47s. Had he worked at his trade, he would have earned 42s. for a 47-hour week.

Demobilization had brought the need for many 'homes for heroes,' but at first few were built. Later they spread out in ribbon development estates outside the towns, eating up the countryside. Most of the new houses were of red brick, or what Osbert Lancaster called 'bypass Tudor' design. London's subsoil could not support tall buildings, according to the experts, so the metropolis spread outwards into rows of neat little houses. Everyone, it seemed, wanted an individual private strip of garden, a lawn, a tall fence as protection from neighbours, a house exactly like the one next door, except for the name, *Mon Repos*, *The Laurels*, *Hill View*, *Simla*, *The Sheilings*.

Although most of the new houses were cheaply constructed, perhaps in doubtful taste, often 'jerry-built' by speculative builders, erected in rows without being planned on a larger scale, few people minded. *Ours is a nice 'ouse, ours is* ran the popular song—*the front's at the back, and the back's at the front*. Only a few people took in the view from a distance, and disliked it.

In 1927, J. B. Priestley found these houses:

very ugly indeed, square little boxes that look as if they had been nailed on to the landscape, and so ugly that even time will not beautify them. As the years pass and sun and rain come to tint the walls and roofs and the creepers climb to the eaves, these houses will mellow a little but they will never be beautiful . . . is it necessary that most of the houses should look so unpleasant? All I can say is that I do not understand why there is such a general passion now for building semi-detached or detached little houses . . . I am convinced that it is this detachment that is responsible for a great deal of the ugliness. This is what peppers the countryside with little brick boxes.

Inside these houses, families were listening to the new wonder of the age, the wireless. The popularity of this craze, as it still was in 1921, led to regular broadcasting next year. In 1922 six equipment makers formed the British Broadcasting Company Ltd., which started a daily service on November 12th. As we shall see, their programmes were a tremendous influence on the post-war generation. And in 1926, in an upper room in Frith Street, Soho, J. L. Baird gave what he claimed was the first demonstration of modern television.

But thistles were growing in many of the wheat-fields of England as more and more farm labourers left the land to seek higher wages and shorter working hours in the towns. The heavy industries that had made Britain prosperous and powerful were being replaced by the manufacture of 'consumer' goods—motor-cars, wireless sets, electrical apparatus, bicycles, artificial fabrics, cosmetics and luxuries. To sell these to one another, more and more people opened shops. Large sections of the public became employed not in producing but in organizing, in bookkeeping and accounting, selling, and advertising. Thus there grew up the great new middle class of office workers.

It was to this large and increasing public that the 'never never' system of hire-purchase, or payment by instalments, appealed. Most of the suites of furniture (and everyone wanted suites) which went into the little pepper-box houses were bought over a long period, by weekly or monthly instalments. *No Deposit!* announced the placards, or *Yours for only 2s. a week!* This was the age of Mr. Drage and his customers, Mr. and Mrs. Everyman. Mass production had replaced craftsmanship, quantity was more important than quality, but Mr. Everyman did not care. There was a suite of furniture in the 'lounge' of his semi-detached house, a mirror hung on chains above the mantelpiece, new orange curtains set off the bow window, perhaps there was a motor-car in the detached garage. What more could he want?

The first British mass-produced cars were coming off the assembly lines at the Cowley works near Oxford. In 1923 a 13·9 horse-power Morris Oxford two-seater coupé cost £415, and was therefore beyond the reach of the worker of moderate means. But soon cheaper models and the advent of the 'baby' Austin and the Morris Minor brought motoring for the millions.

Meanwhile the population was rising rapidly. By 1930 it was increasing in Greater London at the rate of over a thousand a week. Ribbon development extended from London practically to the south coast. But urbanization brought many new restrictions, even at the seaside.

Preparing to bathe in the sea at Worthing, Dr. C. E. M. Joad found a sheltered place behind an iron pillar, and began to undress. He had taken off his coat, a boot and a sock, when an official arrived and told him that it was forbidden to undress on the beach. The corporation had provided huts and machines, and if he liked to go and stand in a queue he would doubtless be allotted one. The queue, however, moved slowly because it was a hot day and there were not many huts. Dr. Joad did not bathe.

Many other Englishmen deplored the new way of life, the noise of the traffic, the garish garages with green petrol pumps, the vulgarity of the huge advertisement hoardings, the rush of the crowd.

'There are quiet places also in the mind,' said Theodore Gumbril in Aldous Huxley's novel *Antic Hay*, 'but we build bandstands and factories on them. Deliberately—to put a stop to the quietness. We don't like the quietness . . . round and round continually . . . and the jazz bands, and the music-hall songs, the boys shouting the news. What's it for? What's it all for?'

GEORGE LUNN'S TOURS

MOUNTAIN MAGIC

Have you seen the Chamois frolic on the rocks and glaciers of the Wetterhorn through the telescopes of the Bear Hotel, or felt that exhilaration engendered by the tonic crystal freshness of a September morn at Grindelwald, or have you on a fine summer's evening seen the *pièce de résistance* of the evening meal deserted by the guests as if in panic to catch the "Alpine Glow," which bathes the snow-covered peaks only for such moments as may never fade from memory? Take GEORGE LUNN'S TOURS to the LAKES and MOUNTAINS of SWITZERLAND and ITALY, or AUTUMN CRUISES to the MEDITERRANEAN.

17 Days Lugano Tour, Hotel du Lac	£14 2 6
10 Days Lugano Tour, Grand Eden	£12 3 6
All rooms with balcony, and facing lake.	
17 Days Lugano, Grindelwald Tour	£17 2 6
17 Days Montreux, Lugano, Lucerne Tour	£15 12 6
17 Days Montreux, Grindelwald Lucerne Tour	£15 2 6
15 Days Lucerne, Lugano, Venice, Paris	£20 10 0
17 Days Axenfels Palace, Lake Lucerne	£15 10 0
Ideal for Golfers, reductions in September.	
23 Days Lugano, Venice, Dolomites, Engadine	£30 12 6
11 Days Montreux, Paris Tour	£11 10 6
10 Days Lucerne. Grand Hotel du Lac	£11 2 6
5 Days Paris, Versailles Tour ...	£ 6 6 0
21 Days Milan, Genoa, Rome, Naples, Florence, Venice, Lucerne. Escorted throughout	£34 0 0
14 Days Paris, Montreux, Venice, Lugano	£22 10 0

Reduced fares from the Provinces to London.

Apply for Illustrated Programme 52L. 600 Escorted Tours. 12 Weekly Departures. Independent Travel Arranged by private interview for preference, or by letter.

74, Wigmore St., London. W.1. No Agents

2

Early in 1923 the British School of Archaeology discovered at Luxor in Upper Egypt the unrifled tomb of the boy king Tutankhamen. When Lord Carnarvon, the leader of the expedition, suddenly died at the entrance to the tomb after being bitten by a mosquito, it was immediately reported that *the curse of the Pharaohs* had stricken him down. The daily newspapers expected Howard Carter, the deputy leader, to fall at any moment. But Mr. Carter carried on, while the world marvelled at the reports of the glittering splendour of the discoveries, the state chariots covered with sheet gold beautifully embossed and inlaid, and the models of Nile craft three thousand years old. On January 24, 1924, it was announced that Mr. Carter had opened the doors of the remaining three shrines. 'With the opening of the final door,' said the official message from Cairo, 'came an exciting moment. As the panels gradually swung outwards there was revealed to the gaze of the spectators a stone sarcophagus, colossal in size, magnificent in workmanship, and beyond any question intact.'

Inside the first shrine was a second shrine with doors bolted, corded and sealed with the day seal of the royal necropolis. The seal was intact, just as it was when placed there 3,270 years before. Between the doors of the two shrines lay or stood a large number of beautiful objects. Foremost among them was an alabaster vase mounted in silver and gold. There were two 'Hapi' (God of the Nile) figures, one on each side, crowned with the emblems of Upper and Lower Egypt. Not for centuries had eyes beheld such splendour.

The discoveries started a minor cult in Egyptology among fashionable women in Britain. The *Illustrated London News* reported, 'Women who desire to be in the Tutankhamen fashion can now wear real ancient gems in modern settings as personal ornaments.' Cartier, the Bond Street jeweller, sold ornaments, many dating from 600 B.C., made up as hat-pins, earrings, pendants, brooches and belt clasps.

The thrill of awe experienced by Mr. Carter and his helpers when they saw the sarcophagus for the first time was shared by millions of people who had followed the progress of the search with mounting interest. Its vastness, the superb decoration, the dazzling golden doors and the mystic mauve lights which lit the scene, created an awe-inspiring impression.

Later, Mr. Carter was forced to close the tomb 'owing to impossible restrictions and discourtesies on the part of the public works department and the antiquity service.' On February 22 the French Director-General of Egyptian Antiquities, as a sequel to the dispute, forced his way into the tomb and assumed control of the work. The official opening was a political rather than a scientific occasion, the two hundred guests including Lord Allenby (the High Commissioner), Lady Allenby, the Sirdar, Prince Frederick Leopold of Prussia, the Duke and Duchess of Aosta, all the Egyptian ministers except the Prime Minister, and nearly all the diplomatic corps. Mr. Carter, who had renounced all claims to the objects in the tomb, was not present.

In contrast, people in Britain were enjoying an era of cheaper values, of Woolworth's, Marks and Spencer's, multiple stores replacing old-fashioned family shops, and fewer hand-made goods. The Fifty-Shilling Tailors, where one could buy a good suit for 35s., attracted customers by the million, and the music-hall comedian Harry Champion sang a song about Mr. Mallaby Deeley, M.P., who had started the cheaper suits campaign by buying up a supply of government surplus clothing after the war:

In my Mallaby Deeley suit
I fell into the sea
The missus grabbed a boat hook
And began to fish for me—

Even with unemployment figures rising, people still joined in the chorus of another popular song:

Give yourself a pat on the back
A pat on the back
A pat on the back
And say to yourself
'Here's jolly good health,
I've had a good day to-day!'

Or the song of the Frothblowers, carefully encouraged by the brewers:

For your friends are my friends
And my friends are your friends
And the more we are together
The happier we shall be.

In June 1919, all the chorus boys in Albert de Courville's revue at the London Hippodrome were demobilized officers, and several were D.S.O.'s and M.C.'s.

Novelty, sensation, wonder, there was always something exciting happening, while Felix the cat kept on walking, and Captain Malcolm Campbell was racing along the Pendine Sands in his Napier-Campbell at 450 miles an hour. He and Henry Segrave were the idols of schoolboys, who collected cigarette card pictures of them and stuck them into albums along with cards of Jack Hobbs, Maurice Tate, Herbert Sutcliffe, Patsy Hendren and Woolley. In the *Daily Mail* a mouse named Teddy Tail competed with the *Daily Mirror's* ageless Pip, Squeak and Wilfred; Tom Webster's immortal 'Tishy,' the horse which (he said) crossed its legs when it ran, was a favourite cartoon character. And there were great sporting occasions, the fights for the Ashes, Steve Donoghue winning the 1921 Derby on Humorist, Mlle Lenglen being presented to Queen Mary at Wimbledon, Alan Cobham flying from London to Cape Town and back, Charles Lindbergh's lone flight across the Atlantic.

Today we accept international air travel as the quickest, if not the safest, method of moving from one country to another. But in 1924 an air trip to Paris or Hanover or Zurich was a novelty, although there was a regular Imperial Airways service from Croydon to most of the capitals of Europe. And in that year the famous Savoy Orpheans Dance Band broadcast a programme of popular music from an aeroplane circling above Croydon airport.

In London the great town houses were passing into the shadows. Devonshire House and Grosvenor House were demolished, Dorchester House was doomed. Flats and hotels occupied the spaces where great Englishmen and their ladies had dined and wined and danced and sometimes altered the course of British history. Stafford House became a museum, Spencer House a ladies' club, and Montagu House a government office. Park Lane, once a road lined on one side with houses owned by dukes and millionaires, now gave way to blocks of flats and hotels; a bank, then shops appeared. Society overflowed into Bayswater, Westminster and even Bohemian Bloomsbury. The Knightsbridge shops became as fashionable as those of Bond Street.

The so-called West End of London was no longer the exclusive domain of the rich; wealth was now more evenly distributed. A *thé-dansant* at the Savoy Hotel cost 5s. a head, at the Café de Paris 4s., and the same at the Piccadilly Hotel or the Empress Rooms. At the Regent Palace or the Astoria Dance Hall tea with dancing cost only 2s. A supper dance at the Regent Palace cost 3s. 6d., and lasted from ten until twelve-thirty.

It was what David Keir has called 'the Octopus Age,' with everything expanding. During the war there had been a levelling out of the classes, at least superficially. People could no longer be judged by their clothes, which were more uniform. Clerks were now well dressed, there was more choice of clothes. But although conditions of life had improved for large sections of the population, the threat of unemp oyment and 'going on the dole' hung heavily over the great industrial areas of Britain, where wives queued up—in 1921—for quartern loaves at one-and-fourpence each.

In 1922 many music-hall comedians were playing in low-life 'dole' sketches. Albert Burdon, hailed as 'the new star comedian' was to be seen in *On the Dole*. Fred D. Neilson's productions included *Unemployed*, *Rack and Ruin*, *Work*, *Labour*, and *Brewery*. Miss Gertrude Lawrence had a verse for the women:

It ain't all honey
And it ain't all jam,
Walking round the 'ouses
With a three-wheeled pram.

In many parts of Britain the pawnshops were as busy as the bakers'. But the public bars were, somehow, nearly always full, and only the cotton mills were idle. Sometimes a war pension was used to supplement the precious 'dole,' but the pensions awarded to ex-servicemen were little enough, and even by 1955 a married veteran of 67 who had lost a leg on the Somme or at Mons was drawing only £2 0s. 6d. a week. In 1920 he was fortunate if he had a job and a home. Many sang in the street. But for the British Legion the position of some of these veterans would have been even more desperate.

Under a new housing act, the Government arranged in 1923 to pay local authorities £6 a year for twenty years for each new house. Each subsidized house or flat had to be provided with a fixed bath, 'except where otherwise approved by the Ministry of Health on the recommendation of the local authority.' The joke about keeping coal in the bath was an old one, but the truth is that as late as 1955 only half of the houses in Britain were equipped with separate bathrooms.

It was not until 1925 that the number of new houses exceeded the demand. Then, with the housing estates encroaching on the fields, children began to look around for playing fields and parks, and the nation awoke to the fact that no provision had been made for recreation. In hundreds of situations, builders and architects had planned street after street with gardens backing on to one another but no open spaces, not even a line of trees, nowhere to walk but on the pavements, nowhere to play cricket or football or toss a school cap up in the air just for the fun of it.

'Our streets are unbearable,' said James Bridie. 'Does nobody care? In Copenhagen they plant their new housing schemes among the trees instead of tearing up the trees that interfere with their ugly geometrical figures. In Leicester they make their shopkeepers behave, and insist on simple signs and decent windows.'

There had been little planning, nothing had been arranged on a grand scale. Some of the new suburbs were shanty towns, miserable dormitories with meagre narrow roads. There was no spaciousness, no hint of the countryside which had been swallowed up. Instead, fish shops, tobacco shops, a chemist, a fruit shop, all stood in a row labelled *The Esplanade*.

In 1929 the London County Council received applications from a thousand clubs for cricket pitches, but they could provide only 350. Eighty-five hockey clubs competed for the use of 26 grounds, and 65,000 tennis players in the London area strove to play on 676 grass courts and 139 hard ones. There was little room to breathe, and the boy or girl without a few shillings could not play tennis.

After overcoming many difficulties, Mr. George Lansbury succeeded, in November 1930, in opening a single playing ground for poor people in London. But in 1925 the position was much more desperate; most of London's children were playing in the streets.

To solve the problem the National Playing Fields Association was founded, under the presidency of the Duke of Sutherland. An enthusiastic first meeting was held at the Royal Albert Hall, attended by the Duke and Duchess of York and many representatives of youth clubs. Sir Arthur Crosfield announced that they hoped soon to cover the country with branches. A resolution was passed pledging the Association to promote and encourage the provision of open-air recreation facilities in and around every city, town and village.

It was only at the end of the twenties, when the pattern of the new towns became apparent, that it became clear that a great opportunity had been lost. At Winchester in 1928 Stanley Baldwin complained at 'the destruction of all the beauty and charm with which our ancestors enhanced their towns and villages.' Two years earlier *Country Life* had complained:

> In the midst of the loveliest surroundings in the very heart of rural England . . . it is ten chances to one that we alight upon a tin or asbestos bungalow or a choice assortment of hideous advertisement boards . . . Kent and Essex are destroyed, and Sussex threatened . . . first the glaring advertisements, and last, worst of all, the brightly coloured, flimsy bungalows. The advertisements are the least serious . . . a few spirited inhabitants, like certain Cambridge undergraduates, could lay them low in a night . . . but what can happen to the bungalows? The great estates might have exercised some control in certain districts, and no doubt did for a time, but they are fast breaking up, if they have not already done so.

At Hove, Sussex, on January 25, 1925, Mr. Louis Ginnett, the landscape artist, and the Earl of Chichester, gave evidence before magistrates when the East Sussex County Council summoned five defendants for exhibiting advertisements 'disfiguring the natural beauty of the Downland.' On one of the hoardings a poster boldly declared, '*Watch and pray; the time is short. Man brings about his own destruction. The air battle will be the end of the world.*'

Advertisements now occupied a large part of the contents of popular newspapers. Sometimes a whole page was devoted to a well-known product. Laxatives, patent medicines, elastic stockings, cigarettes, gin, beer and whisky, it was the advertisements which brought profits to the newspapers. Many firms made use of theatrical names in their announcements; Phyllis Monkman, Leslie Henson, Madie Scott and

George Robey testified to the excellence of Reudel Bath Saltrates 'for the cure of rheumatism without dosing.' Mr. Robey's signature appeared beneath the words:

> I needed these Saltrates long before commencing to use them. Oh! *How* can I tell you my feelings in those days? Now I have no more tired feet or muscular strains. Do I still travel to Continental Spas? No! *No*—n' n' n' NO! I take my cure at home!

It was an age of patent medicines and cures. In 1924 a product called Yadil was advertised as an almost universal cure for everything from cancer to consumption. It was claimed that it contained oil of garlic. When the advertisers became involved in a dispute with the *Daily Mail*, that newspaper had the medicine analysed and found no trace of oil of garlic. Instead, formaldehyde was present, which doctors considered dangerous. Later, it became obligatory to state the ingredients on medicine bottle labels, and illegal to claim that a preparation could cure cancer, consumption, and other diseases.

Even the old familiar railway names were changing, as L.B. & S.C.R. gave way to Southern, and L. & N.W.R. to L.M.S. Under the Railways Act of 1921, the many railway companies were formed into four big groups:

LONDON MIDLAND AND SCOTTISH (L.M.S.) London and North Western; Midland; Lancashire and Yorkshire; North Staffordshire; Furness; Highland; Caledonian; Glasgow and South Western; Maryport and Carlisle; Cockermouth; Stratford-upon-Avon and Midland Junction.

LONDON AND NORTH EASTERN RAILWAY (L.N.E.R.) North Eastern; Great Central; Great Eastern; Great Northern; Hull and Barnsley; North British; Great Northern of Scotland.

GREAT WESTERN RAILWAY (G.W.R.) Great Western; Midland and South Western Junction; Cambrian; local South Wales railways.

SOUTHERN RAILWAY (S.R.) London and South Western; London Brighton and South Coast; South Eastern and Chatham; Isle of Wight.

The railways were amalgamated to increase their efficiency. The date for the completion of the grouping was July 1, 1923;

the Government's wartime control of railways had ended at midnight on August 15, 1921.

In London the 'omnibus war' involved vigorous competition between the various private companies which plied for hire. Because the London General Omnibus Company was the largest group it was generally considered to be 'official'; and its many rivals were termed 'pirates.' These smaller groups, some owning many vehicles and others only one, painted their transport in brightly contrasting colours.

The L.G.O.C. Livery was red and broken-white, with black lining, and these colours were adopted also by their associates—Metropolitan, Southern, East Surrey, and National. Thomas Tilling 'buses were red and ivory. These were some of the other colours:

Birch Bros.	Light brown and ivory
City Omnibus Co.	Light brown and ivory
United Omnibus Co.	Light brown and ivory
Overground	Red and white
Public Omnibus Co.	Dark blue and ivory
Westminster Omnibus Co.	Chocolate and ivory
Premier Omnibus Co.	Chocolate and ivory
Chocolate Express	Chocolate and ivory
Admiral Omnibus Co.	Red and white

Roads were being widened and adapted for motor traffic and for several years during the twenties they were considered among the best highways in Europe. The old days of stones and dust and frequent punctures had almost gone. Cars were improving in quality, and as the urge to drive farther afield became greater, more families ventured out on to the roads of Britain. Country hotel-keepers now discovered that their trade was being revolutionized by the internal combustion engine, especially at week-ends, when the rush to reach the sea or get out of town brought travellers racing through the villages. England had become smaller, there was no part of the country to which people could not travel quickly.

But as motor transport increased, so did the accident

figures. The war between the motorist and the pedestrian had started. In 1922 London still had 15 hansom cabs and 375 horse cabs or 'clarences,' but there were also 7,191 motor taxis, 4,103 motor buses, and 2,795 tram-cars, besides 8 remaining horse buses. And as the motor licences increased, up went London's accident figures:

	Killed	*Injured*
1922	2,768	67,429
1927	5,329	148,575

3

There were vast changes in social behaviour. In pre-war days it had not been considered correct, in polite society, to dance more than once with the same partner. But during the war these strict bonds of etiquette were relaxed, and after the war they were abandoned. Chaperons vanished, and a man could now take a girl to a dance and be her partner for the whole evening. The rules of sex were greatly relaxed. In fact sex was now openly discussed, especially in the newspapers.

In January 1922 Professor Julian Huxley of New College, Oxford, announced that there was perhaps a third sex. 'It is not only perfectly possible,' he said, 'but even probable, that maladjusted sex factors may exist in man as in moths . . . several results follow, the first the distinct possibility that cases of sexual perversion may be cured by injection or grafting. I believe this is being tested in Germany. The second is legal. It is highly probable that human intersexes are neither male nor female, but definitely intermediate. If so, then it must be wrong to assign a normal sex to them, for they belong to a third category.'

Sex and sin were now widely reported in the popular press. It was an age of frank confessions, of sensational statements, of headlines growing larger each year. More newspaper space was devoted to sport and entertainments, and well-known characters in all walks of life became the subject of articles. An eager and ever-increasing public sought information and gossip about the likes and dislikes and daily habits and private lives of actors and actresses, ex-kings, boxers, criminals, and wireless and cinema celebrities. Almost everything they did was news, and was presumably fit to print.

The boxer Jack Dempsey was reported to have been paid £100,000 for a fight that lasted only four minutes. This must have proved interesting reading to many thousands of unemployed Englishmen who read that before his championship fight with Jess Willard, in July 1919, Dempsey had prayed to win, and prayed again just before the bell sounded for the contest.

'I never went to bed in my life and I never ate a meal without saying a prayer,' he said. 'I know my prayers have been answered hundreds of times.' Such confessions were a feature of popular journalism in the twenties, but they were to be surpassed by the feature articles and gossip columns of the thirties. Steadily, the press was becoming more sensational. Entertainment, and not education or the presentation of news, was the new order of the day.

Conventions were changing, but in 1922 a young University of London don was dismissed for kissing a girl student against her will at a University dance.

Certain conventions have to be observed by a lecturer whose classes are attended by both sexes,' observed the *Daily News*. This harmless escapade was reported on the front pages of several popular newspapers, sharing prominence with the retirement of P.C. Beck of the Surrey Police, who claimed that between 1903 and 1922 he had caused from 9,000 to 10,000 motorists to be summoned before the Kingston-on-Thames bench. The Portsmouth road had provided him, especially at week-ends, with thousands of motoring offenders, a team of officers being responsible for catching 'road hogs' and fast drivers in speed traps. The average motorist objected to the speed traps as much as he disliked the 'road hogs'; the Automobile Association and Royal Automobile Club helped drivers by warning members of the presence of the police.

4

Every year the influence of the American way of life became more apparent. The cinema, popular music, the theatre, literature, the press, all were becoming more 'Americanized.' More vulgar, some people thought. It was not until the coming of sound films in the late twenties that the majority of English people heard the American voice regularly, and began to adopt transatlantic slang, but during 1921 twenty million people in Britain went to the cinema every week, and most of the films they saw were American.

With the advent of the 'talkies' new expressions entered everyday conversation, especially among younger people. American film slang included the nouns *the bunk*, *sugar daddies*, *boloney*, *raspberry* and the verbs *to bump off* and *to fix*. Events were no longer *all right* or *acceptable*, they were *O.K.* Girls were *dames*. Youngsters playing in the back streets of Hull or Newcastle threatened one another with *the works*. *Oh yes* became pronounced *yeah*, and a foolish person was a *dope*. A whole new vocabulary was introduced. Gradually even singers in English theatres, and on the wireless, adopted American accents, in direct contrast to the news announcers, who persisted in speaking with what became known as 'Oxford accents.' The B.B.C. tradition of Savoy Hill, which moved in the late twenties to Langham Place, involved gentlemanliness and what Compton Mackenzie called 'finicking, suburban, synthetic, plus-fours gentility.' He thought the worship of uniform speech, encouraged by the B.B.C., was a sign of decadence, and said, 'For reasons which have nothing to do with beauty of speech, but only with worldly success, we accept as the ideal voice one which has been damped down first by the fogs of Eton in boyhood, then by the fogs of Oxford in youth, and finally by the fogs of London in maturity.'

New words were creeping into everyday use. Fortunately some of them soon vanished. A Reading firm produced the 'Cottabunga,' described as 'an ideal permanent home, artistic, convenient and durable'; open touring cars were described as 'torpedo models.' The 'bright young things,' as they were called, had a language of their own. Parties were 'simply *too* dreary' or '*too* tired-making'; shopping with mother was '*too* boring'; P. G. Wodehouse's young heroes were 'smooth,' his villains or cads were '*too grisly for words.*' According to Ivor Brown, it was the age of the 'tired monotonous drawl, of tired monotonous metaphors, such novelty as there is coming mainly from America.'

The end of the world was constantly predicted in the Sunday newspapers. 'The world is to end next summer,' observed Hilaire Belloc. 'I don't believe it. It is too good to be true.'

In 1921 great interest was aroused by the arrival in London of Emile Coué, who delivered a series of lectures on suggestion and autosuggestion. He told his listeners that it was the imagination which gained the victory over will-power whenever the two forces met, and that it was perfectly possible to make 'suggestions' to persons without first hypnotizing them. There was, he said, no illness within the realms of possibility which would not yield to suggestion and autosuggestion if properly administered. 'Remember, I cure no one,' he announced. 'I teach you to cure yourselves. Come back and tell me you are cured—that is all the recompense I ask.'

During his second visit, a year later, Monsieur Coué gave lectures both in French and English at the Wigmore Hall, and held morning meetings for collective treatment. An address which he published began, 'Every morning before you are fully awake, and every evening as soon as you are in bed, close your eyes and murmur twenty times in succession the following phrase: *Day by day in every way I grow better and better*. It is well to be provided with a piece of string with twenty knots tied in it, so that the counting may be mechanical. Let this autosuggestion be made with confidence, with faith. The greater the conviction, the more rapid and certain will be the results.'

At his headquarters in Grosvenor Gardens, reported the *Illustrated London News*, 'a lady with an affliction of the knee walked with ease after treatment.'

'Modernism' was the order of the day, and most of the old pre-war inhibitions were thrust aside. Before the war most Britons had enjoyed their entertainment at home but now young people, attracted by the cinema, theatres, dancing, ice and roller skating, and public-houses, spent less time at home. Youngsters took up cycling and hiking, and there was an urge to move out of town during the week-ends. Golf, tennis and competitive sports were now more freely enjoyed by women as well as men. In 1921, at a meeting of the Lord's Day Observance Society, Sir Herbert Nield protested, 'We have gone recreation-mad!' He pointed out that the conduct of the public was seriously deteriorating, parental control was diminishing, family life was losing its strength, the press was becoming as vulgar as in America. There was, he said, a lack of morality. Increasing numbers of people were cheating the railways by travelling first-class with third-class tickets, and Hampstead Heath was crowded until midnight with young men and girls up to no good. Sunday had become a casualty, and the world was moving in the wrong direction.

The new name for the modern young girl was 'flapper.' It was really a pre-war expression, but it had acquired respectability and was used to describe the short-haired, boyish girls who rode pillion on the 'flapper-bracket' of a motor-cycle and, with shameless abandon, smoked cigarettes in long holders in the manner of Noël Coward. They drank cocktails, went to innumerable dances and crazy parties, arrived home with the milkman, and enjoyed the latest 'crazes.' The Savoy Orpheans and Paul Whiteman were their idea of heaven, syncopation and sophistication had entered their bright young lives. Lipstick and make-up, which had been used sparingly before the war, were now used freely. Sex could be openly discussed. Flappers always had latch-keys.

5

Wonder after wonder. In 1922 Major J. C. Savage flew in a single-seater biplane above Epsom Downs on Derby Day, and wrote the words *Daily Mail* in the sky. In the same year the catering firm of J. Lyons introduced the ice-cream brick to Britain, and installed a plant capable of producing four hundred gallons an hour. Ice cream had been regarded as a hot weather luxury, but in time it was hoped that the public would eat it also in the winter. It was only a part of the expansion of the enormous catering organization which was bringing clean, wholesome, cheap food to ten million customers a week. At Kensington a factory covered eleven acres, and another at Greenford covered thirty acres, producing tea, cocoa, coffee, chocolates, and confectionery on a colossal scale.

If one was interested in sport, the English Channel was usually in the news during the summer months. The craze to swim the Channel affected many people. The first woman to complete the crossing was Miss Gertrude Ederle, who swam across in 14 hours, 39 minutes, in 1926. In October 1927, Miss Mercedes Gleitze, who had been trying since August 1922, also succeeded. She had made eight attempts. A small, slim girl in her 'teens, she had saved money to achieve her object, and after her first attempt had tried twice in 1925, twice in 1926, and twice more in 1927. On one occasion she was eleven hours in the water and was almost exhausted, but refused to give up her terrific struggle against the tide. Constantly repeating the words, 'I must succeed and I *will* succeed,' she was only 2 miles from Dover when she had to be taken out of the sea.

On October 7th she started out again from Cap Gris Nez at two fifty-five in the morning, her pilot rowing 5 yards ahead. For the greater part of the way there was fog, so the nearby fishing boat could not see her. It was the first attempt made so late in the year, and the water was very cold. She afterwards said that during the last three hours she suffered terrible pain. At ten minutes past six she touched the rocks near the South Foreland and collapsed, awaking two hours later to find herself the national heroine of the moment.

Women were especially proud of Miss Gleitze, as they were later of Miss Amy Johnson. The elders of the nation and the clergy in their half-empty churches might thunder against the modern girl, but here were girls as capable and as brave as any man.

But if the churches lacked their pre-war congregations, religion was not forgotten. This was made apparent by a phenomenon which gained great strength during the late twenties, the Oxford Group, a religious revival movement with no membership list, subscriptions, badges, rules or definite location. It started as a name for a group of people recruited from every rank, profession and trade, in many countries. These people announced that they had decided 'to surrender their lives to God and to endeavour to lead a spiritual life.' The Oxford Group did not claim to be a religion, there were no temples, endowments or salaries, but its members boasted that they were heading a campaign for the renaissance of Christianity. They were sometimes confused with the Oxford Movement, a Catholic renaissance within the Church of England. A large following was attracted by its four aims:

1. Absolute Honesty
2. Absolute Purity
3. Absolute Unselfishness
4. Absolute Love

The cult was founded in the early twenties by Dr. Frank Buchman, an American Lutheran minister who came to England feeling dissatisfied with conditions in the United States. It had nothing to do with Oxford, but the established Church saw it as an earnest effort to revive religion. Young people, mostly of the upper and middle classes, attended week-end 'house parties' and publicly affirmed their belief in God. One of its practices was the 'sharing of sins,' the telling and talking over of misdemeanours in response to the command 'Confess therefore your sins one to another, that ye may be healed.' The Buchmanites claimed that the spirit of anti-Christ had reared itself more blatantly during the post-war years than ever before. 'Millions,' they said, 'are verging on starvation or are disillusioned by the rosy dreams of the future which, held out to them by self-seeking so-called Christian politicians, have never materialized.'

In his book *What is the Oxford Group?* Professor L. W. Grenstead, Oriel Professor of the Philosophy of the Christian Religion, explained the objects of the movement:

> People are not only talking glibly about war, but are working for it. The universe is a huge munitions factory. Fear and spiritual negation keep that factory always at work piling up armaments ready for use at any moment. Humanity spends £200 every minute on armaments, and that in what is supposed to be a period of peace . . . the trenches may not be visible, but the spirit of war is there . . . we know that until God is the deciding factor in the negotiations for peace among nations, the League of Nations will remain earth-bound . . .

Another religious revival, but on a smaller scale, was introduced to Britain by the American evangelist, Aimee Semple McPherson, who arrived in 1928 with a company of feminine 'angels' and hired the Royal Albert Hall for mass meetings of her Four Square Gospel Alliance. Although the newspapers wrote a great deal about her crusade, most of the seats at her meetings were empty. She appeared dressed in white, with white silk stockings and a white college badge on her blazer. She was preceded by a chorus of 'hot' gospellers.

'We want less pie and more piety,' she announced during her second appearance, when less than two thousand people went to see her.

The truth was that the masses kept away from the churches and from religious gatherings. 'You are all a lost generation,' said novelist Gertrude Stein. But in 1927 and 1928 the all-important question was the revision of the Church of England's prayer book, which was opposed by the low church and severely criticized as being Anglo-Catholic. The House of Lords would have accepted it, but the Commons rejected it. In 1928 a modified version was proposed, which the Lords accepted. But in the Commons, Sir William Joynson-Hicks, the Home Secretary, led the movement to oppose it, and a compromise was reached which permitted churches to use either the new or the old prayer book, according to the wishes of the congregation.

6

Although Britain was no longer as rich and prosperous as before the war, there was still evidence of great personal wealth. When John Reddihough, of Baildon, Yorkshire, died at the age of 83 he left a fortune of over £1,500,000, made out of wool. Alfred Straker, a colliery owner of Oakham, left over half a million; Joshua Wheatley of Coventry left £1,379,490; Sir Alexander Hambro, a director of the Bank of England, left £2,323,710; Sir Edward Hulton left £2,220,471; Brenton Halliburton Collins, barrister, left £1,975,494; Viscount Leverhulme, the soap maker, left £1,000,000. In 1922, H. H. Wills left £2,750,000; in 1927 F. M. H. Wills left £5,053,360: and in 1928 Sir George Wills left £10,000,000. In the years 1921–22 there were some 28,000 people in Britain with incomes exceeding £5,000 and with an estimated total income of £367,000,000 a year. About 80,000 people were paying super-tax, and a year later this figure rose to 89,000.

Under the Churchill budget introduced on April 28, 1925 the financial year ended with a surplus of £3,659,000. Income tax was reduced from 4s. 6d. to 4s. in the pound, and super-tax was also reduced.

Those who had expected the end of hostilities to bring a return to the old order had been surprised, even indignant, that by the end of the war income tax had risen to 6s. in the pound. Since the beginning of the century the standard rate had fluctuated, but whenever it was reduced it soon rose again:

	s.	d.
1900–01	1	2
1902–03	1	3
1903–04		11
1904–05 to		
1908–09	1	0
1909–10 to		
1913–14	1	2
1914–15	1	8
1915–16	3	0
1916–18	5	0
1918–22	6	0
1922–23	5	0
1923–25	4	6
1925–26	4	0
1929–30	4	0
1930–31	4	6
1931–34	5	0
1936–37	4	9
1937–38	5	0
1938–39	5	6
1939–40	7	0
1940–41	8	6
1941–46	10	0
1946–51	9	0

The battle of the death duties was pushing the wealthier landlords out of the big country estates. Their families, hunted and harassed by taxation, were driven out in large numbers. Some of the houses became schools, hospital or local government offices; others tumbled into ruins, mute testimony to better times and a more spacious way of life, their formerly immaculate drives, flower-beds and lawns reverting to jungle or making way for housing estates. The old houses were often pulled down. In pre-war days they had formed the hub of a large and contented community of outdoor and indoor servants and workers who grew up in the shadow of the house without fear or want. It was a dignified and essentially British way of life. The younger generation knew nothing about these things, and could not realize the loss, but there were many who regretted the passing of a way of life and a standard of conduct which would never return.

In 1922 the cost of living fell, but it soon rose again. Compared with modern prices everything in the twenties now seems cheap, but hundreds of thousands of families were then living on less than four pounds a week. And the cost of living, after 1922, continued to rise.

In December 1955, the Chancellor of the Exchequer told the House of Commons that one pound sterling was now worth 8s. 8d. in internal purchasing power, compared with 20s. in 1924. This illustrates the rising cost of living in thirty-one years.

Post-war prices certainly look reasonable, from a distance. In 1918 the charge for an ordinary inland letter was raised from a penny to 1½d., and in 1920 it became 2d. Two years later it fell, in line with other price reductions, to 1½d., but by 1940 it was 2½d.

Soon after the war a thirteen-day summer pleasure cruise in the Norwegian fjords cost 20 guineas. But for this sum a whole family could stay at Brighton for a fortnight. What is more interesting is that a 1925 tour of the Holy Land, inclusive of all expenses, cost 49 guineas. Fourteen days' golf on the Belgian coast inclusive of rail and hotels cost £10, and a fortnight at Montreux cost £15.

In the spring of 1922, the year that Princess Mary married Viscount Lascelles in Westminster Abbey, and the King and Queen paid a State visit to Belgium, a big Knightsbridge store was selling the 'Brompton' lounge suit, tailored in all-wool Scotch tweed and lined with alpaca, for 4 guineas. Patterns could be sent on approval. A 'sports' tweed or homespun suit with plus-fours (described as 'knickers') cost 3 guineas. Flannel trousers made of pure wool cost 27s. 6d. The quality of 'off the peg' clothes of this type was definitely superior to those of today. An Austin Reed 'Summit' white wing collar cost 1s., or six for 5s. 6d., a pair of silk pyjamas cost 30s., and a pure silk shirt with two collars to match cost 25s.

In March 1924 the household department of a big Oxford Street store was offering canteens of electro-plated cutlery, six of everything including cheese knives and an oak cabinet, at £5 10s. 6d. In the book department most of the latest novels, such as *Poirot Investigates* by Agatha Christie, *Dust to Dust* by Isobel Ostrander, *Wanderlight* by Ernest Raymond, *The Heavenly Ladder* by Compton Mackenzie, *The Honourable Jim* by Baroness Orczy and *David of Kings* by E. F. Benson, were selling at 7s. 6d. In this year, when British mountaineers reached a height of over 27,000 feet on the third Everest expedition, and the British Empire Exhibition was opened at Wembley, the King and Queen of Rumania and the King of Italy paid state visits to England.

7

Because the threat of unemployment hung heavily over many industries, large numbers of families emigrated. The new and richer territories of Canada, Australia, New

Zealand and South Africa offered hope where Britain could promise only the dole and little prospect of work. A large percentage of those who sailed away were skilled craftsmen, but many were youngsters who had never been allowed to work in their own country. These were the occupations of the emigrants who left Britain in 1922, 1923, and 1924:

	1922	1923	1924
Agricultural	12,937	26,223	18,984
Commercial	9,706	12,960	9,438
Professional	4,404	4,387	3,761
Mines & Quarries	4,836	7,300	2,774
Engineering	10,536	24,724	7,742
Labourers	7,002	19,017	6,834
Others	8,462	10,495	8,240

The figures rose after the slump of 1922, and then dropped in 1924. In April 1925 a group of Scotsmen who had spurned the dole, sailed from Glasgow for Canada on the Canadian Pacific liner *Minnedosa*. On board they displayed notices declaring *We've got jobs in Canada! We don't want the dole!*

In comparison, home agriculture attracted few newcomers. In 1919 Lloyd George had promised more food production, with guarantees for the farmer. A year later this promise was implemented by the Agricultural Act. But prices then fell, and the acreage of land under cultivation steadily declined. Soon the housewife found it cheaper to buy eggs, tomatoes and tinned foodstuffs from abroad. Farming in England was not a paying proposition. It was to help home industry and the farmer that Baldwin proposed tariff protection.

Whatever the men back from the war did, few of them worked on the land. Some of them put their gratuities, more generous than after the Second World War, into small businesses and shops. Many emigrated. And there were also young ex-captains and ex-majors who had perhaps dreamed of what England would be like, but who now found it quite different. These were the men who went drifting in and out of saloon bars, seeking a lost comradeship, constantly moving on for another drink and fresh company, looking for the ghosts of yesterday in a world which seemed always cold. In spite of the bright neon lights, and the speed of the noisy open sports cars which took them off on endless pub crawls, their world was dead. Time had passed them by.

Writing of the young men who had come back to the free-for-all of the twenties, Alec Waugh has observed, 'We were exposed after the war to far less keen competition. It is the best who are the first to fall. The same number of posts were vacant and the men in quest of them were fewer. Twenty-five years later in every country in Europe there was a deficiency of first-class men. The men who should have been their country's leaders were no longer there. There will be the same deficiency in 1970.'

CHAPTER FOUR

The First Labour Government

I

FEW WOULD have believed, before 1914, that a Socialist, the son of a Scottish crofter, a former conscientious objector, a man born out of wedlock, would be Prime Minister of Great Britain. At that time it was almost inconceivable that Britain would ever be ruled by a Labour Government. In 1900 there had been only two Labour Members of Parliament, but during the war the party had gained many new supporters, especially from the fighting services. It was the only group that included in its programme a policy of avoiding war, and to the men home from the front it offered hope for the future, some prospect of safeguarding the interests of the working classes.

On January 22, 1924, the King asked James Ramsay MacDonald to form a government. 'Gentleman Mac' he had been called by some of his colleagues, but according to G. M. Young, the biographer of Stanley Baldwin, the new leader was a mystery, a bewilderment, self-centred, self-devoted. The names of the Cabinet were announced next day.

On the previous day the Liberals had supported a Labour vote of censure, and the Government had been defeated. A packed House, with the Prince of Wales and the Duke of York among the visitors, had taken part in the drama. Now, for the first time in her long history, Britain had a Labour Government. In later years it was described by John Gloag as 'that strange, uninspiring amalgam of hope, class-consciousness and determined respectability.'

The City of London viewed the new Government with alarm, and it was reported in the Conservative newspapers that MacDonald did not want to be Prime Minister, but this was not true. Although his position was insecure, because he must rely on the Liberals for strength, he was delighted with his success. But no really constructive Labour policy was possible, because the Liberals were determined to keep the Government strictly under control, and because the new Ministers found themselves unprepared for the role they were required to play. Thus, when the country awoke to discover that a Labour Government was in power, no one was more surprised than its leaders.

Ramsay MacDonald was described in the popular right-wing newspapers as 'a self-made man, educated at a board school, and in early life a pupil teacher and an invoice clerk.' This was one way of sneering at the new regime. But even his most severe critics found very little of the Socialist touch in the behaviour or actions of the new Ministers, and it soon became obvious that the Labour policy did not, or could not, differ greatly from that of the previous Government.

MacDonald himself remained an enigma. According to Lord Brabazon of Tara, he could speak for an hour yet convey no single message or positive thought of any kind. Sir Patrick Hastings, the new Attorney-General, saw him as a man of striking appearance and many good qualities, a powerful and attractive speaker whose enthusiasm for the Labour cause was completely sincere. But he thought him unable to move quickly from his own sphere of life to become the first citizen of the land. 'He did great service to his country at a very difficult time, and his very human faults have been much exaggerated. I think the harshest criticism that could be made upon him is that he was not always loyal to his friends.'

The new Prime Minister's task was certainly difficult. In 1923 the unemployment figures had risen by a million, and one and a half million workers now formed up every week to draw the dole. In Lancashire hundreds of cotton mills were idle; coal mines were closing because they could not be worked economically. It was perhaps hardly surprising that the country's workers had returned to power the party which they believed would most genuinely represent their interests, which wanted the mines nationalized and modernized, and the Versailles Treaty revised. Suppose Labour had been able to persuade the other Powers to revise the Treaty, would it have ensured peace in Europe? There was so much to be done, but whether Ramsay MacDonald was the right man for the task is another matter.

His life had been hard. At 18 he had left his Lossiemouth home to seek his fortune in London. Lodging in tenements off Gray's Inn Road, he worked as a clerk in a warehouse for 15s. a week. Determined to be a schoolmaster, he studied science at night classes, but then became a journalist. Finally he entered on a Parliamentary career as private secretary to Thomas Lough, the Liberal Member for Islington.

On August 3, 1914, Sir Edward Grey had announced to a crowded House that 'in the present crisis it has not been possible to secure the peace of Europe.' Before he sat down the House was gripped with war fever. Ramsay MacDonald, now a Member of Parliament, was one of the few who did not support Sir Edward. When his turn came to speak he said, 'The right honourable gentleman, to a House which in a great majority is with him, has delivered a speech the echoes of which will go down to history. The speech has been impressive. However much we may resist the conclusion to which he has come, we have not been able to resist the moving character of his appeal. I think he is wrong. I think the Government that he represents and for which he speaks is wrong. I think the verdict of history will be that they are wrong. We shall see.'

A self-confessed pacifist, deserted by most of his colleagues, he became the most unpopular man in politics. In the 1918 election he lost Leicester by 14,000 votes. In 1921 he contested Woolwich, regarded as a safe Labour seat, but a winner of the Victoria Cross was put up against him and he lost by 683 votes.

'I realize now,' he wrote at the time, 'that my public career is over.' But within two years he was Prime Minister. His experience had made him a dour, sombre, difficult man. He could not forget or forgive, and it was typical of him that he never rejoined the Lossiemouth Golf Club, from which he had been forced to resign, although he received several invitations. In 1911 the death of his wife, to whom he was devoted, had dealt him a severe blow.

Winston Churchill summed him up, 'Urbane, cultured, incorruptible, he is willing to drag the car of Empire down every slope, social, military and political, so long as he can put on the brakes and be praised for his skill in applying them.'

Yet now, in January 1924, this was Labour's hour. And, surprisingly, Mr. MacDonald, dressed in a top hat and morning coat, or photographed in court dress, did not fulfil the popular conception of a Labour Prime Minister. He seemed too prosperous, almost too Conservative. But there they were, the Socialists, driving in big cars up to the palace to see the King. Conservative supporters wondered what would happen next, with the 'Reds' in power. And when someone asked the King how he was getting on with his new Government he is said to have replied, 'Very well. My grandmother would have hated it; my father would have tolerated it; but I march with the times.'

The new statesmen were mostly men of very humble birth, drawn from a new social class. They had gained their positions by ability and hard work. Philip Snowden, the crippled Yorkshire Chancellor of the Exchequer, had known poverty; Arthur Henderson, the Home Secretary, had been a Tyneside iron-founder; J. H. Thomas, the Colonial Secretary, had been the leader of the railwaymen's union; Sidney

Webb, the great Fabian thinker and writer, was the new President of the Board of Trade.

But social differences were quickly swept away by the King's immediate understanding and acceptance of his new ministers. Indeed, according to Winston Churchill, it was the King who 'reconciled the new forces of Labour and Socialism to the Constitution and the Monarchy.'

2

The remarkable feature of the new regime was the mildness of its Socialism. Doctrinaire Socialists spoke bitingly of the 'betrayal' of the Labour programme by MacDonald. Philip Snowden's 1924 Budget was described as 'an orthodox Gladstonian Budget,' and it was well received by the Liberal leader, Asquith. In the end, MacDonald's Government pleased hardly anyone. But it is interesting to recall that there was one member of the Government, almost unknown to the public, who was one day to be Prime Minister.

It was in 1922 that Richard Clement Attlee had entered Parliament as Labour Member for Limehouse. Now he was Under-Secretary for War. Later, in 1930, he was to become Chancellor of the Duchy of Lancaster, and then Postmaster-General. He had been educated at Haileybury and University College, Oxford, and was afterwards called to the Bar. In 1908, he became a Fabian, and in 1910 secretary of Toynbee Hall, a pioneer settlement in London where young men explored the problems of poverty at first hand. During the war he served with distinction with the South Lancashire Regiment and the Tank Corps in Gallipoli, Mesopotamia and France. In the Second World War he was to prove an invaluable deputy to Winston Churchill, and later he was to be Prime Minister, responsible for an orderly return to a better way of living; a slow process involving the retention of unpopular controls in order to give Britain a firm foundation on which to build her economy.

The mistakes of the early twenties would not be repeated in 1945. Demobilization, rehabilitation, the problems of emergency housing, the return of prisoners of war, the care of the homeless, the treatment of the enemy, the gradual return to more normal conditions, all these immense problems, much greater than they had been in the twenties, would be solved. Perhaps wisely, the people of Britain would choose a Labour Government to help them through the first difficult years of peace. A Government which they would grumble about, which offered no sugar on the pill, but methodically, even sternly, guided men and women out of uniform into civilian clothes. When the United States suddenly abandoned Lease-Lend, Attlee's Government would win a loan worth a billion pounds; the greatest loan ever made. It could be compared with Stanley Baldwin's abortive visit to Washington.

Hugh Dalton thought Clement Attlee the exact opposite of Ramsay MacDonald, who was 'showy, rhetorical, vain, jealous, snobbish, petulant, self-pitying, with a chip on his shoulder and an inferiority complex in his heart.' In contrast Attlee was 'splendidly free of these defects, straightforward, a real Democrat, a convinced Socialist, a good comrade and a loyal team man.' He would be remembered for giving freedom to India, Pakistan, Ceylon and Burma, a bold and wise decision taken on his own personal initiative.

But in 1924 Clement Attlee occupied a back seat in the Government, and all eyes were on MacDonald, who was Foreign Minister as well as Prime Minister. For a short time the League of Nations, in which Europe had gradually lost interest, was given a new lease of life through his energetic influence. The opening of the Assembly at Geneva on September 1, 192[illegible], was made memorable by his speech and by the address of M Herriot, the French Prime Minister. MacDonald urged arbitration as the only alternative to war. Next day, M. Herriot declared that arbitration must have force behind it. Thirty-one years later, in 1955, after a second tremendous war which was due at least partly to the failure of the members of the League, and the absence of a strong police force, the leaders of Russia, France, the United States and Britain met again and reached exactly the same conclusion, in the same place.

Diplomatic and trading relations with the Soviet Union were now re-opened, but the proposal that the Russians should be granted a loan raised Liberal opposition. At the same time it was revealed that the Prime Minister had been granted 30,000 £1 shares in McVitie and Price, the biscuit company. His friend, Sir Alexander Grant, the company director who had made the gift, had subsequently been created a baronet and had presented the Prime Minister with a Daimler car. MacDonald had no difficulty in explaining that they had been boyhood friends, and that the dividends on the shares, which were settled on him only for life, were to be used for the upkeep of the car. Further, Grant's name had been put down for a baronetcy during the Conservative regime. But the savage attacks made by the more Conservative newspapers greatly embarrassed the Government.

The final straw which broke the Government and turned the Liberals, not unwillingly, against it was the mishandling of the Campbell case. J. R. Campbell, acting editor of the Communist *Worker's Weekly*, had been arrested and his prosecution had been ordered for the publication of an article which, it was alleged, was intended to incite members of the armed forces to mutiny. When Labour Members protested, the prosecution was withdrawn. Sir Patrick Hastings, the Attorney-General, then made a feeble excuse for the change of policy, saying that Campbell was a wounded ex-serviceman. But the Government found it difficult to deny the accusation of political interference with the normal course of justice, and after a little over eight months of rule the first Labour Government fell. Perhaps its greatest achievement had been the encouragement of the building of municipal housing estates by the granting of a State subsidy.

But it had been unable to achieve what was expected of it, because it was controlled by the Liberals, and was plainly unprepared for power.

The general election which followed was made hopeless for Labour by the publication in the *Daily Mail* of a copy of a letter alleged to have been sent from the Communist International in Moscow to Communists in Britain. It urged an uprising among the workers and sought to undermine the armed forces. The *Daily Mail* headlines bore the words:

COMMUNIST PLOTS IN BRITAIN

RUSSIA PLANS TO CAUSE A REVOLUTION

ATTEMPTS TO SUBVERT ARMY AND NAVY

The document, called the 'Zinoviev Letter' and stated to have been signed by Zinoviev, the President of the Third (Communist) International, and counter-signed by the President of the Communist Party of Great Britain, appeared in the *Daily Mail* only four days before Britain went to the polls.

On October 10th Sir Eyre Crowe, the Permanent Under-Secretary to the Foreign Office, had been handed a copy of the letter. It was examined by the Foreign Office, who thought it genuine. Eleven days later a draft letter of protest, addressed to the Russian Ambassador in London, was sent to the Prime Minister for his approval. That afternoon the Foreign Office learned that the *Daily Mail* had another copy of the document, which they intended to publish next day.

Although it is now difficult to see how the letter could have affected Labour's cause, even if it were genuine, it must be remembered that the popular Press confused the Labour Party and Socialism with Communism, and lumped them all together as 'reds.' The 'Zinoviev Letter' was therefore used as an election device to create a 'red' scare. And although at the Queen's Hall in London MacDonald announced, 'Communism, as we know it, has nothing practical in common with us—it is a product of Tsarism and war mentality,' his opponents branded Labour as 'red.' Unionist election posters claimed that unemployment had risen under Socialist rule, and stated, '*Russia already owes us £722,500,000. Don't risk another £40,000,000, but vote Unionist!*' On other posters John Bull was warned that his pockets would speedily be emptied by Bolshevism. The *Illustrated London News* published a map of Britain showing Labour's rise to power and labelled the Socialist constituencies 'Red strongholds.' Although there was no connection between Labour and the Russian 'bogy,' the public rushed to vote for the Unionists, and for Mr. Baldwin.

For two days after its publication Mr. MacDonald gave no public explanation of the mysterious Zinoviev affair, and when at last he referred to it, only two days before polling day, he left the matter still in doubt. On the day that the letter was published Mr. J. H. Thomas said simply, 'We're bunkered.'

The Unionists swept the country with an overall majority of 210 seats. Labour, although they increased their total vote by a million, lost 42 seats. But the principal losers were the Liberals, who had forced them out of office. Their poll fell by more than one and a quarter million votes and they lost 119 out of 158 seats. It was the end of power for Liberalism in Britain. Stanley Baldwin's appeal for a 'sane, commonsense Government,' together with the 'Red scare,' had won the day.

It was several years before the Labour movement regained its full strength, indeed, had the Conservatives made a better job of their task during the next five years they might have stayed in power indefinitely.

For the first time the leaders of the three parties made use of broadcasting in their electioneering. Mr. Baldwin, however, was the only one who delivered a special address into a microphone at 2 LO, the Savoy Hill headquarters of the B.B.C. According to Lord (then Mr. J. W.) Reith, he was the only one of the three who took the opportunity seriously, going to Savoy Hill to see exactly what to do, asking intelligent questions, and preparing himself for the broadcast. Stuart Hibberd, the B.B.C. announcer, has recalled that he was always impressed by Baldwin's 'humanity and friendliness, also his great concentration while speaking at the microphone.' Apart from Hugh Walpole, Baldwin was the only person who ever spoke without a manuscript, and Hibberd felt that a manuscript would have bothered him, not helped him. He spoke slowly and deliberately, without using much voice, from a few headings written on a piece of folded paper which he kept twisting and turning nervously around his fingers. He remained all the time looking directly at the microphone, as though engaged in earnest conversation with a man immediately opposite him in the room. As soon as the broadcast was over Baldwin would start filling his cherrywood pipe, ready to light up immediately he got outside. While waiting for the engineer's report on the broadcast he laughed and joked like a schoolboy, talking in a homely and natural way.

Mr. Asquith, speaking from Paisley, was clearly heard in London, but Mr. MacDonald did not broadcast well, raising and lowering his voice, turning from side to side and striding about on the platform away from the microphone. 'Work, work, work for a majority!' he had urged his party leaders, and he was untiring in his efforts, addressing twenty-seven meetings in one day, so that he was exhausted at the end of the campaign.

When the election result was known the popular music-hall performers Norah Blaney and Gwen Farrar sang the verse:

Since Ramsay Mac
Has got the sack
It ain't gonna rain no mo'.

MacDonald's extraordinary silence over the fatal 'Zinoviev Letter,' which had contributed to the defeat of his party, led to attempts to remove him from the leadership. But Arthur Henderson, secretary and chief organizer of the party for over a generation, loyally supported MacDonald and insisted that his colleagues must not divide the opposition. Many Socialists blamed the Liberals for their fall. One of the characters in Alec Waugh's novel *Kept* said, 'No words can express my contempt for the treachery of the Liberal Party. They have sold themselves to Toryism. They have betrayed us. From 1910 to 1914 we, the Labour Party, kept the Liberals in office. We held the balance of power, and we held it honourably. The Liberals have held it, and they have betrayed their trust. We shan't forget. They shall pay for this, the traitors, when our turn comes.'

3

With the fall of Liberalism came the decline in the power of Lloyd George. In 1919 he had been the best-known Briton in the world. History books of the time set him above Pitt. Prime Minister since 1916, he looked like leading the country almost indefinitely. But in 1922, when the Coalition was suddenly dissolved, he was left out in the wilderness; never to return to power. Perhaps too many people remembered the pledges which he was unable to fulfil. Perhaps not enough people forgot Northcliffe's Press campaigns against the war leader.

In February 1919, Lloyd George had told his friend Lord Riddell, 'If I had considered my own happiness and my own place in history, I should have resigned when the Armistice was signed, but I could not do it. I was bound to go on.' Before 1922 the cartoonist David Low had drawn 'L. G.' as a fiery, inspired, active leader; in the late twenties and thirties he drew him as a little old woman wearing absurd hats, a ridiculous figure of fun without power. A major criticism of his period of rule was the generous sale of honours, peerages, baronetcies and knighthoods, which were exchanged for contributions to party funds. Of his work as a war minister John Buchan has said that it was 'in the class of Cromwell and Chatham.' He never quite lost his magic, and he still possessed it in 1940, towards the close of his life, when in one of his last speeches he called upon Neville Chamberlain to sacrifice his seals of office and contribute to victory in the war by resigning.

In March 1928, the old question of the 'Zinoviev Letter' was debated in the House of Commons, but hardly to Ramsay MacDonald's advantage. With a great show of dates, he complained that the letter had been published fourteen days after it had been received by the Foreign Office. True, said Mr. Baldwin, *but what had you intended to do about it?* Was it your intention to publish the letter then or at all if your hand had not been forced by the *Daily Mail?* To this penetrating but unfair question Mr. MacDonald replied evasively. As a result he came under suspicion of having been saved by the *Daily Mail* from practising a little diplomatic concealment on his own. Mr. Baldwin then produced a statement volunteered by a city man with no political loyalties to the effect that he had secured the copy of the letter from a Communist and had passed it on to the *Daily Mail*. *Punch* joked, 'It is thought in the best humorist circles that Mr. MacDonald considers the Zinoviev letter a fraud, because it isn't.'

Throughout his political career MacDonald continued to assert his dislike of anything to do with the Soviet Union. It should never be confused, he said, with Labour. Even the song, *The Red Flag*, was not good enough for Labour. At Newport he declared, 'We still want our great Labour song—a song which is not a ditty. *The Red Flag* is too much of a ditty, a "Lahdi, lahdi, lahdi da." ' George Bernard Shaw was less complimentary, comparing it to the 'funeral march of a fried eel.'

MacDonald now announced that in opposition the Labour Party 'would give the State, the people, the Commonwealth their fullest service.' They would serve the nation as they had served it as a Government—'It shall be a fight of gentlemen.'

And Liberalism? Soon after Mr. Asquith was created Lord Oxford he announced that the Liberals were still one and undivided. *Punch* suggested that perhaps he had underestimated their number. Could it not be as much as two, or a few more? Some years later A. P. Herbert wrote, 'I hope that no one in the Liberal Party suggests that I am one of those who would see it crushed out of existence. No, no. There is not so much fun in the world that we can afford to be without it. No, no. The Liberal Party must march on, two or three hearts that beat as one, though they vote as four or five.'

On November 4, 1924, Stanley Baldwin became Prime Minister for the second time. With him in the Cabinet were Sir Austen Chamberlain, Lord Birkenhead, the Marquess of Salisbury, Lord Balfour, Sir Laming Worthington-Evans, Sir Samuel Hoare, and Sir William Joynson-Hicks. The old guard was back. Winston Churchill was First Lord of the Treasury, and it is said that when he received news of the appointment tears came into his eyes. His return to the gold standard in 1925, criticized for the Opposition by Philip Snowden as likely to aggravate the existing grave condition of unemployment and trade depression, but advised by Montague Norman, led to the coal owners' attempt to reduce the wages of miners and lengthen their working hours, which in turn led to the General Strike. In April 1925, in *Punch*, Bernard Partridge depicted Mr. Churchill struggling with a monster serpent marked 'Trade depression and wasteful expenditure.' It was to occupy the Government's attention for its full term of office.

CHAPTER FIVE

Trouble with Germany

I

THE FIRST COUNTRY to enter into trade relations with Soviet Russia was Great Britain. It was Lloyd George's hope that an alliance with Russia would end the period of industrial depression from which Britain had suffered since 1920. On March 16, 1921, an agreement was signed, providing for the resumption of commercial relations, pending the signing of a peace treaty which would regulate future relations. By 1922 Russia had made similar arrangements with Germany, Norway, Austria and Italy. And the Soviet Government, which had previously repudiated all Russia's war debts, now suggested that it was willing to consider foreign claims at an international congress where recognition of the Soviet Union should be established.

Lloyd George therefore arranged with the other nations of Europe that a great economic conference should be held at Genoa. It was to be 'the largest gathering of nations that has ever met in the history of the world.' Privately, he admitted that he had no programme for the conference. Russia would be the feature of the discussions, and Lloyd George was confident that much would be achieved, although he was disappointed to learn that Lenin would not lead the Soviet delegation, as had been expected. At the last moment the Soviet leader had decided not to attend, announcing at a Press conference that Russia would not raise political problems at Genoa. 'We shall go as businessmen,' he said. 'In all bargaining there is an element of bluff. We, too, know how to bluff.'

The conference opened in April 1922 with thirty-four

states in attendance, these being all of Russia's creditors except the United States. At first the delegates confined themselves to the opening speeches, which were fully reported only in their own countries. After several weeks of discussion the talks finally broke down because the demands and counter-demands prevented any agreement. The negotiations were later resumed at The Hague, but no positive agreement could be reached. Bankers, industrialists, journalists, financiers, all the leading statesmen of Europe—except one—went away without having achieved the purpose of their journey. The one exception was Walther Rathenau, the German Foreign Minister.

Rathenau was a Jew, the son of Germany's biggest industrial and financial magnate, who had inherited great wealth. He was determined to help his country. The question of war guilt did not affect the economic situation, which was desperate. Germany's prosperity was, in his view, essential to Europe. The purchasing power of the world had fallen by forty per cent because of the war. He had a good case.

Opposite him across the table sat M. Chicherin, the Soviet Commissar for Foreign Affairs. To the casual observer it seemed that they had little in common, for no one imagined that Russia would support Rathenau's claim, that the Allied stranglehold on Germany should be relaxed. But no one knew which way the Russians would jump.

Rathenau was nervous. From the first day at Genoa it seemed certain that the Allies and the Russians were conspiring against him. He tried to speak privately to Lloyd George, without success. Then, suddenly, the Soviet delegation decided it was ready to make a pact with Germany. Rathenau was informed secretly, and was instructed that it must be signed at once, that day. He jumped into a car and drove to Rapallo, where the Russians were staying. Too late, Lloyd George telephoned to him for a talk; Rathenau was already on his way to sign the treaty. Next day the conference was stunned by the news that the pact had been concluded.

'I do not remember, even during the war itself, a sadder ending to an Easter day,' said Lloyd George's secretary, Edward Grigg. The Prime Minister insisted that only the cancellation of the pact would stop him returning home. But, realizing that he could hardly go back and admit defeat, he changed his mind and wrote a strong note of protest to Germany. A few days later his daughter Megan was dancing with a leading member of the German delegation. In France, Poincaré fumed. He was determined to safeguard Europe, and particularly France, from the ambitions of Germany.

When they parted, Rathenau said to Lloyd George, 'We shall never meet again. Within three months I shall be a dead man.' Two months later he lay in a pool of blood, shot by young extremists who believed him to be a Bolshevist and a traitor to his country. There was an uproar in Germany at the news of his death, but his murderers were never brought to justice.

Returning to London, Lloyd George was greeted by a large crowd at Victoria Station. The Duke of Atholl, representing the King, brought a royal message. Later the Prime Minister revealed that on several occasions the conference had nearly broken down, and only much energy and tact had prevented it. Poincaré had been anxious to break up the conference, but had not liked to send direct instruction to that effect.

Rathenau was not the only victim of Genoa. Lloyd George's halo was now worn out, and, as we have seen, the Conservatives forced him out of office.

2

One of the main difficulties was to obtain from Germany the reparation payments which she had agreed to make. Because she had no credit, and no other country in Europe would lend her money, it seemed impossible for her to pay. The war and the Allied blockade had destroyed her commercial trade, she could not export her goods quickly enough to buy the essentials which her people needed, and the result was inflation and a depreciation of currency. But the principal reason for her default was the feeling among her people, especially the industrialists, that the reparations were unjust.

In 1921, when Germany refused to sign a reparations plan put before her by the Allies, her representatives went home and were applauded as if they had won the war. The Allies, however, threatened to invade Germany unless she agreed to pay. She therefore signed the treaty, although she intended to default.

The first payment was made on August 31, 1921, but was immediately followed by a serious decline in the value of the mark. By the end of 1921 the German Government, finding itself in financial difficulties, pleaded that further payments would ruin the country.

Britain was particularly anxious that Germany should regain her prosperity because in pre-war days she had been the Empire's best customer. But no one wanted Germany to increase her exports at their expense. In 1922 Lloyd George therefore suggested that the economic stability of the former enemy was more important to Europe than the payment of reparations. People in Britain were becoming increasingly tolerant of Germany's protests that she could not pay. English troops in the army of occupation testified to the miserable condition of the working classes. Only Poincaré considered that Germany was deliberately avoiding payment. Was it not a fact that she was sending gold abroad? In London he told Bonar Law (who had succeeded Lloyd George) that Germany's bluff must be called; but the British policy remained firm, and in Paris, Bonar Law suggested that Germany should pay only one-fifth of the agreed figure.

France, Italy and Belgium angrily disagreed. And on

January 11, 1923, Poincaré's threat to take action came into force, and the occupation of the Ruhr began. French and Belgian forces marched into Germany, meeting with no resistance. But if she had no army, and could not push the invaders out, Germany could make things very unpleasant for them. She immediately stopped all delivery of reparations goods to France, forbade the inhabitants of the Ruhr to pay custom duties or coal taxes, and made it an offence to assist the occupying forces. The vast railway network of the Rhineland was put out of commission. In retaliation, France imposed severe restrictions, including censorship, and seized private property. Fighting broke out; 76 Germans were killed and 92 wounded by the Allies; 20 Allied soldiers were killed and 66 wounded by the Germans.

In April 1922 a French newspaper reported:

> Upper Silesia remains a secret arsenal of arms and war material which German military organizations maintain despite the vigilance of Allied troops of occupation.

In a suburb of Gleiwitz a secret store of munitions was found under a chapel. When French soldiers started to move it, an explosion killed twelve men and wounded eleven. In two years, forty-one French soldiers had been killed in this district. They were, said the French authorities, 'the victims of German reprisals.' Evidence was difficult to obtain because of the existence of many secret organizations.

In retaliation against the invasion the German authorities ordered all cafés and restaurants to display notices stating that Frenchmen and Belgians would not be served. German newspapers whipped up hatred against the French by printing absurd atrocity stories. The *Deutsche Allgemeine Zeitung* published an account of a negro sentry in Essen who, it was alleged, had been seen smashing open a German boy's head with his rifle and then eating his victim's brains.

As far as the invasion of the Ruhr was concerned, Britain blamed France, and read the newspaper reports with pious horror. But this was nothing new. France was usually blamed for most of the troubles in Europe, especially if Britain was not concerned.

According to Poincaré, the Germans could pay what they owed if they would only stabilize the mark by taxation. But Germany had no intention of doing this. Instead, she pushed her inflation to extremes by printing millions of extra marks with which to pay the resisting workers in the Ruhr, and to buy essential foodstuffs. It was clearly her intention to sabotage the reparations agreement; she hoped that her financial chaos would force the Allies to abandon their claims. Sooner or later, she was sure, America or Britain would persuade the French and Belgians to withdraw. But meanwhile the country was on the verge of ruin.

In 1914 a pound sterling had bought 24 marks. In June 1922 it bought 1,200 marks. On November 23, 1923, the rate stood at 95,000,000 marks to the pound, and only a week later a pound note could buy no less than 18,400,000,000 marks—if anyone wanted them. Millions of people were ruined, tens of thousands were facing starvation. To prove her plight to the world, Germany issued photographs showing people using mark notes as wallpaper.

Poor Germany. In Britain the Labour party believed that the resistance of the Ruhr workers was right and just. They even sent a sympathetic delegation to Germany, which embarrassed the French. Ramsay MacDonald and Arthur Henderson spoke in favour of their 'fellow workers.' Philip Snowden claimed that the Allies were behaving 'like beasts' towards Germany. *The Times* was openly pro-German. Most people agreed. The Liberals demanded that France should be compelled to evacuate the Ruhr at once, and should be brought before the Council of the League for causing a breach of international peace. Not unnaturally, the French Government gasped. Who had won the war, the Allies or the Germans? And whose side was England on?

Bonar Law, compelled by public opinion to take action,

persuaded Italy and Belgium to break with France. His successor, Stanley Baldwin, carried on the battle of words on behalf of Germany, whose economic collapse was at least partly responsible for British unemployment and the depression in Europe.

Millions of Germans were dreading the approach of the winter of 1923, for there was no coal and the factories and railways of the great industrial areas were at a standstill. French and Belgian sentries guarded the occupation camps. Then, suddenly, the collapse came. Nearly bankrupt, Germany gave up the unequal struggle and ordered the people of the Ruhr and the Rhineland to resume work. France sighed with relief, for the cost of maintaining the army of occupation had been heavy.

With the help of Dr. Hjalmar Schacht, a brilliant banker, Germany started to put her house in order. September 23, 1923, was the turning point, the day on which millions of German workers streamed back to the factories, to the coal mines, steel works and railways. It was the day on which the new Germany was born. The issue of the Reutenmark and later of the Reichsmark, with the revival of trade, backed by the American Dawes plan, helped to stabilize her finances. Germans, always hard workers, began to work harder than anyone in Europe in order to rebuild their national prosperity. And on July 31, 1925, new treaties guaranteeing future German payments were made, and the last of the French troops withdrew.

The Dawes plan, which provided for a loan of £40,000,000 was introduced at a conference of financial experts held in Berlin and presided over by the American banker, General Dawes. The plan was adopted at a subsequent conference in London, and came into force in September 1924. It was superseded by the Young Plan, drafted in Paris in 1929 at a conference presided over by Owen Young, of the United States. The plan was negotiated and accepted with certain modifications at the two Hague conferences in 1929 and 1930, and operated from September 1930. It was later replaced by the Hoover Plan.

Under the Dawes Plan, Germany paid the Allies 8,000,000,000 marks, and under the Young Plan some 3,500,000,000 marks, a total of 11,500,000,000 marks between September 1, 1924, and July 15, 1931. Her payments during the Ruhr occupation are valued at about 1,750,000,000 marks. An American estimate gives the total German payments between 1919 and July 15, 1931, as about 39,000,000,000 marks.

3

In December 1925, a pact was signed between Germany, Italy, France, Poland, Czechoslovakia and Britain. This was the Locarno Pact, an unimportant treaty bringing no tangible advantage or disadvantage, except to Germany.

The Allied Powers had decided to magnify the event into a great occasion, claiming that it was the 'final peace settlement.' This announcement led Dr. Gustav Stresemann, who had become Germany's foreign minister during her financial crisis, to plan that Germany should be well represented at the conference. Under his foreign policy, which continued until his death in 1929, Germany gradually gained all her objectives. First, the American Dawes Plan brought economic stability, leaving the way clear for commercial treaties with France, Britain, Belgium and Luxembourg. Then came Stresemann's great triumph, the signing of the Locarno Pact, which gave Germany the recognition she sought. For the first time since the war the representatives of all the major European countries sat together as equals, and not as victors and vanquished. This was Stresemann's chance to show that Germany was at least equal to the others. It was an opportunity that must not be missed.

In Britain and France the announcement that a treaty was

to be signed at Locarno which would safeguard world peace was greeted with great enthusiasm. In Germany, however, the new National Party, which had nominated the aged Field Marshal von Hindenburg as President of the Reich, at first led public opinion against the pact. But they reckoned without Stresemann.

The meeting place for the conference was chosen as Locarno, on Lake Maggiore, out of deference to Mussolini. The pact hardly concerned Italy, but the other statesmen desired his company, wishing to draw him closer into European affairs, and he was anxious to attend in order to impress the Italians. It promised to be the greatest international event since Versailles, and Mussolini, whose position was still insecure, welcomed the chance to strut and be photographed with the statesmen of Europe.

On the third day of the conference Stresemann electrified the meeting by saying that he hoped it was not only Germany who would have to make sacrifices in the cause of peace. Had not his country, by her example, assured Europe of a permanent peace? And if this were so, had not the time come to change some of the things which were injuring Germany, which she found dishonourable? Germany needed colonies. Why could she not have them? She should also be freed from Allied control, and from the stigma of occupation. Germany alone had disarmed; surely other countries should follow her example?

Sir Austen Chamberlain raised his arms in surprise. M. Briand, the French Prime Minister, nearly fell off his seat. Then, in a brilliant speech, he persuaded the Germans not to cause difficulties at such a critical moment. The creation of a spirit of harmony was surely the most important purpose of the conference. Later, he said, he hoped that the pact would bring results 'in this sense.'

This promise of more generous treatment, of recognition, was exactly what Stresemann wanted. It was the perfect finish to twelve days of negotiation. On October 16, 1925, the pact was provisionally signed in Locarno; on December 1, it was definitely signed in London. Four arbitration treaties between Germany and France and between Belgium, Poland and Czechoslovakia were signed, and two treaties of guarantee between France, Poland and Czechoslovakia. The treaty was to come into force as soon as Germany became a member of the League. Triumphantly, Dr. Stresemann returned home.

With the signing of the pact a great wave of joy spread over Europe. In Switzerland the church bells pealed out their message of hope. In Britain people flocked to church to thank God, at special services.

In the Mansion House in London, M. Briand had said, 'The spirit of solidarity now takes the place of distrust and suspicion. Opposite me sit the German delegates. That does not mean that I do not remain a good Frenchman, as they remain, I am sure, good Germans. But in the light of these treaties we are Europeans only . . . we must collaborate in a common labour of peace, and our nations, which on the battlefield showed equal heroism, will discover in other phases of human activity means of emulation no less glorious.'

In Germany, Chancellor Luther announced, 'The German people will approve of the Locarno agreement only when they concretely experience its practical steps.' He demanded the evacuation of the Rhineland by the Allies, as proof of the Locarno spirit. But he and the other leaders of Germany knew that this was the beginning of the revival of their country as a Great Power. A year later the first of the three occupied zones of the Rhineland was returned to Germany. Soon a date was fixed for the complete evacuation.

'This treaty,' said Sir Austen Chamberlain, 'is the dividing line between the war years and peace.'

M. Briand set the mood for many similar pacifist outbursts. 'Away with rifles, machine-guns, cannon,' he exclaimed. 'Clear the way for conciliation, arbitration, peace!'

Slowly but surely the way was being cleared for the new Germany, and Hitler. But in London the 'Arbitrate First' League sent out vans carrying notices referring to the new spirit of peace created by the Locarno Treaty.

1000 Miles
up the
AMAZON

In an Ocean Liner.
Fare from **£90**

The R.M.S. "**HILDEBRAND**" will sail from Liverpool on **MARCH 12th,** July 14th, Sept. 15th, Nov. 17th.

Write for Illustrated Booklet of these Six Weeks' Cruises to Dept. I.L.N.

THE BOOTH LINE

11, ADELPHI TERRACE, LONDON. CUNARD BUILDING, LIVERPOOL.

CHAPTER SIX

Trouble in Ireland

I

THE WAR had postponed the settlement of the Irish problem, which had existed since 1801, when Ireland had been absorbed into the United Kingdom. Twice during the latter part of the nineteenth century Gladstone had introduced a bill to give the Irish Home Rule, but each time it was defeated. Between 1912 and 1914 a third bill had brought the country to the verge of civil war. The Protestants in Ulster were determined not to become a minority in an Irish Catholic Parliament. The majority of Irishmen, however, were equally determined that the whole country should be ruled by one house of representatives, free of English control. This constituted the Irish problem.

In 1916 a republic had been declared in Dublin, but strong action was taken and fifteen revolutionary leaders were executed. Two years later the position, apart from the Ulster question, had resolved into a struggle between the Irish Nationalist Party, which wanted home rule, and the Sinn Feiners, who demanded an Irish Republic completely independent of Britain. Eamon de Valera, Arthur Griffith and Michael Collins were the leaders of the Sinn Fein, or Irish Republican Party.

At the first meeting of the illegal Irish Parliament, the Dail Eireann, in January 1919, delegates were chosen to represent Ireland at the Versailles Conference. But at Versailles the status of the 'so-called Irish Republic' was not recognized. Next day, de Valera was elected first

President of the Irish Republic, and ministers were appointed under him to govern the country.

In Britain there were strong feelings against the complete independence of Ireland, especially if Ulster was to be included in the new State without being allowed to choose her own future. The average Englishman found it difficult to believe that Ireland felt no loyalty to King George and the throne, and he did not really understand the position.

Lloyd George's Government of Ireland Bill of 1920 provided for two Parliaments, one for the six northern counties and the other for the rest of the country. Although a measure of Home Rule was granted, the ties with the Crown were still strong. Northern Ireland readily accepted the plan, and at Belfast on June 22, 1921, King George opened the Parliament of Northern Ireland. In his speech he said:

> 'The eyes of the whole Empire are on Ireland today—that Empire in which so many nations and races have come together in spite of ancient feuds, and in which new nations have come to birth within the lifetime of the youngest in this hall. . . I speak to you from a full heart when I pray that my coming to Ireland to-day may prove to be the first step towards an end of strife amongst the people, whatever their race or creed. In that hope I appeal to all Irishmen to pause, to stretch out the hand of forbearance and conciliation, to forgive and forget, and to join in making for the land which they love a new era of peace, contentment and goodwill.'

But it was not to be. Outside Ulster the Act of Partition was not accepted. The Sinn Feiners refused to recognize the new Southern Parliament, which met in June but never met again. Sinn Fein now took over control of the island, except for the six northern counties, and formed a Republican Army which was much stronger than the British forces. The Royal Irish Constabulary immediately started recruiting volunteers to oppose the new army, fitting out their men with khaki uniforms, black hats, and police armbands. They became known as the 'black and tans,' and were certainly far more violent than the regular police.

IV. *War in Ireland: Street fighting in Dublin, July 1922.*

M. Briand, David Lloyd George and Marshal Foch at Chequers, February 1921.

Mr. and Mrs. Stanley Baldwin, 1924.

V. *Watching the motor-racing at Brooklands, Surrey, 1922.*

Ladies like the "Standard."

A LADY likes to own a "Standard" because she knows that whatever company she may be in she will be proud of her car. People know its reputation, its quality, and its complete dependability. And driving a "Standard" is so easy. It means simplicity, ease of control and freedom from all trouble.

Comfiness and ample protection against the weather add zest to the pleasures of the drive. Naturally, ladies like the "Standard."

Registered Trade Mark.

"Count them on the Road"

The All British

Standard

Light Cars: 11 h.p. & 14 h.p.

£235 and £375

Saloons from £450

Dunlop Tyres.

Send for particulars.

The Standard Motor Co., Ltd., Coventry.
London Showrooms: 49, Pall Mall, S.W.1.

ECCLES

TRAILER CARAVANS

Completely Furnished from £105

The IDEAL HOLIDAY.

CARAVANS, GOSTA GREEN, BIRMINGHAM.

Write for Literature.

"ECCLES have hundreds on the road."

Women were the new customers, eagerly wooed by motor manufacturers—and the new trailer caravans were all the rage—from £105 each.

A reign of terror now swept over Ireland, dividing families and villages. During the first half of 1921 there were two Governments, and the forces of both were out of hand. Gangster tactics were employed by both sides. There was rioting in all the big cities, expecially in Dublin, Cork, Belfast, and Londonderry, with serious disturbances across the border. In the first seven months of 1921, 244 police and 94 soldiers were killed, and 428 police and 204 soldiers wounded. On May 25, 1921, soldiers of the Republican Army seized the Dublin Customs House and set it alight. In the battle six Irish soldiers were killed, twelve wounded and seventy captured. All over Ireland army officers were ambushed and attacked by the 'rebels,' police were killed, armoured cars were overturned, trains were derailed. The vengeance of the armed forces was swift, and not always just. The report of the Labour Party's commission on Ireland, published in 1921, concluded with the words, 'Things are being done in the name of Britain which must make her name stink in the nostrils of the whole world.' The party was not alone in thinking that the British Army should be withdrawn.

In October 1921, a conference was held in London to attempt to solve the problem. The Coalition was still in power, and the British representatives included Lloyd George, Winston Churchill, Sir Hamer Greenwood, Sir Austen Chamberlain, and Lord Birkenhead. The Sinn Feiners sent Arthur Griffith, Michael Collins, Eamon J. Duggan, and Gavan Duffy. All sat nervously together around a large table in 10 Downing Street. The Irish delegates, walking through crowds in Whitehall, had been met at the door by the Prime Minister. Only a year previously barricades had been erected in Downing Street as a protection against Irish rioters.

After eight weeks of anxious argument and discussion a document was signed which established the Irish Free State as having the same constitutional status within the Empire as Canada. Northern Ireland was not to be included in the Free State if she wished to remain independent.

The treaty split the ranks of Sinn Fein. De Valera, who had not attended the meetings in London, strongly opposed it, saying that Ireland was too near Britain for the plan to work. Arthur Griffith accepted the arrangement, and finally it was agreed to in the Irish Parliament by a vote of 64 to 57, whereupon de Valera resigned as President, and Griffith succeeded him.

2

Ireland was now plunged into civil war. The opponents of the new regime vowed that they would destroy the 'Irish Government working under British authority.' De Valera's irregular Irish Republican Army spread terror throughout the country. Opposing them, the regular Free State Army, under Michael Collins, attempted to preserve law and order. Declaring war on England, de Valera's men destroyed houses, railways, roads, bridges, and summarily executed all 'traitors.' On August 16, 1922, Michael Collins was ambushed and killed.

By January 1923, order had been restored, largely due to the discipline and initiative of William Cosgrave and Kevin O'Higgins, the leaders of the provisional Government. Reprisals were severe, and law and order were drastically enforced. On December 6, 1922, the Irish Free State was established by Royal Proclamation, and by the new year all British troops had left.

In England the Irish troubles and the murder, pillage, burning and looting which had devastated the island were soon forgotten. Perhaps they had never been fully appreciated. But in London an echo of the troubles stirred the country when Field-Marshal Sir Henry Wilson, the former Chief of General Staff, was murdered by two Republican gunmen. Dressed in his Field-Marshal's uniform, he had just returned from unveiling a war memorial at Liverpool Street Station when he was shot on the steps of his Eaton Place house. Six bullets struck him, and he died on the pavement. His murderers were chased by policemen and civilians, and were finally caught, but only after they had shot a policeman in the leg, another in the stomach, and had wounded a chauffeur. After a short trial they were hanged.

The murder, it was revealed, was a reprisal for the shooting of a Roman Catholic publican in Ulster. Sir Henry, as a member of the Northern Parliament, had been judged responsible.

From 1922 to 1933 the Irish Free State prospered under its Prime Minister, William Cosgrave. There were often troubles over the boundary, but relations with Britain gradually improved. The water power of the River Shannon was harnessed in a great electricity scheme, Englishmen invested money in Ireland. But when de Valera replaced Cosgrave many of the links between the two countries were cut. In 1932 a bill was introduced in the Dail which abolished the oath of allegiance to the British Crown, and withheld land annuities due to Britain, who retaliated by placing heavy duties on Irish farm products entering Britain. The Free State then imposed similar duties on British cement, coal, iron, and steel. Three years later the British Nationality Acts were repealed, depriving Irish Free State citizens of the advantages of British citizenship. Finally, in July 1949, the Republic of Ireland came into being, the last ties with Britain were officially broken, and both countries could settle down to regard each other with respect across the Irish Channel, and forget the past.

CHAPTER SEVEN

The Wonderful Wireless

I

AT THE END of the First World War broadcasting did not exist. By the end of the second war it had spread like a net all over the world. It was destined to alter the daily habits of Britons more than anything that the decade produced.

In 1899 the young Italian inventor Marconi had transmitted Morse signals across the English Channel. A primitive aerial fixed to a flying kite on the coast of Newfoundland picked up signals sent three thousand miles across the ocean, from Cornwall. Two years later, Marconi, on board the *S.S. Philadelphia*, received signals over a distance of 2,099 miles, from shore to ship. With the development of the thermionic valve, perfected in 1904 by Professor Ambrose Fleming, it became possible for speech and music, as well as Morse, to be relayed by what was now known as wireless telephony, or wireless for short.

According to P. P. Eckersley, the first time that speech was relayed to an aeroplane in flight was about 1915, at Brooklands, Surrey. A year later the Irish Republicans transmitted a message from the wireless station in Dublin, announcing the proclamation of the Republic. This message, published in newspapers in America after being picked up by ships at sea, was probably the first of its kind, conveying news.

Broadcasting as we know it did not start in Britain until 1920, when the Marconi Company's experimental station at Chelmsford was opened. On February 23rd, Marconi employees started transmitting readings, and then music.

The first broadcasts were readings from catalogues, or recitals of extracts from train time-tables, relayed in order to test reception. Thus, a sentence like 'The London, Brighton and South Coast Railway trains to Brighton leave London from Victoria Station' would be repeated several times during an hour, being picked up by many amateur wireless enthusiasts who had made their own receiving sets. Broadcasts started with the words, 'This is the Marconi valve transmitter from the Marconi works at Chelmsford.' At first no one thought of using the new medium for entertainment, but after a few weeks of reading, singers were asked to perform, and were paid for their services. These early broadcasts aroused considerable interest among amateurs, and the novelty of 'listening in' and twiddling a knob in order to hear Chelmsford spread across the country.

On June 15, 1920, Dame Nellie Melba sang from the Marconi station, at the invitation of the *Daily Mail*. Her voice was clearly heard in Paris and Berlin and within a radius of a thousand miles. More than any other, this broadcast drew the attention of the public to the possibilities of the wireless. The *Daily Mail*, which had paid a fee of a thousand pounds to the singer, reported next day that it was 'a wonderful half-hour, when art and science joined hands.'

By the end of 1921 over three thousand wireless amateurs had asked the Post Office, who controlled wireless telegraphy in Britain, to provide regular programmes. In the following April the Postmaster-General announced that he was considering 'what additional facilities may be granted for "broadcastings" of general interest.' In America, public interest in the new phenomenon was so great that nearly a million people now owned receiving sets on which they heard concerts, bands, speeches, lectures, sermons, weather forecasts and market prices. In Britain it was possible, on most afternoons, to listen to recitals from the Eiffel Tower; on Tuesday evenings at seven there was a Marconi concert from Chelmsford; on Thursday evenings there were musical selections from the Hague, and on Sundays from 3 to 5 p.m. a concert. Many amateurs were also transmitting music, songs and speech, but in Britain there were still no broadcasting organization, no regular programme. The Hague radio band, a quartet, played into an enormous, man-sized cardboard horn.

After considerable deliberation the Post Office entrusted the task of entertaining the nation to a single company, the British Broadcasting Company, which was formed with a capital of only £100,000, mainly subscribed by six wireless equipment manufacturers. It lasted for four years, and set the standard for the public corporation which followed.

Listeners were required by the Postmaster-General to pay 10s. for an annual listening licence, half of which went to the B.B.C. Many felt that the new medium would challenge the newspapers and the newsreels. Would people listen to the news instead of reading it? Lord Northcliffe feared broadcasting, which he said would eventually enable people to subscribe to all the sporting, financial, political and general news, 'spoken in any room you choose in your own home.'

By December 1922, the B.B.C.'s forty hours a week consisted of three hours of news, five and a quarter hours for children, forty-five minutes of talks, an hour of religion, and the rest music. By 1923 nearly half a million listeners were licensed, but the B.B.C. estimated that some further two hundred thousand had no licences.

Although the first sets were crude and reception was unreliable, these difficulties were soon overcome. Headphones and the cat's whisker gave way in time to loudspeakers, and batteries to power from the mains. At first long poles were erected at the end of gardens, or on roof-tops, to hold elaborate aerials. 'Listening in, was a solemn ritual, like watching television in later years. Crystal sets and headphones could be bought for only a few shillings, and a complete set for under ten shillings. The wireless set was accepted as a feature of the average house, and soon the coils, wires, loudspeaker and controls of the primitive sets were combined into one box or cabinet. Indoor aerials were installed in attics.

Perhaps it was Lord Northcliffe's fear of rivalry that led the *Daily Mail* to enter the commercial radio field in 1922, by renting an amateur station in Holland and broadcasting to Britain. Many other newspapers and industries considered that the monopoly granted to the B.B.C. was wrong, and demanded a commercial station in England. By the end of 1923 there were B.B.C. stations in London, Manchester, Newcastle, Cardiff, Glasgow, Aberdeen, Birmingham and Bournemouth. During 1924 ten 'booster' or relay stations were built. As new stations covered more parts of the country, so the number of listeners grew.

The first wireless-telephone conversation between the United States and Britain took place in the early hours of the morning of January 15, 1923. Mr. H. B. Thayer, President of the American Telephone and Telegraph Company, spoke from his office in Broadway, New York, to journalists assembled at the New Southgate works of the Western Electric Company. Communication was maintained for two hours, a transmitter having been installed at Rocky Mount, Long Island, connected with New York by telephone. At new Southgate a special receiver with eight valves was used, the indoor frame aerial being about six feet square. Both headphones and a loudspeaker were used.

Schoolboys were among the keenest of the amateurs. When the Prince of Wales visited Mill Hill School he said, 'I was interested the other day to hear that Mill Hill had got America. I think this school is among the first of the schools to wireless the Atlantic, and I congratulate you.'

To others the 'magic box' remained a mystery. When the Archbishop of Canterbury heard a wireless set for the first time, in March 1923, he asked if it were necessary to leave a window open in order to hear the programmes.

In 1924 King George had his own set, presented by the B.B.C. and designed by Captain P. P. Eckersley. The cabinet was of mahogany with ebony panels and inlaid ivory lines, and it was mounted on an ebony stand. Four pairs of headphones, described as 'head-telephones,' were contained in a compartment above the loudspeaker.

In July of that year the new wonder had been demonstrated for the benefit of blinded soldiers from St. Dunstan's at an exhibition of their work in the Strand. The *Co-optimists*, appearing at the Royalty Theatre in Dean Street, gave two performances of excerpts from their show, which were transmitted to the exhibition from the Marconi laboratory in St. Anne's Court, Dean Street. Some entertainment bodies, notably theatrical managements and concert agents, were opposed to broadcasting from theatres, and decided to stop concert artistes from broadcasting in the studios. If they could be heard on the B.B.C., argued the managers, who would pay to see and hear them on the stage? The National Opera Company, however, allowed their performances to be broadcast.

Confusion had arisen over licences, no provision having been made for their issue to people who had made their own sets or assembled them. The Postmaster-General having failed to settle the question, a government committee was set up, which decided that constructors' licences should be issued at 15s. a year, out of which the B.B.C. would receive 12s. 6d.

By the end of 1925 it was estimated that since the opening of a new high-power transmitter at Daventry, 85 per cent of the population could hear programmes on a crystal set. Great improvements had been made in transmission, and theatre managements had agreed that excerpts from twenty-six stage shows could be broadcast each year, each lasting for thirty minutes. No objection was now made to theatrical artistes being engaged by the B.B.C., but no agreement had been reached with the concert industry, and many eminent performers were unable to broadcast.

There were, of course, many unrehearsed incidents during

the early days. One afternoon announcer Freddy Grisewood, having put on a *Tannhauser* gramophone record, was horrified to discover that it was going round 'at about a hundred miles an hour.' He was too inexperienced to stop it, apologize, and begin again, so he let it run on—hoping that no one would notice. Next day there were several letters, and one listener said it was the most exhilarating piece of music he had heard, a great improvement on the original. The listener was Sir Thomas Beecham.

On another occasion Grisewood announced His Holiness Pope Pius, for some unaccountable reason, as 'His Holiness the Pipe.' Later, when making an announcement about Scotland Yard equipping policemen with motor cycles and side-cars he announced, 'The police are changing their combinations this winter, as they are not suitable.'

While it was still at Savoy Hill the B.B.C. was a lively and informal company. There was a certain amount of irregularity about the programmes, and on one occasion the Bishop of London was heard to end a religious address with the words 'I *don't* think!' He had been cut off while remarking, 'I *don't* think that was too long, do you?'

From the earliest days Mr. Reith insisted on the announcers wearing evening dress. A man of strong religious conviction, he was determined that broadcasting should be conducted as a national service, with definite standards, and not used for entertainment alone. He wanted the service to reach the greatest possible number of homes, and to provide 'all that is best in every department of human knowledge, endeavour and achievement.'

One of the developments of broadcasting was the production of a weekly magazine containing the B.B.C. programmes. When London newspapers refused to publish the programmes unless they were paid for, the London programme was printed in Selfridge's advertisement column in the *Pall Mall Gazette*. The newspapers immediately lifted the embargo, but plans were made by the B.B.C. to produce their own *Radio Times* with the co-operation of George Newnes. The first issue appeared in September 1923, a quarter of a million copies being distributed. At least half a million could have been sold.

In 1925 the B.B.C. broadcast symphony concerts conducted by Sir Edward Elgar and Sir Landon Ronald, and a series of popular concerts was arranged in collaboration with leading newspapers, including the *News of the World*, the *Evening Standard* and *Answers*. Madame Tetrazzini sang in the *Evening Standard* concert.

The radio correspondent of the *Illustrated London News* now advised his readers that 'with all types of receiving sets, broadcasts must be "tuned in" by turning the controlling knobs until the apparatus responds to the wavelength of the broadcasting station. With a simple crystal set, tuning is accomplished by turning one knob, and by adjusting the crystal detector until broadcast sounds are heard clearly.' Most multi-valve sets, he explained, were turned by rotating two condensors until their dials were in proper relationship for reception. The correct setting could be found only by 'careful and slow adjustment.'

But still the new wonder of the age remained a mystery to many people. A lady who bought a set early in 1924 telephoned the shop two days later demanding that an engineer should call immediately, because she could not alter the speed of the dance music.

'How soon shall we be able to see by radio?' asked a newspaper correspondent in 1925. 'Already photographs have been transmitted and received by radio; but that feat has been improved upon by Mr. J. L. Baird, a Scotsman who has demonstrated in London recently the transmission of animate objects.' As early as January 1925 a demonstration had been given by Dr. Fournier D'Albe, in which the word 'Hullo' was relayed on to a screen. Baird's first full demonstration was given on January 27, 1926, in an upper room in Frith Street, Soho.

At the second Wireless Exhibition, held in 1924 at the Royal Albert Hall, the 'Fitton One' set was displayed. With only one valve, this operated a loudspeaker in a small room, and could receive stations within a radius of twenty miles, although with an outdoor aerial the radius was about a hundred miles. The instructions issued with the set stated, 'The two tuning knobs must be turned *very slowly*, otherwise the spot at which reception occurs will be missed.'

On January 2, 1924, the *Rand Daily Mail* announced that a reader, Mr. G. Bekker of Port Elizabeth, had 'listened in' to a wireless concert 'broadcasted' by the B.B.C. London station, 2 LO. The music and other items were loud enough to operate a loudspeaker. The average listener, however, found that programmes were constantly interrupted by oscillations, atmospherics and other strange noises. When the Northolt station sent out Morse, it was claimed, many sets tuned in to 2 LO received nothing but 'howls' and 'wheezings.'

At this time the principal stations in Britain were:

London 2 LO
Chelmsford 5 XX
Hull 6 KH
Leeds–Bradford 2 LS
Manchester 2 ZY
Liverpool 6 LV
Newcastle 5 NO
Sheffield 6 FL
Belfast 2 BE
Aberdeen 2 BD
Dundee 2 DE
Edinburgh 2 EH
Glasgow 5 SC
Nottingham 5 NG
Bournemouth 6 BM
Cardiff 5 WA
Birmingham 5 IT

The opening of the high-powered transmitter at Daventry in July 1925 was an important step forward, because it gave the country a national programme. In the same year Bransby Williams, Norah Blaney and Gwen Farrar, and that great favourite of the music-halls and the gramophone, Sir Harry Lauder, broadcast for the first time. By 1927, when broadcasting lasted for ten hours a day, many reputations had been established by the microphone. The voices of Stuart Hibberd and Rex Palmer were probably the best-known in the country and such names as Wish Wynne, Norman Long and Christopher Stone were famous. Christopher Stone had arrived at Savoy Hill, the 2 LO studio, to deputize for his brother-in-law Compton Mackenzie, but had stayed on to become one of the most popular wireless celebrities of the time, and continued broadcasting for over thirty years. His quiet, engaging and confidential conversations with listeners while selecting gramophone records endeared him to millions.

New comedians were discovered by the wireless, Leonard Henry, Stainless Stephen, Clapham and Dwyer, Tommy Handley and Vivian Foster (the Vicar of Mirth) reaching a great new public which later wanted to see them on the stage. The power of the microphone brought sudden fame to Reginald Foort, the cinema organist, J. H. Squire and his Octette, and Albert Sandler, the violinist; the Savoy Orpheans and Savoy Havana bands became the most famous in the country. Mabel Constanduros and Michael Hogan, partners for nine years, appeared in the *Mrs. Buggins* sketches, a series of extraordinary family adventures in which father, mother, Grandma and Alfie enjoyed hilarious adventures.

In addition to entertainment, the B.B.C. provided a full measure of instruction. There were seldom less than three talks a day, on every imaginable subject. In time, broadcasting made good music popular, and raised the national standard of musical appreciation. It also created employment in the musical world, which was hit by the coming of sound films and the disbanding of cinema orchestras.

When the B.B.C. took over the Promenade Concerts at Queen's Hall, orchestral music was assured of a lease of life which astonished even Sir Henry Wood. The B.B.C. Symphony Orchestra, conducted by Adrian Boult, helped to raise the standard of music, and the formation in 1928 of the first B.B.C. Dance Orchestra and the appointment of Jack Payne as resident leader added dignity to the 'jazz band' craze and brought ballroom dancing into the home. When, in 1932, Jack Payne was succeeded by Henry Hall, his famous signature tune 'Say it with Music' was less frequently heard on the wireless; he took his band around Britain on a series of personal appearance tours which attracted hundreds of thousands of listeners.

A broadcasting personality of the late twenties who retained his popularity and widened his interests, Payne appealed to family audiences by providing a band show full of variety. Fox-trots, the latest waltz, a novelty number, the newest comedy song, all could be heard in his programmes. His gramophone records, like those of Jack Hylton—whose orchestra was mainly a stage show band—sold in hundreds of thousands. Broadcasting was not a highly paid business, but the reputation which could be established through regular programmes ensured success for many years to come.

In 1924 Madame Galli-Curci, the American coloratura singer, whose fame had been built up by gramophone recordings, received £20,000 for a six weeks' tour of Britain. In America she regularly received from £1,000 to £1,500 for a single concert. She was now one of the singers whose recordings could be heard, over and over again, on the wireless. The magic of Caruso filled the humblest room; listeners could listen to Paderewski giving a ninety-minute piano recital from Savoy Hill, and in the same week hear the finest orchestras in the country from London, Birmingham, Manchester, Bournemouth and other stations. The Bournemouth Municipal Orchestra, conducted by Sir Dan Godfrey, became well known throughout the country.

The first regular news bulletin and the first Children's Hour programme had been heard in 1922. In January 1923 the first act of *The Magic Flute*, relayed from Covent Garden, had marked the first outside broadcast. In the same month the first variety programme was presented, and a month later came the first wireless appeal and the first complete dance band programme, provided by Marius B. Winter.

It was in August 1923 that the first time-signal had been heard, and a month later came the first S.O.S. message. That October, dance music was relayed from the Savoy Hotel in London, leading to the popularity of the Savoy Orpheans and Savoy Havana bands. By 1924 the most popular items in the programmes were the relays of operas, with the Savoy bands a close second. The talks, however, were less popular.

The wireless had now replaced the parlour piano, and five-finger exercises next door had given way to the music of the Boyd Neel String Quartette. Over 20,000 pianos had been imported every year before the war, mostly from Germany, but in 1928 there were only seventy-five imported. Although in some Welsh homes the black upright piano with the runner along the top was still a sign of respectability, and might be played when visitors called, its day was dwindling. The radio had made it almost obsolete. As *Country Life* observed,

> There is no need whatever to have the wireless set in one of the main living rooms. It can be kept in the telephone room or some other place where its wires and its batteries are out of the way. Points similar to those used for plugging in electric standard lamps or radiators may then be fitted up in the drawing-room, dining-room, library and so on. Further, if the receiving set has that margin of power to which reference has been made in previous articles, reception is not limited to one room at a time. It is simple, for instance, so to arrange matters, that loud-speakers may be used simultaneously if desired, in the drawing-room, the nursery and the servants' hall.

When, on April 16, 1926, Father Ronald Knox broadcast a humorous account of a mythical unemployment riot in London, many listeners were alarmed. Speaking from Edinburgh, he let his imagination run riot as he described a fictitious revolution. Hundreds of listeners telephoned to

Savoy Hill, thinking that the Houses of Parliament had really been attacked, and that, as Father Knox had told them, people were being roasted alive in Trafalgar Square.

In the autumn of 1926 visitors to the Radio Exhibition at Olympia were able to see a specially-built broadcasting studio from which programmes were being relayed. The walls were of glass, and all day an endless stream of visitors passed by, watching the performers. On Armistice Day 1927 the new short-wave transmitter at Chelmsford was used to broadcast the British Legion Rally from the Royal Albert Hall to the world, and Stuart Hibberd, the announcer, was able to say in the opening announcement:

> This is the British Broadcasting Corporation calling the British Isles, the British Empire, the United States of America and the Continent of Europe from London, England, through Coventry 5 XX, and through Chelmsford 5 SW. . .

In America the programme was received in New York and was distributed through the network of the National Broadcasting Company.

In January 1929 the B.B.C. published the first number of *The Listener*, in which was printed every week a selection of the talks delivered during the previous week. The first edition contained contributions by Sir Walford Davies, Sir Oliver Lodge and the Archbishop of York.

With the coming of the thirties, and the move from Savoy Hill to Broadcasting House, Langham Place, the B.B.C. was fast growing up. Its finest hour was in the 1939 war, when it became the voice of Britain and the spokesman of the free nations of the world. But its record during the twenties was distinguished, and it set a high standard of entertainment, education, enlightenment and taste.

Established 1808
Dunville's
AND V R
WHISKIES
13/6 Bottle 7/- Half-bot.
12/6 Bottle 6/6 Half-bot.
Read what The Lancet (the leading Medical Journal) of 20th August, 1921, says of Dunville's Whiskies :—
"Evidence of a proper degree of maturation. . . . . Particularly smooth, pleasant, and characteristic of the highest grade of Irish Whisky. . . . . Odour and flavour maintained. . . Examined in 1908 and 1914. No falling off in their good qualities.
DUNVILLE'S
SPECIAL LIQUEUR
WHISKY
DUNVILLE'S
V R
WHISKY
BELFAST
On sale at leading Hotels, Restaurants, and Bars, also all Wine and Spirit Merchants for home supplies.
DUNVILLE & CO., LTD., Royal Irish Distilleries, BELFAST.
LONDON OFFICES—239 & 241 Shaftesbury Avenue, W.C.2.
S.V.22A

CHAPTER EIGHT

Wembley

I

UNDER THE INFLUENCE of Rudyard Kipling and through the tireless devotion of generations of servants of the Colonial Office and army officers, most of whom had made considerable contributions to help the welfare of those born under the Union Jack, the British Empire had been, up to the early twenties, almost a cult. Dr. C. E. M. Joad recalled it as being, in his younger days, 'unique in history, a testimony to an immense and continuing patriotism, a monument of disinterested self-sacrifice, a witness to racial superiority, which, conscious of itself, willingly accepted the burdens which its superiority imposed.'

Bernard Shaw, however, disliked the Empire for its 'imperial aggression, in which, under pretext of exploration and colonization, the flag follows the filibuster and trade follows the flag.'

The truth lay somewhere between. To millions of underprivileged people, incapable of governing themselves, the Empire on which the sun was said to never set was a safe, sure shield; they knew their own rulers would fall short of the British in ability and honesty. In 1924 Viscount Milner, with many years of experience behind him, thought the Empire 'the most powerful bulwark in the world against the spread of discord.' And this was still the popular view during the twenties, before the so-called bonds of Empire were withdrawn and the policeman at the gate was retired. The people of the world knew that a British passport still held great advantages, that at its best the English way of life was something to be respected among the teeming millions of India, Africa, and the outposts of Empire.

In 1924 the spirit of Empire was crystallized by the gigantic British Empire Exhibition at Wembley. In January some 220 acres of land in this north London suburb were covered with giant buildings, vast lakes, the largest sports arena in the world, and several miles of roads and pathways. It was the greatest enterprise of its kind ever planned by man.

At a cost of over £10,000,000 the great exhibition was preparing for its opening in April. Building had begun in 1922, and the sports stadium had been opened in April 1923. It was to be a comprehensive survey of the power and wealth and immense resources of the Commonwealth of Nations, where visitors could walk around the world and pass within a few minutes from continent to continent.

The roads between the pavilions were named by Rudyard Kipling, 'Anson's Way,' 'Drake's Way,' 'Commonwealth Way,' and so on. Six huge lions guarded the Government pavilion, each bigger than Landseer's famous lions around Nelson's column. The Palace of Engineering, the largest concrete building in the world—six and a half times as big as Trafalgar Square—housed shipbuilding, marine and mechanical exhibits, and was a paradise for boys. Here were the rich cream-coloured royal saloon railway carriage built for the King of Egypt, the model of the armoured cruiser *Kongo* built for the Japanese navy, an 1825 locomotive next to the latest L.N.E.R. giant, and a sixteen-inch naval gun weighing 117 tons which could throw a one-ton shell six miles.

In the Palace of Arts a splendid collection of paintings was displayed, lent by the King and other owners, together with specimens of many other arts, including furniture, pottery and jewels. So great was the attraction of the exhibition that until August it was almost impossible to secure a passage to Britain from any of the Dominions. The Tower of Babel could not have competed with the confusion of tongues.

A reconstruction of Old London Bridge included one of the original arches; the East African building, with an entrance copied from a doorway in Zanzibar, contained halls devoted to exhibits from the Sudan, Zanzibar, Nyasaland, the Seychelles, Tanganyika, Kenya, Uganda and Mauritius. In the Hong-Kong section visitors walked along a Chinese street and could eat birds'-nest soup, sharks' fins and other delicacies in a Chinese restaurant. The British Government pavilion contained the Royal apartments, several military exhibits, and a huge water stage for naval displays. The picturesque Union of South Africa pavilion was built in old Dutch style, with white walls, red roof, and gables over the entrances, stoep and loggia. In contrast, the Gold Coast pavilion was designed on the lines of one of the famous castles built by the Danes, Dutch and Portuguese. The doors had been carved by African students at Accra.

The Indian pavilion was housed in a replica of the Taj Mahal. Crossing the courtyard, the visitor found himself watching carpet-weavers from Baluchistan, and saw an ingenious model containing twenty-five thousand miniature figures, representing a pilgrimage to Hardwar. Carpets from Samarkand, silks from Kashmir, brasswork from Benares, carvings in ivory and jade, and silver representations of the Hindu theocracy—Vishnu, Siva, Krishna—down to the elephant-headed god Gunniputty, were all displayed. The magic of the East had come to Middlesex.

In the Canadian pavilion a proscenium showed what Vancouver Harbour would look like in 1930, when the system of grain elevators would be added to the port. Next to it was a representation of Jasper Park, with actual waterfalls and wild game, including bears and silver foxes. In nearby booths visitors saw the great Wheat Belt, the Niagara Falls and a Canadian experimental farm. The eastern end of the building was fragrant with thousands of apples.

Ceylon displayed a collection of pearl necklaces insured for a million pounds. In the South Africa pavilion there was a huge model of the Karoo landscape, with hartebeest, springbok and eland. Every South African industry was represented, gold and diamond mining, diamond cutting, cotton and wool production, agriculture, vine growing and ostrich farming. Visitors could lunch or dine on South African fare in a restaurant car standing in a specially built station. The history of the country was retold in the relics of the Voortrekkers, their cap-tent wagons, their veldt-skoen, a wooden plough, and weapons and candle moulds.

The walls of the Nigerian pavilion were made of sun-dried clay, with doorways decorated with Arabic patterns. The Mata-Atua, a carved Maori house in the New Zealand pavilion, had been built in 1874 to ratify peace between two fierce Maori tribes. Eighty feet long, it was the finest example of Maori art ever discovered. The house, after being exhibited in Sydney in 1892, had been brought to London and shown, but had been stored in a vault in the South Kensington museum until it was re-erected at Wembley.

At night the grounds were brilliantly lit by floodlights, transforming the white buildings into a magic city. In the amusement park, under the fluttering flags of many nations, were a giant scenic railway, boating lakes, and hundreds of side-shows. There was also a colliery complete with pit ponies, underground stables, and coal. People were lowered in a two-decked cage to the bottom of the shaft, stepping out into the underground workings.

The amusement park had cost one and a half million pounds, and it offered lively entertainment. A huge green caterpillar, writhing on the ground, contained miniature trains of forty cars riding on a circular track; as they revolved a hood covered the passengers. At intervals, said the official description, '*surprises* are caused by blasts of air coming up from the floor.' Women's skirts were blown high over their heads, causing screams from under the covering.

On the double-track mountain water chute small boats were raised by electric lifts through the centre of a plaster mountain, to slide down chutes into a lake. In 'Over the Falls' the passengers ascended a gangway, entered a dark chamber, and sat in a row on a form; then the seat fell away beneath them and they found themselves sliding helter-skelter down a moving belt which landed them, with squeals of delight, at ground level.

The 'Derby Racer' was a circular track carrying nine double-seated wooden horses in groups of five, each group racing the other. In 'Jack and Jill' a jaunting car carried passengers to the top of a tower, where the seats dropped away, shooting them out on to slides. A giant switchback, river caves, a mountain railway, a huge globe representing the earth, and a non-stop scenic railway were other amusements, in addition to hundreds of side-shows and shops.

The Exhibition represented seventy-eight different governments or 'more or less independent national and racial entities.' But there were already signs that the word 'Empire' was beginning to fall out of favour.

On St. George's Day, April 23, 1924, in the presence of about one hundred thousand people, the King-Emperor opened the Exhibition. A barony had been conferred on Sir James Stevenson, Bart., the chairman of the standing committee, and knighthoods on the principal engineers and architects. Replying to an address of welcome delivered by the Prince of Wales, the President of the Exhibition, the King said that Wembley 'may be said to reveal to us the whole Empire in little, containing within its 220 acres of ground a vivid model of the architecture, art, and industry of all the races which come under the British flag . . . we believe that this Exhibition will bring the peoples of the Empire to a better knowledge of how to meet their reciprocal wants and aspirations . . . and we hope further that the success of the Exhibition may bring lasting benefits not to the Empire only, but to mankind in general.'

A microphone was suspended just above and to the right of the King's head. Through this, 2 LO broadcast the royal speech, the first time that the King's voice had been heard by the mass of his subjects, the first broadcast by a British sovereign. After the speech the Bishop of London read a collect and the Lord's Prayer, and then massed choirs sang *Jerusalem*, *Land of Hope and Glory*, and *Soul of the World*. The broadcast created tremendous interest, and listeners turned on their wireless sets again that evening to hear a recording made by the Gramophone Company.

After the opening ceremony Wembley settled down to its task of entertaining and instructing the millions of visitors who were expected during the summer. They crowded to see the reconstruction of the tomb of Tutankhamen, the diamond-washing plant where blue soil yielded gems which were cut and polished in front of them, and they watched Burmese boys play the game of Chin-Ion, which the Prince of Wales had just taken up.

In the gardens there were a hundred thousand British-grown Darwin tulips, and five thousand delphiniums. By July 9th, nearly a quarter of a million pounds was being spent at Wembley every day. From all over the world immense crowds flooded the gates.

Empire Day, May 24th, was celebrated with a great parade in the stadium, the first of a series of massed band performances, followed by fireworks. As the Duke of Connaught took his place in the royal box a band of six hundred musicians struck up the National Anthem, and ensigns dipped in salute. A procession headed by a hundred pipers included a drum and fife band of three hundred, and eight thousand London school children.

Next day nearly a hundred thousand people assembled, in the presence of the King and Queen, the Prince of Wales and other members of the royal family, to attend thanksgiving service. In an address the Archbishop of Canterbury, Dr. Randall Davidson, reminded his vast congregation that this was the largest religious service the world had ever seen. As he spoke, rain began to fall. In the royal box were the

King and Queen, the Prince of Wales, Prince Henry, the Princess Royal, Princess Helena, Princess Marie Louise, Lady Patricia Ramsey, the Duke of Connaught, Princess Beatrice, and Mr. Arthur Henderson, the Home Secretary.

On May 30th the Queen paid a private visit to the Exhibition, with Prince George. They toured the Indian and Burmese pavilions, lunched at the Lucullus restaurant, and then visited Ceylon and South Africa. After tea they went to the amusement park, where they travelled on the scenic railway, to the delight of a tremendous crowd. Later the Queen talked to the driver, Alexander Martes, who told her that he had, some years before, driven her on the scenic railway at the White City Exhibition.

On Whit Monday, in spite of dull weather and an unofficial Underground strike, 321,232 went to Wembley, exceeding by 75,000 the number which had visited the Great Exhibition in Hyde Park during the whole of its first week, in June 1851. At ten o'clock that night a maroon rocket gave the signal for the joining of hands in a 'Link the Empire' handshake, after which festivities continued until late with music, dancing and fireworks.

2

One of the most popular exhibits at Wembley was a life-size statue of the Prince of Wales, made of butter. It was displayed in the Canadian pavilion, but when the Prince saw it he said he thought the legs were too fat. Nearby, in the Palace of Industry, a gas exhibit included a large black and white china cat lying curled up on the mat of a model room occupied by an old lady with white hair. The old lady was stated to typify 'The seven ages of women,' and everyone who visited the room was invited to stroke the cat for luck. Nearly a million people did so.

Australia followed the example of Canada by exhibiting a tableau in butter, showing Jack Hobbs batting. There was also, at a nearby pavilion, a complete factory where a Ford car was assembled in front of the crowds. Sixteen models were turned out every day. But perhaps the most popular of all the novelties was a structure only 102 inches long, a complete mansion in miniature, with almost everything inside made in the scale of one inch to a foot. This was the famous Queen's Dolls' House which was presented to Queen Mary.

Furnished and decorated in the style of a royal palace, it had been created by Sir Edwin Lutyens, R.A., and Princess Marie Louise, and leading artists, authors and craftsmen had taken two years to prepare it. The outside walls were made to rise, so that each room could be seen. The garden, with every type of flower, folded up like a writing desk and slid into the basement, just as the garage, containing miniature Rolls-Royce, Daimler, Sunbeam and Vauxhall cars, did at the other end. The centre of the main front was taken up with a great staircase hall, 31 inches broad; the paving was of lapis-lazuli, and the walls were painted by William Nicholson in blue and white.

The Queen's bedroom, with a black, red and yellow ceiling by Glyn Philpot, A.R.A., was only 22 inches high, yet its grey silk hangings and bed, walnut furniture, carpet, and even the blue-enamelled toilet-set and the photograph of the King, all were perfect. In the dining-room the ceiling was by Professor Gerald Moira, there was a portrait group of Queen Victoria and the Prince Consort with their children, by McEvoy, and above the chimney-piece hung Alfred Munnings's portrait of the Prince of Wales out hunting. Every detail, down to the salt-cellars and the rolls on the table, was complete.

The library, 28 inches high, was wainscoted in walnut. The 170 books were bound in red or grey leather, and many of them were written in manuscript by their authors. Rudyard Kipling, Robert Bridges, John Galsworthy, John Masefield, Thomas Hardy, Arnold Bennett, Joseph Conrad,

Sir James Barrie, Ian Hay, Hugh Walpole and W. W. Jacobs were represented. On one table were writing materials, including a fountain pen half an inch long; and on another were pipes and tobacco. On a third table lay the dispatch cases of ministers of state. The ceiling was by William Walcot.

The nursery, painted by Edmund Dulac with fairy stories, was 8 inches high, and contained every toy a child could want, including lead soldiers the size of mosquitoes, a toy train, a model theatre and a scooter. The ordinary bedrooms were 10 inches wide and 8 inches high, each completely furnished down to tooth-brushes three-quarters of an inch long.

There were four bath-rooms, a box-room, a strong-room with the Crown jewels (set with real gems), a housemaids' closet with sinks and Dutch tiles only half an inch square. Underneath were store-rooms and a cellar, with cases of real Johnnie Walker whisky, and dozens of real claret and champagne, bottled and binned. In the store-rooms were chocolate boxes, soaps, and tiny pots of genuine jam and marmalade.

Electric light was fitted in every room, and the tiny taps in the bath-rooms worked. Never had such perfection of detail been seen by the public.

The only thing lacking at Wembley was fine weather. A cold spring was followed by a wet and singularly sunless summer, and the curtailment of daylight saving shortened the days.

In January 1925 Sir Travers Clarke, Chief Administrator, explained why the Exhibition would be continued for a second year. The transport figures, he said, showed that although Greater London had been tapped, it had not been fully exploited. Many students of the economic resources of the Empire had not found the first six months sufficient for study. One visitor had claimed that although he had been to Wembley 142 times he had only just finished the Palace of Engineering when the Exhibition closed.

'We had lovely gardens in 1924,' said Sir Travers. 'We shall have more gardens and more flowers in 1925, more music, more light, and more variety in our restaurants.'

Where had the money come from, to build this vast Exhibition? In March 1924 the Minister for the Overseas Trade Department told the House of Commons that the contributions had been raised as follows:

Great Britain	£175,000
India	£180,000
Canada	£200,000
Australia	£200,000
New Zealand	£ 80,000
South Africa	£ 80,000
West Africa	£100,000

This left some £10,000,000 to be found by commercial firms and private enterprise. Originally it had been estimated that a £1,000,000 would cover the cost of the fun fair, but this proved inadequate. The Mountain Water Chute and the Globe and the Derby Racer together cost nearly £150,000. The coal mine cost £100,000.

The decision to open the Exhibition for a second year was taken after considerable discussion. But the numbers who attended in 1925 were considerably less than in the first year, under ten million. When Wembley finally closed in October 1925 there was some talk of a third year, but when it was pointed out that it would be run at a severe loss, the idea was abandoned, and speculation began about the future of the buildings. A *Punch* cartoon depicted the Wembley lion, which had been the trade-mark of the Exhibition, as a white elephant. Suggestions ranged from a permanent Palace of Industry, or a British Hollywood of film studios, to a sports centre and a garden city. Eventually it was decided to sell the site and the buildings and to wind up the company.

The Wembley Stadium and Greyhound Racecourse Ltd., was then formed, the stadium being bought for some £150,000. It had cost £750,000 to build. This now became the home of greyhound racing and international sport. Nearly £90,000 was spent on making the track suitable for greyhound racing, and in providing a car park for four thousand vehicles and covered seating for thirty thousand spectators. There were also a cocktail bar, restaurant, luxury smoking lounges and a dance floor. 'Going to the dogs' soon became a national pastime.

The man who developed the Wembley stadium into a centre for football cup finals, speedway and cycle racing, horse shows, indoor lawn tennis tournaments, swimming and ice-skating championships, basket-ball, hockey, water carnivals and even ice pantomimes, was Arthur James Elvin, who had started his career without advantages of birth, wealth or education, but had risen to give the unwanted buildings an even more prosperous lease of life. Yet his association with Wembley had started only in the Exhibition's second year, when he took over some shops and was able, by hard work, to save his first thousand pounds.

There was one other attraction at Wembley which set a fashion which continued throughout the twenties and thirties, and vanished only with the Second World War. This was the presentation of a Military Tattoo, the fore-runner of many famous pageants presented later at Aldershot, Tidworth and elsewhere, in which men from thirty-five regiments took part. Then spectacle began at dusk with buglers sounding the retreat. Then the whole pageantry of British military history from the days of Waterloo up to modern times was re-enacted under searchlights, for the benefit of the immense crowds who, every day, flocked to Wonderful Wembley.

CHAPTER NINE

A Day in 1925

I

THE DATE is Tuesday, April 14, 1925, the day after the Easter holiday. It is a warm spring morning and Mr. Everyman is wearing a light raincoat as he leaves his semi-detached house, *Mon Repos*, in Wimbledon to go to his office in the City. It is nearly eight o'clock.

Mr. Everyman is thirty, he has been married for five years, and he earns £4 15s. a week as head of the contract department in a stockbroker's office. He has a son of three, and he hopes for another child later. His choice of house has been governed by his pocket; there are houses for sale at New Malden for £1,475 freehold, or £1,325 leasehold, but his will have cost him £850 when he has finished buying it on the 'never never'; it is semi-detached, has four bedrooms, a bathroom with beige tiles, two reception rooms, a long, narrow garden surrounded by a high wooden fence, a tiny workshop, electric light and gas. And it is only seven minutes' walk from the railway station.

The Everymans came to Wimbledon because it is so close to London, and yet retains its semi-rural character. Its great unspoilt common, with its windmill, gives the illusion of being almost in the country, and its shopping centre caters for all tastes. Wimbledon's houses in 1925 are modern and quite well built, and the colour of the big main street compares favourably with the drabness of some of the suburban centres nearer London.

Mr. Everyman walks to Wimbledon station and arrives in

the City by eight-forty. The train fare from Wimbledon to Waterloo by Southern Railway is ninepence, and the journey takes fifteen minutes. The season-ticket rates are as follows:

Wimbledon–Waterloo

	1st Class			*3rd Class*		
	£	s.	d.	£	s.	d.
One month	2	5	0	1	1	0
Three months	4	10	0	2	16	0

Wimbledon–City via Waterloo

	£	s.	d.	£	s.	d.
One month	2	11	0	1	7	0
Three months	5	5	0	3	8	3

Weekly season tickets are not issued. The Metropolitan District Railway runs frequent electric trains to the Mansion House via Earls Court and Putney Bridge. There is no need to travel by General omnibus or one of the many 'pirates,' but Wimbledon is served by three services: No. 22 (weekdays); Nos. 51a (51 on Sundays); and 130 (Sundays only). L.C.C. trams (services 2 and 4) run to Charing Cross and Blackfriars, the journey of nearly ten miles taking less than an hour. Between 10 a.m. and 4 p.m. the fare for this trip is 2d., and an ordinary return tram fare from Wimbledon to the Embankment costs 4d. Fares for 7½ miles on the trams are 3d. single and 5d. return, and for 8d. one can buy a return ticket which will take one 18¼ miles, and back. An all-day ticket on Saturdays or Sundays costs a shilling.

Sitting in his seat in the railway carriage, Mr. Everyman opens his *Daily News* (price 1d.) and glances at the headlines. He has left the *Daily Mirror* at home for his wife. What is happening in his England on this spring day in 1925?

His ten pages of newspaper give him all the news. The main story on the front page is devoted to a spirited speech by Mr. Ramsay MacDonald, strongly defending Labour's short term of office, which ended in November. Mr. Everyman is a Liberal, and likes his *Daily News*, but he sometimes wishes that less space was given to the Labour Party, and especially to Mr. MacDonald, who, he thinks, made a mess of his short term of office. He suspects Mr. MacDonald of being a snob.

'When the history of those eight months comes to be written,' the Labour leader has said, 'it will not be written by small-minded critics, but by men who will be compelled to pay a tribute to the work of that administration in the life of this country and of Europe.'

The other main items on the front page include a report of Easter crowds returning to London from the seaside. In six hours on Sunday 2,617 cars used the new road to Southend. At Preston in Lancashire 30,000 children and adults made merry rolling coloured eggs down the green slopes of Avenham Park in an orgy of 'egg jarping,' and then enjoyed pitched battles with eggs and oranges. At Newport the hero of the hour is William Thomas, the brother of J. H. Thomas, M.P., who has risked his life descending a well to rescue a fox-terrier. Lloyd George has arrived at Madeira in the *Kenilworth Castle*. In France there is still no Cabinet, but M. Briand hopes to form one. Meanwhile, severe masculine lines mark the new Paris fashions; women are wearing short, straight-cut skirts, flesh-coloured stockings, low-heeled shoes, and coats like men. The only concession to femininity is a bright scarf or a broad-brimmed hat. At the Colombes Stadium in Paris, England has beaten France at Rugby by 13 points to 11, fifty thousand people having watched the match.

Page two is devoted to an article entitled *Keep Out the Damp* with recipes for home builders and details of how to 'make your own tennis togs and save money.' A tin of Ronuk polish, says one advertisement, costs 2d., 4d., or 6d. Bournville Cocoa costs 7d., 1s. 1½d., or 2s. 2½d. a tin. Wolfe and Hollander offer loose covers for their 'Wembley' three-piece furniture suite at £5 19s. 6d.

Page three reports unrest in the teaching profession (will they accept the new Burnham Award scales of pay?) and

Mr. Everyman notes that Tom Mix, the film star, is expected to arrive at Southampton today, with his wife, mother-in-law, and four-year-old daughter, Thomasina. The Mayor and Council will greet him, and later the party will travel to London by train, to meet the Lord Mayor. At 10.45 p.m. Mr. Mix will broadcast from 2 LO. Such is the power of the cinema.

The main news story on page five concerns a statement made by an eighteen-year-old valet who has been charged with murdering a sixteen-year-old dancing teacher in West Kensington. He is reported to have said, 'I did it because she was always teasing me and nodding to other fellows. I lost my head.'

No. 10 Downing Street is being spring-cleaned; Mr. William Woods, of Brixton, the last of the Christy Minstrels, has died; so has Dame Clara Butt's father. In Belgium the Zeebrugge Memorial is to be unveiled by the King of the Belgians. Yesterday Brighton enjoyed 4·5 hours of sunshine, Clacton 7·3, Torquay 0·5, Weymouth 1·1, Blackpool 4·5, and Ramsgate 8·1. Bognor, where the Everymans hope to go in August, is not listed, being still a relatively remote resort.

A young critic and essayist named J. B. Priestley is one of the book reviewers on page six, criticizing *Charles Dickens and Other Victorians*, by 'Q,' Sir Arthur Quiller-Couch. In an adjoining column, Robert Lynd, writing from Rome, describes a visit to the Capitol and Trajan's Forum.

Mr. Malcolm Cherry, an actor of whom Mr. Everyman has never heard, has died at South Kensington. The familiar signature 'E. M. Harvey' will soon disappear from Bank of England notes, and will be replaced by 'C. P. Mahon.' But, reads Mr. Everyman, treasury notes will still be signed by Sir Warren Fisher. Mr. Everyman reflects that he sees too few treasury notes, and turns to page seven where an advertisement for Wills's cork-tipped 'Jack Scott' cigarettes gives the price as 5½d. for ten, or 11d. for twenty.

VI.
Suzanne Lenglen at Wimbledon, July 1922.

Steve Donoghue on Captain Cuttle, *the 1922 Derby winner.* 'Come on Steve!' *shouted the crowds.*

The horse which crossed its legs—Cartoonist Tom Webster's Tishy *in the* Daily Mail.

VII. *The height of fashion in London's Oxford Street 1926: a cloche hat, pointed shoes, and a revealing leopard-skin coat.*

The sports columns are more interesting. Chelsea and Manchester United have drawn, without scoring; West Bromwich Albion is leading in the First Division; Jimmy White's horse Cloudbank has won the Queen's Prize at Kempton Park. Rain has postponed some of the motor racing at Brooklands, the highest speed of the Bank Holiday meeting being achieved by Lieutenant G. Kidston in his 1,990 c.c. Bugatti at an average of 96¾ miles per hour. The Easter Private Competitors' Handicap was won by Jack Dunfee, and the 90 miles per hour Long Handicap by Captain Malcolm Campbell. Mr. Everyman enjoys a quick mental picture of himself roaring down to Bognor in the 'baby' Austin with the aluminium sports body which he has seen every day in the window of the garage near Wimbledon station. But how can he afford a car on £4 15s. a week?

Mr. Everyman thinks the new electric services from Victoria are excellent. He has an aunt living at Sutton, and the electric line now takes him to see her more quickly than the old steam train. Extensions to the suburban electric system, covering some 650 miles of track, are going to cost the Southern Railway nearly £8,000,000. Guildford, Dorking, and Orpington will be reached in July; Hayes and Chislehurst in December, Dartford early in 1926. The fifteen miles from Coulsdon North to Victoria now takes 35 minutes instead of an hour by steam.

If he looks around him, Mr. Everyman might notice signs of some improvement in the general health of the people, especially children. Neither the clothing nor the conditions of the children shows the extreme destitution of pre-war days, but the homes of the very poor are still appalling slums, outside the world of Mr. Everyman, who is unlikely to be on the dole, or unemployed. His *Daily News* this morning tells him that State relief is slowly, gradually, laying the spectre of poverty in its ugliest forms.

Mr. Everyman will have lunch with some of his fellow-clerks in a Lyons' teashop in the City. His lunch never costs him more than 2s. 2d., including 2d. tip for the smart 'Nippy' who serves them. If he wishes, he can have quite a good lunch for 1s. 6d.

	s. d.		s. d.
Stewed Lamb's Heart	8	2 Fillets of Fish	1 2
Mashed Potatoes	3	Mashed Potatoes	3
Apple Pie	4	Bread & Butter Pudding	4
Coffee	3	Pot of Tea	3
	1 6		2 0

Stewed Steak & Carrots	9	Soup	3
Mashed Potatoes	3	Steak Pie	8
Boiled Raisin Roll	3	Cabbage	2½
Coffee	3	Roast Potatoes	3½
		Trifle & Custard	4
		Coffee	3
	1 6		2 0

Although it hardly affects him, he is interested in a discussion which one of his friends started during lunch on Thursday. The subject, hotly argued by all four young men with some feeling, concerns Labour's attempt to abolish the death penalty in the Army, a question which has been debated in the House of Commons. One of his colleagues pointed out that soldiers who break down under battle conditions are not criminals—like Frederick Bywaters was—and should therefore not be executed. Another clerk disagreed, saying that if men are cowards in the front line an example must be made of them, because cowardice is contagious. The discussion was purely academic, because there had been no fighting since 1918, but these matters interest young men, whose thoughts often turn to the next war, which must sooner or later break out.

It was Mr. Thurtle, the Member for Shoreditch, who raised the question in the House, asking if there was any such thing as 'real cowardice,' as distinct from nervous breakdown? During the war, he said, 287 white officers and men in the British army had been executed by shooting. He quoted the following cases:

1. A private soldier with a working party in the trenches ran away on the bursting of a shell and did not rejoin his party. Executed.
2. A private soldier, after going over the top with his company, 'absented himself while the attack was in progress,' and remained absent until next day. Executed.
3. The accused, 'from motives of cowardice,' left the trenches during a gas attack. Executed.
4. A private soldier, aged 18½, ran away from a trench that had been heavily bombarded for six days, the battalion holding the trench having sustained heavy casualties. The lad enlisted when only 17. Executed. Later it was admitted that the authorities did not know his real age when he was shot.

Out of 287 men shot, more than 30 had been under 21. The Labour argument pointed out that there was no death penalty in the Australian Army, 'and did they fight any the worse?' Mr. Everyman expects to continue the discussion over his fillets of fish.

2

What else is happening in Mr. Everyman's Britain? Lord Balfour has recently stated, 'I believe that the preposterous suggestion that the Jews and Arabs cannot live together in harmony will be finally exploded, and will not be admitted in rational political controversy.' But Palestine is a long way from England, and few people care about the problem.

On April 28th Chancellor Winston Churchill will present his Budget; it will cut the standard rate of income tax by 6d.—to 4s.; it will put up death duties; and it will promise Government economies. Mr. Churchill, during his term of office from 1924 to 1925, will show great ingenuity in balancing budgets without increasing taxation.

On May 9th the King, accompanied by the Queen, is

going to open the British Empire Exhibition's second season at Wembley. At present the King, recovering from influenza, is cruising in the royal yacht in the Mediterranean. Prince Henry, the Archbishop of Canterbury, the Lord Chancellor, and Mr. Baldwin are acting as Councillors of State during his absence. The Prince of Wales is in West Africa, bound for Cape Town, where he will be installed as Chancellor of the University.

Mr. Massey, the Prime Minister of New Zealand, will die on May 10th, and be succeeded by Mr. J. G. Coates. In the United States, where Mr. Coolidge has been inaugurated as President, a tornado has swept over five States, killing 645 people and injuring 1,945. In December, Australia wins the first test match at Sydney by 193 runs; in January they win the second at Melbourne by 81 runs. The matches are fully reported in all the English papers. In March, ten thousand people are thrown out of work in Lancashire as a result of a lock-out organized by the Co-operative Societies. A fire at Madame Tussaud's, in London, has completely gutted the famous waxworks and destroyed many historic relics.

Nearer home, what is Mr. Everyman's own borough of Wimbledon like?

There is some excitement in the district because of the arrival of the Maharajah of Jodpur, Major His Highness Sir Raj Rajeshwar Maharadhijara Umed Singh Banadur, K.C.V.O., who came to the town on Easter Sunday. An enormous crowd waited for him at Wimbledon District station, and throughout the week-end Belmont House, a palatial mansion facing the common, has been the centre of attraction. The Maharajah is twenty, and rules two million subjects. He claims to be the direct descendant of Rama, the deified King of Ajodhya, and as befitting one of India's wealthiest ruling princes he has brought with him to Belmont House not only his wife, the Maharanee, and their infant son, but also twenty secretaries and servants. The house, whose gates are locked and guarded day and night during his visit, is owned by the Duc de Vendôme, the brother-in-law of the King of the Belgians, and stands in eleven acres.

Wimbledon in 1925 is a centre of sporting activity. The new ground and Centre Court Stadium of the All-England Lawn Tennis and Croquet Club was opened in June 1922, and has brought fame to the town; the Royal Wimbledon Golf Club, with a membership of six hundred, is the second oldest in the London district; there are seventeen tennis courts run by the Ramblers Lawn Tennis Club, to which Mr. Everyman pays an annual subscription of £2 12s. 6d. for the pleasure of playing tennis on Sunday afternoons and sometimes in the evening. In cricket, hockey, polo, swimming, football, and boating—all of which can be enjoyed in the district—he is not interested.

This afternoon Mrs. Everyman plans to go shopping in the town, and then, perhaps, to a cinema. She has first to visit the showrooms of the Wandsworth, Wimbledon, and Epsom Gas Company, in Hill Road, to ask them to call and inspect the gas cooker, which is faulty. The company charges ¾d. a unit for gas in the summer and 1d. a unit in the winter. Electricity in the house costs 4½d. a unit (ordinary meter), and coke for the kitchen boiler costs 34s. 2d. a ton. As for the Wimbledon rates, they are 10s. 4d. in the £.

Mrs. Everyman has seen an evening gown at Lefevre's which she would like to buy, but she wonders if she can afford it. Made of soft satin with feather trimming, it costs 25s. 9d. Her shoes, which she has bought at Treadwell Brothers in Merton Road, have cost her 8s. 11d. On a total family income of £4 15s. it is very seldom that she can buy herself an evening gown, and she reluctantly decides that she must wait. Perhaps, one day, she will win the crossword puzzle prize which they offer every week in the *People*. Then all her dreams will come true. Even the magnificent new Bean Fourteen five-seater, price £395, which she has

Lady (suffering from the heat). "I SAY, ISN'T THIS PERFECT WEATHER TOO AWFUL FOR WORDS?"

seen in the window of the Wimbledon Motor Works, might be theirs . . .

For the present she must be content, after buying meat and groceries, with a visit to the pictures. Her *Wimbledon Boro' News* tells her what is showing. At the King's Palace she can see Eleanor Boardman in *Wine of Youth*, with Creighton Hale and Pauline Garon, and *The Butterfly Nun*, with Fannie Ward as an added attraction; her seat will cost 5d., 8d., 1s. 2d., 1s. 10d., or 2s. 4d. At the Raynes Park Cinema there is *Zeebrugge* (stalls 4d. to 1s. 2d., circle 1s. 2d., and 1s. 6d.), but this cinema does not open until 5.30 p.m., and she will probably go to the King's Palace. If she chooses the Elite, Wimbledon, she can see John Lowell in *Floodgates*, and Harold Lloyd in *Hot Water*, while farther afield, at the Hippodrome, Putney, there is Pola Negri in *Lily of the Dust*, and *Gold Heels*—a racing drama starring Peggy Shaw.

The three-year-old infant Everyman is being cared for by Mrs. Everyman's mother, who has been staying in the house during Easter. One day he will probably go to King's College School, Wimbledon Common, and then—so Mr. Everyman declares—to London University. But all that is a long way off, and just at present the boy's mother can see no farther ahead than the gas company's showrooms and the afternoon visit to the pictures. Meanwhile his father travels on towards his City desk, looking out of the window at an express train, drawn by one of the new 'King Arthur' class locomotives, rushing towards Bournemouth.

3

Mr. Everyman plans to stay at home tonight and listen to the wireless. He turns to page eight to see what the B.B.C. will offer him for entertainment. His loudspeaker set can pick up either 2 LO or Chelmsford, and he has a choice of programmes:

LONDON (Call 2 LO)

1—2	Luncheon music from Holborn Restaurant.
4—5	Books to read; talk by Ann Spice. Organ and orchestral music from Shepherds Bush Pavilion. Talk, Famous Old Castles: Alhambra in Spain, by Helen Townroe.
6	Children: When the Fairies Spring-cleaned, Nancy M. Hayes. Progress through the Ages: Roads, W. J. Claxton. Lucy Hughes, soprano.
6. 30	Children's letters.
6. 35	Sybil Thorndike appealing for the Royal Waterloo Hospital.
6. 45	Light music.
7	Big Ben: Weather: General News. John Strachey, Literary Critic.
7. 25	Light music (to all stations).
7. 35	Mr. H. E. Powell-Jones: Our Telephones: Local news.
8—9	Ballad concert (to all stations except 5 XX) with Elsie Suddaby, Edith Penville, Walter Hyde, Mary Foster, Thorpe Bates.
10	Time (Greenwich); Weather; General News. Talk by Mr. T. G. Landincruce: Shipwrecked; Local News.
10. 45	Tom Mix, the Western cowboy film star, broadcasts to all stations.
10. 30— 10. 45 & 10. 50— 11. 30	Savoy Orpheans and Savoy Havana Band from Savoy Hotel all stations).

From Chelmsford (Call 5XX) there is the Charles Woodhouse String Quartet and a one-act comedy entitled *Entertaining Mr. Waddington*, by Vernon Bartlett, with Raymond Trafford, Phyllis Panting, Henry Oscar, and Mabel Constanduros. At 9.15 there is a play, *The Dweller in the Darkness*, by Reginald Berkeley, and at 9.45 a Brahms concert.

Let us leave Mr. Everyman reading his newspaper, as the train takes him towards the City, in this first of five years of Conservative rule. Although he reads that the Stock Exchange is confidently looking forward to a return to more prosperous times, the general strike is only a year off. If only he could foresee what is to come—the great depression of the thirties—but there is no way of telling. Like millions of others, he must trust in Mr. Baldwin and hope that the man with the pipe will guide the country to prosperity.

CHAPTER TEN

The General Strike

I

BRITAIN'S PROBLEM was how to pass from the unbridled extravagance of war to a normal life of prosperity. But the war had left a hideous industrial mess to be cleared up. Her great advantage lay in her coal and her workmen. Most of her raw material had to be imported; she could not feed herself, and was dependent on outside demand for her workshop goods. Thus, a population too large to be fed by home supplies gained its living by passing raw materials through the industrial workshops and selling the finished product to other countries for money which bought food and more raw materials.

Most English manufacturers had kept pre-war costs down by paying low wages. But this was resisted, especially after the war, by a trade union organization which was the most efficient in the world. The conflict between employer and employee was renewed with vigour when the war ended.

England's great customer was the continent of Europe, but since the war this market had been sadly disorganized, the transport systems were run down, and in most countries there was financial chaos. The delicate commercial and industrial mechanism of Britain was therefore thrown out of gear. The country's ability to regain her old markets hinged on the recovery of European industry, especially in Germany. And meanwhile she could not employ all her own workmen. But prices kept rising, and the trade unions tried to raise wages.

In a sense, Germany had won at least one of her war aims, the industry of northern France and much of Belgium having been destroyed. No matter what reparations the Germans were forced to pay, the lost industries could not be replaced until she was able to absorb their products.

Many parts of Europe had been devastated by the war. Great industries in Poland had been destroyed, a tract of land some two hundred miles broad and four hundred miles long being fired by the Russians in the face of the advancing Germans. Here four hundred thousand Poles had died without food, clothing, or shelter. In Hungary and Rumania there was almost no farm machinery left. Pre-war Rumania had been one of Europe's greatest exporters of grain, but in 1920 less than one-third of her fields were planted. Serbia, utterly devastated, was left with nine locomotives and all her industries paralysed.

How was Britain to regain her markets, and so employ her workers? This was the problem facing people who demanded an increasingly high standard of living and higher wages than their opposite numbers in other countries. In order to see if wages could be cut, a Royal Commission under Sir Herbert Samuel was appointed in March 1926, to report on the condition of the coal industry. It revealed that three-quarters of all Britain's coal was produced at a loss, and it decided that miners were paid too much, while mineowners were taking too much money out of the industry. It also recommended nationalization.

During the Commission's proceedings Mr. Herbert Smillie cross-examined the Duke of Northumberland, and drew public attention to the Duke's mining income—some £82,000 a year—and his indifference to the conditions of the miners.

The heavy industries, especially coal, iron, and steel, were using equipment long out of date. Many of the pits were among the most antiquated in Europe. There was very little mechanical extraction; wooden pit-props were still used, and not all of the valuable by-products were being developed. Only about 25 per cent of the coal was washed mechanically, whereas in Germany the figure was 80 per cent, and in France it was 85 per cent.

How had this happened? In England the mining leases usually lasted for limited periods, so that the lessees were often unwilling to sink capital. There were some 1,400 independent coal producers working 2,000 pits, and the older mines acted as a drag on the industry. How could unity of action be obtained from hundreds of separate mines which had never co-operated?

Nationalization was recommended by the Royal Commission as the cure. But Baldwin's Government, ignoring this solution, supported the owners in their claim that wages should be cut and demanded a 13½ per cent reduction in miners' wages. The powerful Trades Union Congress immediately threatened a strike, whereupon the Cabinet demanded that the threat be withdrawn. A deadlock followed, which was resolved on Monday, May 3, 1926, when the strike began.

Extreme Socialists had for long argued that Capital was defrauding the workers of the produce of their labour. Hence arose the idea of a nation-wide 'general strike' of all workers in all industries, to overthrow the controlling power of the propertied classes.

In 1926 the secretary of the Miners' Federation was Mr. A. J. Cook, who described himself as a 'humble follower of Lenin.' His union was particularly dissatisfied with working conditions in the mines, which, as the Samuel report had shown, were far from satisfactory. The Transport workers were headed by a more moderate leader, Mr. J. R. Clynes, supported by Mr. Ernest Bevin; the railwaymen were led by Mr. J. H. Thomas, who had in 1921 curbed a miners' strike by refusing to support them. In the eyes of the rest of the great unenlightened British public these trade union leaders, representing millions of their fellow-workers, were all 'bolshies,' Communist sympathizers who wished to wreck British industry. Actually they were moderate in their demands, except for Mr. Cook, who had more power than the rest, and eventually brought the miners out on strike. The Trades Union Congress then ordered a strike of all railwaymen, transport-workers, and printers, and what has become known as 'the general strike' started.

Strikes were not new in Britain. From 1900 to 1923 over 315 million working days had been lost because of them. The coal strike of 1921 had cost the country 73,000,000 working days, £35,000,000 in wages, and probably £18,000,000 in indirect losses, coming at a time when German and French mines were starting to compete with Britain for European trade.

It was the bankruptcy of the mining industry that had caused the strike. Had the Government accepted the Samuel report and taken drastic and prompt action by nationalizing the mines, there would have been no reason for the strike. But the only part of the report which was considered was the recommendation to lengthen working days and cut wages. The miners, looking back, remembered the Sankey report of 1919, which had condemned the attitude of the mineowners towards modernization, and they reflected that miners in France and Germany were now capturing their markets at the expense of England's old-fashioned, ill-equipped mines.

In fairness, Baldwin stated that not only the miners but also all other classes of workers would have to accept wage reductions. He knew that if wages could be reduced in industry then unemployment figures would be lowered. But the workers regarded this as the result of mismanagement of foreign affairs by the Government, and were not willing to lower their standard of living. Wives at home needed money for shopping, there were children to be fed, there were rents to be paid. What man would accept a lower wage and work longer hours for it?

Baldwin's proposals were rejected with the slogan *Not a minute on the day, not a penny off the pay*. But before the strike began the Prime Minister made the position clear, from his point of view, by circulating the following private note to all newspapers, through the Conservative Party Central Office:

> The Government are particularly anxious to draw the attention of the public to the serious economic position of the coal industry as disclosed in the statistical table given in the House of Commons last week, showing the percentage of coal which is raised at a loss. Reference may also usefully be made to the question of hours, upon which it is desirable to concentrate attention rather than upon the reduction of wages.

Ramsay MacDonald had warned his fellow-Socialists: 'The general strike is a weapon that cannot be wielded for industrial purposes. It is clumsy and ineffectual. It has no goal which, when reached, can be regarded as victory. If fought to a finish as a strike it would ruin Trade Unionism, and the Government in the meantime could create a revolution.'

When, however, there was no doubt that the battle was on, MacDonald supported the strikers, saying, 'If constitutional means fail, we are there with you, taking our share uncomplainingly until right and justice have been done.'

On April 29th the Cabinet had advised that a state of emergency should be declared; troops were moved into Lancashire, Edinburgh, South Wales, and London, and eight battalions were held in reserve in barracks. From now on the war was between the orderly forces of the Government, with power and communications behind them, and the disorderly, unprepared, unorganized workers led by men without the means to carry the strike through. But there was courage on both sides.

Three days after the strike had started, on May 6th, Sir John Simon stood up in the House of Commons and declared that it was illegal, and that every trade union leader behind it was 'liable in damages to the uttermost farthing of his personal possessions.' A move to make the use of trade-union funds an indictable offence was abandoned only when the King counselled the Prime Minister not to provoke the strikers, who had until now 'been remarkably quiet.'

The strikers were taking very little action, being mainly content to stay at home or collect on street corners and watch the forces of law and order protecting lorries driven by volunteers. There were a few demonstrations, rowdy scenes in several cities, stones and bricks were thrown, but this was the exception rather than the rule. At Plymouth a football match between the police and strikers was reported as an extraordinary event, as if there was some fundamental difference between the players. On the fifth day the Plymouth strikers attended a special service at St. Andrew's church.

Meanwhile the average citizen bore the inconvenience of the strike with good humour. London trams and omnibuses, driven by volunteers and guarded by police, bore chalked inscriptions *Here we are again! Ladies of the normal size 3d. We keep quite sober*, and *Slow but sure*. Hundreds of drivers and other volunteers were housed and fed at Earls Court in the Empress and Queen's Halls by the Underground Railway company and the 'bus companies. Petrol and food were the most vital commodities, but during the short period of the strike there was no lack of either. Motor launches took London's office workers to the City. There was a legendary story of a volunteer who drove an express train into Waterloo station twenty minutes early with two level-crossing gates on the buffers. 'Flappers' in small cars gave people lifts, manners suddenly improved, the average citizen became more thoughtful.

The Government, finding that it could not publicly brand the strikers as anarchists because there were now few newspapers being printed, decided to publish its own propaganda news sheet, which would present the official point of view. One of the first actions of the strikers, which precipitated the strike, had been the refusal of the printers of the *Daily*

Mail to produce the edition of Monday, May 1st, which contained a leading article stating that the strike was 'a revolutionary movement intended to inflict suffering upon the great mass of innocent persons in the community.' This seemed to the printers a monstrous absurdity, because the men who were going on strike up and down the country were in fact part of the masses of Britain; and although they and their families were prepared, if need be, to suffer the immediate consequences of the strike, which they believed to be just, they had no revolutionary feelings and no anti-national feeling. Yet the headline on the *Daily Mail* read 'For King and Country.'

Although the presses were ready, the men in the machine room angrily refused to go to press with the paper. Politely, a spokesman told the management that they would print the newspaper, but only if the offending leading article was cut out. The *Daily Mail* did not appear next day.

The Government newspaper was called the *British Gazette*, and was published in the offices of the *Morning Post*. Edited by Winston Churchill, it represented the views of the Government, and was widely distributed. The first issue on May 5th described the strike as 'an effort to force upon some 42,000,000 British citizens the will of less than 4,000,000 others.' Next day, Stanley Baldwin called the strike 'the road to anarchy and ruin.'

The B.B.C. under the management of Mr. Reith, made an effort to preserve its tradition of accuracy and fair play, and broadcast information about both sides. The speeches of the trade-union leaders were quoted on the wireless, and the news was presented dispassionately. The timings of trains were given at length, and a newspaper cartoon by David Low showed people listening to a loudspeaker from which the following words appeared:

> Mr. Baldwin has eaten a good lunch and is hopeful . . . it is denied that the Albert Memorial has been wrecked . . . There will be several trains to-morrow and the other six millions of you can walk.

Some newspapers were printed abroad, but the absence of normal deliveries prompted many people who seldom listened to the wireless to crowd around sets to listen to the strike news. In these nine days the B.B.C. set itself a standard which was, in retrospect, greatly admired. It had been the Government's intention to use the B.B.C. to inform the public of the official stand against the strikers. But Mr. Reith pointed out that the strikers and their sympathizers formed a considerable part of the listening public, and that the B.B.C. should be used only for a just and unbiased presentation of all points of view.

The strikers produced their own newspaper, the *British Worker*, under the guidance of Ernest Bevin. There were willing workers to print and distribute copies, but there was difficulty in obtaining ink and paper. The ink was made by volunteers, but paper could not easily be manufactured. In his biography of Julius Salter Elias, *Viscount Southwood*, Mr. R. J. Minney describes how 'every night reels of paper were found lying in a side street, just around the corner from Odhams, as though left there inadvertently.' Many people believed, says Mr. Minney, that this was done on the instructions of Mr. Elias, to counterbalance the facilities available to one side but not the other. Lord Beaverbrook, in helping to start the *British Gazette*, had suggested that Elias might well be given a knighthood, even a baronetcy, if he would print the paper for the Government. But Elias had refused, feeling that he ought not to oppose the strikers during their desperate struggle.

2

One of the main difficulties in ending the strike was the fact that the Government refused to negotiate. Instead, the armed forces and special police were instructed that they could take 'any action necessary' in an honest endeavour to aid the civil power. The Government refused the publication of an appeal by the churches for a peaceful settlement, although it was backed by the Archbishop of Canterbury. Publication was withheld in the *British Gazette*, until the matter was raised in the House of Commons. Cardinal Bourne's statement that the strike was 'a sin against God' was given wide publicity by the Government. Meanwhile the average citizen walked to work, or begged a lift, and—apart from the inconvenience—rather enjoyed the novelty and excitement of the situation.

'Strange how things happen!' wrote E. V. Lucas in the *Sunday Times*, when it was all over. 'Three weeks ago who would have said that within the month we should see London omnibuses driven by youths from the Universities, with policemen on the box to protect them from attack? Who would have dreamed of travelling in trains driven by amateurs, with amateur guards, amateur porters, and amateur signalmen, and arriving safely at the other end? Who would have guessed that medical students would leave their hospitals in order to unload vessels in the docks? Who would foresee Ranelagh and Hurlingham and Roehampton projecting their best polo players into the streets of London as mounted patrols? I have not consulted Old Moore or Zadkiel for the current year, but I suspect them to be dumb on these matters.'

Just after mid-day on May 12th, the ninth day of the strike, a deputation of the General Council of the Trades Union Congress went to 10 Downing Street to discuss the end of hostilities. The strike was called off on the understanding that negotiations should proceed to ensure a lasting settlement of the dispute.

It soon became clear that the miners had been betrayed. Very few, if any, of their claims were going to be realized. According to Allen Hutt, in his *Post-War History of the British Working Classes*, 'a vast army had entered battle with incomparable *élan*; but at its head stood generals anxious above all to avoid decisive actions, fearful of victory, concerned to bring the war to an end on any terms.'

The *Daily Mail*, in announcing the end of the strike, proclaimed the 'Surrender of the Revolutionaries,' and revealed, somewhat surprisingly, that *five hundred* Soviet agents had planned the strike. Men returning to work found themselves victimized, many being asked to accept terms which included a reduction in wages, although Mr. Baldwin had stated that he would not countenance any such action. Nearly forty-five thousand railwaymen did not return to work for another five months, and the coal dispute, which had caused the strike, continued. The miners held out for seven months before accepting a reduced wage. Many of the smaller pits were forced to close down, and when the majority of miners had returned to work others were forced through continued unemployment to find other work, migrate, or live on the 'dole.'

The strike had been a personal triumph for Mr. Baldwin. The *Sunday Express* hailed him as 'the man who emerges from the crisis with the greatest enhancement of reputation. Next comes Sir William Joynson-Hicks . . . who gave a remarkable exhibition of tact, conciliation, and efficiency.'

But the strike had cost the country several million pounds and had set industry back at a time when all the other nations in Europe were reorganizing their exports. In Conservative circles it was considered that the elusive character called 'the man in the street' had broken the spirit of the 'revolutionaries' or 'reds' or 'bolshies' and had prevented a possible threat to the security of the country, perhaps even to the throne. But in fact the deadlock had been ended by the General Council within sight of victory for the strikers. The majority of people had believed every word of the *British Gazette*, and had a completely false picture of the strikers, their grievances, and their claims.

The employment of the Army, armoured cars, and the use of the White Ensign on tugs carrying flour in the Thames, sanctioned by the Admiralty, were only part of the mobilization of force against sections of the civil population and their wishes and hopes. Police and members of the specially enrolled Civil Constabulary (wearing plain clothes but with steel helmets and truncheons) sought, in some situations, to break up strike pickets with baton charges. There were many hundreds of arrests, followed by severe jail sentences. A youth who called out, 'Don't shoot the workers!' received three months' hard labour. At every move the strikers were on the defensive. The *British Worker* weakly announced, in reply to the official charges of 'revolution,' that 'the General Strike is not a menace to Parliament, no attack is being made on constitutional government. We beg Mr. Baldwin to believe that.'

In addition to the *British Worker*, the strikers produced several duplicated bulletins and hastily printed leaflets. Many of these were as cheerful as the attitude of the undergraduates who drove railway engines and 'buses. In Kensington a bulletin joked, 'Sir John Simon says that the General Strike is illegal under an Act passed by William the Conqueror in 1066. All strikers are liable to be interned in Wormwood Scrubs. The three million strikers are advised to keep in hiding, preferably in the park behind Bangor Street, where they will not be discovered.'

When it was all over, but not forgotten, a Labour Party publication declared, 'The General Strike has made a united working class.' But it had done more than that. Never before had the ordinary citizen realized that the life of the community depended on the wage-earners. While the strike lasted there had been very few trains, no regular newspapers, and there was a danger that with time essential foodstuffs would run short. Although there had been little personal hostility between the strikers and the rest of the public, the position of the ordinary working man was now more fully appreciated by the governing classes and the 'white collar' workers.

But the failure of the strike to achieve its object seriously weakened the trade-union movement, and membership fell off, just as Ramsay MacDonald had foreseen. In 1927 the Trade Disputes Act declared 'general strikes' to be illegal, but this aroused strong Labour opposition, and when the Socialists came to power in 1946 the Act was repealed.

558 PUNCH, OR THE LONDON CHARIVARI. [MAY 16, 1928.

Mother. "WELL, REALLY, ANGELA, YOU KNOW I'M NOT NARROW-MINDED, BUT—COCKTAILS BEFORE BREAKFAST!"
Daughter. "NOT 'BEFORE BREAKFAST,' MOTHER; AFTER SUPPER."

CHAPTER ELEVEN

Five Years of Baldwin

I

A VERY LARGE Conservative majority had been returned in the general election of 1924 and, in November, Stanley Baldwin started five years of office as Prime Minister. His Foreign Secretary was Sir Austen Chamberlain, who had been Chancellor of the Exchequer in the 1918 Coalition Government. During his term of office there was some hope that the international problems which were engaging the attention might be solved, and he was able to collaborate with Briand of France, and Stresemann of Germany, and in 1925 he was prominent in negotiating the Locarno Pact, But, as we have seen, this did little to further the cause of peace, or to improve international goodwill.

Baldwin's Chancellor of the Exchequer was Winston Churchill, the son of Lord Randolph Churchill, who had held this office in 1886–7 under Lord Salisbury. He had been a Conservative, but had deserted the party to become a Liberal, and had served with distinction at the Admiralty under Lloyd George's war-time Coalition. Churchill's chief task was the difficult one of balancing the country's finances, a job which he tackled with vigour.

One of the Government's first acts was to set up a Royal Commission on food prices, with Sir Auckland Geddes as chairman. After a long investigation the Commission recommended the establishment of a permanent Food Council of twelve, of whom two men and two women would represent the consumer. The Council would have powers to report to

Parliament if any firm or association acted against the public interest. The view was expressed that food monopolies, trusts, and combines should be controlled.

The Council was set up under the chairmanship of Lord Bradbury, and it at once discussed with the bakers the question of the quartern loaf, which now cost 10d. Within a few weeks the loaf was reduced by a halfpenny, owing, so the bakers said, to the fall in the cost of flour. But the Council said this reduction was not enough, and after further talks the price fell to 9d. It then went on to consider the cost of milk and the question of short weights and measures. with some success.

Baldwin, smoking his pipe of peace, said that he did not believe in class wars. Nevertheless, there was still a great deal of class feeling in Britain, as the general strike proved. And this was in spite of the fact that the old order had changed so greatly. Had not King Edward knighted Thomas Lipton, a grocer? Had not Lloyd George raised many industrialists to the peerage? As Alec Waugh put it, 'We began to think that class is a habit that can be changed in half a generation; a man who is a newsboy at seventeen may be a baronet at fifty and a viscount at seventy.' But although one of the main criticisms that the Conservatives made against Labour was that Socialism fomented a class war, Stanley Baldwin, more than any other leader, fostered the division of the classes. But he was such a brilliant speaker that he was able to convince the majority of his listeners that what he said was right. Most of his speeches were extremely moving, so that at times it seemed almost impossible that he would not break down or falter while talking. When broadcasting from 2 LO during the general strike he included in a speech the words, 'I am a man of peace,' thus implying that he was the champion of the people at the mercy of the ruthless strikers; when, in fact, the strikers were on the defensive from the moment the strike began.

Even his political opponents were swayed by him. George

Lansbury said, 'When I listen to the Prime Minister at any time, he almost persuades me that I ought to be his supporter. I think his speeches have a similar effect on a good many other people too.'

George Graves and Alan Hodge, in their book *The Long Week-end*, consider Asquith to have been 'the last politician whose speeches could be printed as decent examples of English prose.' But Churchill's greatest speeches were yet to come, and many of Baldwin's, though hardly in the same category, were outstandingly fine, and very moving. They were published in volume form, and sold well.

Oratory, however, was not enough; neither Baldwin nor his colleagues brought any immediate improvement in the economic situation. The production of coal and the output of the basic industries remained well below the pre-war level; there were always, each year, over a million unemployed. But a genuine effort was made to improve the housing situation, and to employ more workers and provide more homes. In his desire to reduce the unemployment figures Baldwin announced his intention of reintroducing a tariff policy, which Labour had repealed. The Socialists immediately protested that this would be a violation of the Conservative election pledges, and the plan was watered down to include only partial protection.

'What you want,' said a character in a *Punch* cartoon, 'is protection.' Then, seeing the look of alarm which his remark drew, he hastily added—'from rain.'

But even rain could not help British agriculture, which was in the doldrums. Between the years 1919 and 1939 over three million acres of land passed out of cultivation and was used for rearing cattle or went barren. It was on many of these fields, close to the towns, that the new houses were going up, with assistance from the local council.

A good illustration of what could be done by an enterprising local authority was revealed in a scheme adopted by the Loughton, Essex, Council in 1925. Recognizing that the main difficulty lay in finding the difference in cash between the cost of building and the amount of a loan, the council decided to supplement the existing State subsidy with a contribution. Thus, a working man with from £35 to £50 capital could own his own home in fifteen or twenty years. In the case of a house and land worth £675 the Council advanced £520 at 5 per cent. The remaining £155 was reduced by the State subsidy of £75 to £80. Towards this the Council contributed £50, leaving only £30 to be found by the purchaser. Legal costs, say £15, had to be added.

Under the Loughton Council scheme a man could buy a £675 house by paying about 19s. 6d. a week, including rates. The London County Council had no comparable scheme. For a £675 house a cash payment of at least £80 was required by the L.C.C.

In Europe the fear of war continued to poison the peace which had been so laboriously won at the price of so much sacrifice. Each country continued to protest that it wished only for peace, but there was always at least one neighbour whom it distrusted. Until 1914 international foreign policy had been conducted by diplomats and courts and reigning monarchs, parliaments playing a subordinate role. But now each politician took up his own language and withdrew into his own country. At Versailles neither Lloyd George nor Wilson had been able to talk to Clemenceau in his own language; it was fortunate that the older man could speak English. But the League, created at Versailles, did not fill the gap in international diplomacy. The United Nations and N.A.T.O. were yet to come. Meanwhile Europe was so accustomed to the order which she had enjoyed for over a century before 1914 that she forgot the conditions and the methods of international diplomacy which had made those peaceful years possible.

The new statesmen of Europe were not diplomats—or even statesmen—in the pre-war sense. They were politicians, parliamentarians. And few realized that the peace and order which had been enjoyed before the war was not a privilege but a unique prodigy of history which would not be repeated unless the States of Europe made an effort to co-operate, and the United States added her influence.

Unfortunately, the politicians chosen by the people were not of the stature of the pre-war breed. And foreign policy was now left to a single minister, backed by a Foreign Office which was, as events proved, often too incapable. The solution lay in muddling through, while the League went overboard.

How could the responsibility for the remaking of Britain be entrusted to a single politician? G. K. Chesterton sounded the warning note in 1923:

> I was quite prepared to believe in a League of Nations; but I supposed, in my vague theoretical way, that it was a League of Nations. A League of Nations means a League of Nationalists. . . We must have a common principle; it ought to be a religion, but it must be an idea and it must not be a platitude. Above all, it must not be in the hands of anybody so unpractical as a practical politician.

By the middle twenties the majority of Britons had lost confidence in the League, but they clung to it desperately, because there was nothing else. 'What an absurd thing the League of Nations seems to be!' said the young hero of Evelyn Waugh's *Decline and Fall*. 'They seem to make it harder to get about instead of easier.'

Only a minority continued to believe in it, and to support the League of Nations Union, led by Lord Cecil. During the twenties and thirties most young men, reared in the shadow of the 1914 war, presumed that in the event of another war they would all be killed. It did not occur to them that anyone would escape. War, which was by no means uncertain, meant death and destruction on an unprecedented scale. Bombs dropped from aeroplanes would wipe out whole cities overnight; poison gas would destroy millions of people in a matter of hours. This fear increased during the thirties, when large sections of the public joined the Peace Pledge Union and added signatures to documents which stated that war should be 'banned.' Books like Beverley Nichols's *Cry Havoc* emphasized the slightly hysterical but nevertheless sincere pacifist attitude of the country at a time when Germany was starting to re-arm, and Britain, to keep the balance of power and to safeguard the peace of Europe, should have looked to her armaments and the strength of her Army and Navy.

In spite of the prevailing pacifist feeling, and the even more general apathy of the public concerning foreign affairs, there was still a measure of pride in the armed services. In July 1929, nearly two hundred thousand people attended a great aerial display given by the Royal Air Force at Hendon. Two hundred pilots took part, performing many novel and daring evolutions, including parachute descents. At Portsmouth and Plymouth and Chatham there were 'Navy weeks' when His Majesty's ships were on show to the public. Crowds flocked to the military tattoos. But there was no rush to join the Territorial Army, and as little money as possible was spent on keeping the armed services up to date.

Meanwhile Britain's mistrust of the Soviet Union, a fear based largely on hearsay and suspicion, increased. The publication in the *Morning Post* of evidence of 'Bolshevist blasphemy' and a 'war on religion' helped to convince many people that there was much to fear from the 'reds.' Cartoons reprinted from the Moscow anti-religious newspaper *Bezbozhnik* (Atheist) were described as 'revolting.' One was captioned, 'We have done away with the Tsars on earth; now we are going to destroy the Kings of Heaven.'

The Allies had been torn between two courses, either to invite the Bolsheviks to the Versailles meetings, and then to regard them as equals, or else to support the remnants of the White Russian armies still struggling against Bolshevism. Finally the Russian epidemic had been left to take its course, hemmed in by the new States of Finland, Esthonia, Latvia, Lithuania, and Poland. For two years Russia had been gripped by revolution. But by 1925 Communist Russia was firmly established, and was reluctantly recognized by the European States. When Britain officially recognized the U.S.S.R. in 1924, most other countries followed suit. But the fear of Russia remained, and no genuine efforts were made to understand the new regime. By 1926 most countries had decided to leave her alone to work out her own destiny. Her diplomats had taken part in both the Disarmament and World Economic Conferences, and in the thirties she was to join the League of Nations. But just as she was beginning to be accepted by the more moderate countries, the anti-Bolshevik scare was renewed by Nazi Germany, Fascist Italy, and Japan. By 1937, Stephen King-Hall thought that Russia was moving to the right 'at about the same rate as Great Britain and the U.S.A. are moving to the left.'

In 1926 the Imperial Conference was held in London, initiated by Mr. Leopold Amery, the Secretary of State for the Dominions. The Chairman was Lord Balfour. For more than a fortnight the Conference discussed the basis of future relationships between the self-governing Dominions. For the first time the term 'British Commonwealth of Nations' came into use, making it possible for General Hertzog, the Prime Minister of South Africa, to say that the old order had been replaced by 'a free alliance of England and the six Dominions, co-operating as friends.' The countries within the Commonwealth were now 'autonomous communities, equal in status, united by a common allegiance to the Crown, and freely associated as members of the British Commonwealth of Nations.'

But relations with Russia deteriorated. Early in 1927 the Government complained of the Communist propaganda which was being carried on in both Britain and China, and threatened to break off diplomatic relations if it continued. Suddenly, on May 12th, the Moorgate offices of Arcos Ltd., the headquarters of the Soviet trading corporation, were raided by the police. It was believed by the Foreign Office that the organization was being used for subversive action, and that secret documents which had disappeared from the War Office would be found there. Safes were opened by oxyacetylene drills, and although the documents were not discovered, the Government announced that considerable evidence was found of Russian military espionage. As a result, all relations with the Soviet Government were severed.

Stanley Baldwin's ministry ran its full course, from 1924 to 1929, five years in which there was some improvement in international affairs, the highlight being the Imperial Conference. Under the leadership of Neville Chamberlain, Minister of Health, considerable progress had been made in housing, although, as we have seen, many of the houses built were poorly constructed. There had also been a big extension of the 1911 Health Insurance scheme, with the introduction by Winston Churchill in 1926 of a pension grant to widows and their orphan children.

In August 1928, came the Briand-Kellogg Pact, officially called 'The Pact of Paris,' which was no more valuable than the 1926 Locarno Treaty. Its aim was to renounce war as a national policy, and it stated what the Covenant of the League of Nations had declared nine years before. Sixty-one States were represented at this great gathering of politicians and the pact was signed with a golden pen. A week before the conference ended, Monsieur Briand received, at his farm in Normandy, a correspondent of the *Sunday Dispatch*. The French Foreign Secretary granted an interview, but continued to fish during the conversation.

'Henceforth,' he said, 'nations will not be able to launch warlike adventures without reflection and appeal to judges . . . war is still a possibility, but it does not dominate the situation and the destiny of people so completely as it once did. The pact against war is a new obstacle to the frightful calamity which is war.'

The last eight years had seen many international gatherings. Politicians had discussed the future of Europe at San Remo,

Boulogne, Spa, Paris, London, Washington, Cannes, Genoa, The Hague, Lausanne, Locarno, Thoiry and Geneva. Now came another pact.

After the signing of the Pact of Locarno in 1925 Germany was free to enter the League. She had agreed to pay reparations, she had accepted the frontiers imposed on her on the west, and she had pledged herself against war. But as soon as her representatives took their places at the council table the youth of Germany claimed equality of treatment with the other countries of Europe, and protested against their helplessness before the tanks and heavy artillery of the Poles, Czechs and French. The final nail in the coffin of the League and the Treaty of Versailles came later, in June 1935, when Sir Samuel Hoare signed the pact which, in violation of the existing treaties, granted Hitler a larger fleet than France or Italy. Later, Mr. Baldwin boasted of the achievement of this pact, and later still he revealed that he had deceived the people of Britain in the matter of their national defence, so that he could maintain himself in office and his party in power.

But perhaps it was on January 30, 1933, the day the Nazis gained final power in Germany, that the shadow of the Second World War fell across Europe.

A. B. Payne's famous cartoon characters, Pip, Squeak and Wilfred, in the DAILY MIRROR *January 21, 1925.*

CHAPTER TWELVE

Emancipation

I

FOR MANY CENTURIES men had monopolized activities which they were not exclusively fitted to discharge.

At the beginning of the war women had still been in the toils of the long skirt, and very few had discarded the boned neckband. But the war freed them; they were too busy with essential work to be able to stop and adjust long dresses, or perch hats at correct angles. So skirts became shorter, hats more simple, veils vanished, and hair was cut short. Women, feeling free, and being given men's jobs to do, found that they could do them remarkably well.

'The freedom you have got with regard to dress is worth the vote a hundred times over,' declared Sir Alfred Hopkinson, speaking to the girls of Cheltenham Ladies' College. After the passing of the Sex Disqualification Act in 1919 more and more women entered the professions and worked in offices. Their war work had won them the parliamentary franchise, and admission to Parliament. In 1924 there were eight women members. And four years earlier, women began to serve on juries.

By 1923 there were some four thousand women serving as magistrates, mayors, councillors and guardians. In 1919 they were admitted to the legal profession and to Oxford, but Cambridge did not follow suit for twenty years. In 1921 the Higher Civil Service was opened to women, and in 1923 they were allowed to sue for divorce on the same terms as men.

The first Englishwoman to be called to the Bar, on May 10, 1922, was Miss Ivy Williams, a lecturer at Oxford. But although women could now become barristers, men dictated what they should wear in court. Nine women had passed the final examinations of the English Bar, and a committee of judges and benchers of the Inns of Courts expressed a wish that the dress of women barristers should conform to the following rules:

1. Ordinary barristers' wigs should be worn and should completely cover and conceal the hair.
2. Ordinary barristers' gowns should be worn.
3. Dresses should be plain, black or very dark, high to the neck, with long sleeves, and not shorter than the gown, with high, plain white collar and barristers' bands; or plain coats and skirts might be worn, black or very dark, not shorter than the gown, with plain white shirts and high collars and barristers' bands.

In a letter to *The Times* a colonel suggested that 'the masculine wig, grotesque and undignified as it will appear upon a female head, should be replaced by the graceful "coif".'

A striking feature of middle-class life was the increasing number of women who earned their living. The tendency of girls to copy their brothers and fathers, to wear stiff collars and ties, and to call their friends by their surnames, had been noticeable in pre-war days, but all the petty restrictions of those times were not abandoned. The modern girl dressed very simply, and required little material for a scanty frock, which could be easily made. Patterns could be bought to teach the novice the art of dress-making. The 'ready-made' frock was available for those who had no time to make dresses, and could be bought in any size and at almost any price. Feather-weight mackintoshes replaced the old heavy-weight rubber waterproofs; bathing dresses were no longer hideous shapeless navy serge garments trimmed with braid, but were simple and more revealing; light stockings which had to be washed every day had replaced black woollen ones. At the end of the twenties the society couturier, Norman

Hartnell, could say, 'English women are dressing better each season; their preference is for simple, well-cut and well-made dresses; they avoid the bizarre and the conspicuous.'

When the first number of *Good Housekeeping* magazine appeared in London in March 1924, the editor wrote:

> Any keen observer of the times cannot have failed to notice that we are on the threshold of a great feminine awakening. Apathy and levity are giving place to a wholesome and intelligent interest in the affairs of life, and above all in the home. There should be no drudgery in the house . . . the house-proud woman in these days of servant shortage does not always know the best way to lessen her own burdens . . . the time spent on housework can be enormously reduced in every home without any loss of comfort, and often with a great increase to its well-being and its air of personal care and attention. . .

Women who read that first number found short stories by William J. Locke, Marie Corelli, Robert Hichens and Kathleen Norris, an article entitled *The Ideal Home* by Herbert Jeans, articles on cookery, health and beauty, fashions, furnishing, decoration, lighting and needlework; Helena Normanton, R.A., contributed an article on *The Law as a Profession*, Viscountess Gladstone wrote on *The Model Housewife*, and Lady Astor's name appeared beneath an article entitled *England and the Dragon*. The dragon was alcohol.

In 1920, revealed Lady Astor, the drink trade had kept for itself nearly three times as much as was spent on education—£97,000,000.

Writing about divorce in the same magazine, Clemence Dane told readers to 'take nothing for granted because the Tory or the Liberal, the priest or the layman, says so. Let us find out the truth of these matters *for ourselves*. Let us question and argue and inquire until our minds are made up, freshly and independently. And then—having rightly or wrongly made up our minds, and knowing that we are represented in parliament, that our voices will be heard if we choose to raise them—*for Heaven's sake let us get a move on!*'

The magazine contained 120 pages. 'Inexpensive artistic furnishings' were advertised, cretonnes 31 inches wide cost from 1s. 0¾d. to 5s. 11d. a yard; lounge chairs cost 8 guineas, a settee 16 guineas. An electric washing machine and combined wringer which washed 'everything from the daintiest lingerie to the heaviest blankets' was claimed to be 'silent, rapid and efficient.' A tube of Gibbs's tooth paste cost 7½d. or 1s.; a forty-one piece leadless glaze tea-set from Heal's cost £1 7s. 6d., a fifty-four piece Copeland Spode dinner set cost 10 guineas.

The 'ideal home' of the time was 'a country cottage of the bungalow type with dining-room, living-room, kitchen, maid's bed-sitting room, loggia, three bedrooms and a bathroom.' This could be built for from £1,450 to £1,600, plus the cost of the land.

Low waist-lines and the 'monk's sleeve' were the features of the early spring costumes. Wide hats and brimmed hats were expected to replace close-fitting hats. Pearls would not be worn so much with black evening gowns as hitherto. And from Paris came an important fashion note—'it is *whispered* that *orange* will play a prominent part in our early summer frocks.'

Daring women bobbed their hair, corsets dragged the stomach in and ignored the waist, zip-fasteners made life easier. Pudding-basin hats, long 'tube' and sack-like dresses with low waists or no waists at all were the fashion. In 1922–23 the skirt had been worn just above the ankles. In 1925 it was just below the knees. In 1926 the knees were freely shown. Women were out to show men that it was not only a man's world.

'Now or never,' said Marie Corelli, 'women must undertake in earnest the task of civilizing man. And they must set about it the right way. Not by soft yielding to every caprice of a creature that has still so much more of the *monkey* than the man in him, but by a gentle yet firm rectitude and purity that shall effectually restrain his simian impulses.'

'Women are the most important persons in the world,' announced Sir William Arbuthnot Lane, the exponent of the 'New Health' movement, which advocated the eating of roughage, uncooked vegetables and 'natural' foods. But the Archbishop of York declared that there was a great tide of feminine restlessness and instability of nerves and passion now forcing itself up against the barriers which preserved the sanctity of marriage. In 1921 the number of divorces had been greater than ever before. In 1927 the figures were almost as high.

For the first time, the subject of birth control was now widely and openly discussed. An American, Mrs. Margaret Sanger, had taken a leading role in the birth control movement in the United States, and had organized a conference at Geneva, but the scientists who had been invited ignored the practical side of the subject. It was a British doctor of science, Dr. Marie Stopes, the wife of the well-known aeroplane designer, A. V. Roe, who first publicly advocated the new doctrine. In 1922 she hired the Queen's Hall in London, for a meeting, but soon encountered strong opposition, especially from Roman Catholics, who regarded the use of contraceptives as almost akin to child murder. Dr. Stopes insisted that by the use of birth control one got fewer but healthier children, and avoided racial disease.

In her book, *Mother England*, Dr. Stopes pointed out that while doctors often told women that to have more children meant death, they seldom, if ever, told them how to avoid having children, except by abstinence. At her birth-control clinic in the East End of London she received in three months more than twenty thousand requests for procuring abortions, mostly from mothers who did not know that abortion was criminal.

In 1923 Dr. Stopes brought a libel action against a writer who suggested that she was making money out of the sale of contraceptives. She proved that her clinic made no profits, and claimed that her work was divinely inspired. This drew a violent attack from the defending K.C., who exclaimed, 'Dr. Marie Stopes will have you believe that God sent down this beastly, filthy message!' She lost her action, but the publicity which it attracted and the free discussion of the subject brought the subject into the open. By the end of the twenties most doctors were giving birth-control information, and contraceptives were publicly sold and discreetly advertised.

Dr. Scharlieb, a leading woman doctor, thought Dr. Stopes was wrong. She told a large meeting of women that most contraceptives were harmful, causing diseased nerves, hysteria and other evils. The only safe method, she said, lay in voluntary continence at certain periods. If family economic problems could not be solved at home, she advised families to go out into the wide open spaces of the Empire to seek a living.

2

The London season of 1922 had been heralded as the most brilliant since 1914. At the full State Courts the women's trains were shorter than at Edwardian Courts, when they had measured 3 yards, making two on the ground. Now they were 18 inches on the ground, and headdress plumes were worn 'just a little bit lower.' Evening Courts had returned, and Princess Mary made her début as a hostess at Chesterfield House, a rendezvous for young people in the Court set.

'What does Miss 1922 see and do in town during her first season?' asked a society magazine correspondent. She went to Court, visited Ascot and Goodwood, attended innumerable dances, saw plays and heard operas, and made friends among the young girls and men of her parents' circle. 'The girl of today is allowed a good deal of liberty, but chaperons for dances have been an acknowledged feature of the entertaining this year.' By 1924, chaperons had almost entirely vanished, at least at dances.

Miss 1922 had breakfast in bed, because 'even glowing youth must take precautions against being over-tired and losing its freshness and capacity for enjoyment.' If shopping with mother did not claim her in the morning then she went out with a girl friend or 'indulged her passion for exercise by taking a swim on ladies' days at the Bath Club.' In pre-war days she would have gone with her mother on an endless round of receptions and afternoon calls. Now she went to polo matches at Hurlingham, Ranelagh or Roehampton, watched lawn tennis at Queen's, or played golf. The *thé-dansant*, a stroll in the park, the trying-on of dresses, and perhaps after-dinner bridge or a game of Mah-Jong were all part of the social round. For some girls there were wild, hectic parties in Chelsea or Bloomsbury or Mayfair.

In December 1924, Violet Bonham Carter described upper-class married women as 'drones, exclusive parasites who consume more money than they could possibly earn in the labour market by the services they render to their homes.' Meanwhile, poorer women and girls were working long hours in factories, as their grandmothers had done, or were trying to feed a family on the dole money which their husbands drew. The men went to the Labour Exchange and the women went to the pawnshop.

Many women found that they could not, as their grandmothers had done, wait for a husband to come along. There were now tens of thousands more women than men, and few families were rich enough to keep daughters at home doing nothing. Sometimes the man of the family had been killed or maimed in the war, and the woman must work. But in May 1922 the society journals were chiefly concerned about whether a débutante should or should not carry flowers when being presented to the King and Queen.

Princess Mary's wedding trousseau was stated to 'combine the qualities of elegance and simplicity.' Her going-away dress reached almost to her ankles and was of powder blue charmeuse, embroidered with coral beads, and worn with a black satin hat adorned with a wreath of blue and pink flowers. There was also an evening dress with a low waist, made of wild-rose pink georgette, embroidered with crystal beads and finished at the waist with bead roses. Another item in the trousseau was 'an exquisite ermine wrap,' the ends of which were turned back to form sleeves, and a swathed toque of gold tissue.

The 'boyish' vogue in women's fashions, which lasted for a short time but made a great social impact, first became popular in 1924, when the hipless and bosomless female figure was something to be desired and achieved. 'Women's fondness for sport fixes the present severe contour,' announced Monsieur Worth. 'Women now prefer simplicity in order not to attract attention. Their emancipation socially and politically has gradually led to masculine severity in line. These masculine lines make women look young, and they go well with shingled heads and short skirts.'

Most women wanted to be flat both in front and behind. Even nude figures in the Folies Bergères were flat-chested, and were chosen for that reason. Straight, chemise-chested, beaded dresses were the vogue. The 'shingle' and the 'Eton crop' accentuated the boyishness of the 'flapper' or 'butterfly' girl. To keep their chests flat, many women wound wide ribbon around their bodies.

In his novel *Crazy Pavements*, Beverley Nichols described one of his women characters as being a 'flat-chested monocled figure, about as feminine as General Pershing when young, to whom, indeed, she bore a certain resemblance.'

Towards the end of the war Mrs. E. Alec Tweedie's book *Women and Soldiers* had enjoyed enormous popularity. It faithfully represented the outlook of large numbers of her readers. Some of her observations are worth recalling:

> Bachelors from twenty to forty should be taxed 25 per cent of their incomes.
>
> Let the Minister of Reconstruction start by putting all feeble-minded persons on farm lands, where there is no possibility of offspring.

Alas! Some really nice girls are afflicted with an unintentional 'glad-eye' that attracts the worst side of the worst men.

Tawdry finery is the hall-mark of the usual working-class girl, while the factory-hand has been known to pull out her mirror, puff-box and rouge, in the middle of a twelve-hours' night shift on a fourteen-consecutive-nights' job.

Let us put the whole nation from sixteen to sixty under conscription —men and women alike—so that babies by dozens may be born into a better-disciplined world.

Nothing, perhaps, so effectually demonstrated the altered conditions of life as the triumphant rise and progress of the ready-to-wear garment. At first good designs were cheapened and made vulgar in the process of copying, but soon several grades of 'ready made' dresses were available, to suit all sizes and pockets. In 1925, 5 or 6 guineas was the average sum to give for a neat serge or tweed suit in a fashionable London store, but attractive summer cotton fabric frocks could also be bought from 37s. 6d., up to £4 or £5. Dainty hand-work was an important feature in the decoration of washing fabrics, and was considered well worth an extra guinea.

The Hon. Mrs. C. W. Forester revealed, in this year, that a woman with an annual dress allowance of £100 would probably spend it like this:

Lingerie	£15
Accessories	£10
Boots and shoes	£10
Tailored clothes (including jumper)	£20
Afternoon dress or three-piece	£15
Evening gowns	£12
Hats	£10
Extras—tea gown, blouse, jumper	£8

Writing about the week-end wardrobe for the society girl, Mrs. Forester advised:

The usual country week-end is an informal affair. Probably you will motor down, or at least be met by your host's car (but it is as well to know if it will be an open or a shut one). On Friday afternoon, let us say, you will leave town in a simple suit with matching jumper of some kind. It can either be the inevitable navy serge or rep, mixed tweed, or suiting. If plainly tailored and not too countrified, such a suit will do admirably for Sunday or a visit to the neighbouring tennis party.

According to this expert, the visitor's two small or one large suit-case, neat canvas hat-box, and reasonably-sized dressing case (three or four pieces!) should contain:

1. A simple tea frock.
2. A smarter dinner-gown.
3. Two dressing-gowns.
4. A bed-jacket and boudoir cap
5. A perfectly plain severe country tweed or knitted suit with jumper or washing over-blouse.
6. For golf—a heavier skirt and woollen sweater.
7. For tennis—a smartly cut plain or pleated skirt in navy or white and a couple of dainty coloured jumpers.
8. A pair of thick-soled low-heeled country shoes.
9. For evening—shoes and stockings to match the best dress.
10. Hats, scarves, gloves, belts, handkerchiefs.
11. Undergarments (woven knickers, either thick or thin, are more or less essential with short country skirts).
12. A warm coat or mackintosh.
13. Parasol, folding or short umbrella.

'Motoring,' said Mrs. Forester, 'has become so general that beyond big leather, tweed and fur-lined overcoats, with well fitted hats or caps, *no special attire* is necessary.'

In June 1922, Miss Florence Fenwick Miller asked when the wedding service was to be revised. In an article claiming that equality with men was what most women wanted, but still did not have, she said:

Is any woman justified in promising to obey her husband when obedience, as the church service explains it, implies absolute subjection of the womanly judgment, will and sense of responsibility to the unexplained orders of the man she has married? Has any woman the right to solemnly vow in church that she will give unquestioning, invariable obedience to another human being?

Many of the women engaged in what had previously been masculine tasks were working only until they found husbands and could 'settle down.' Amateurs had entered all walks of life. Even the professional prostitute's career was threatened. But it was in hat-shops, tea-rooms, secretarial positions, in telephone exchanges and in journalism that the new 'career girls' excelled.

The first woman to sit in Parliament was Lady Astor, the Member in 1919 for the Sutton division of Plymouth. She was introduced to the House by Lloyd George and A. J. Balfour. Her fearlessness of speech and action were matched only by her courage. When, returning from a night meeting at Plymouth, she met a man in the entrance hall of her home who threatened to kill her, she overawed him. When he fled into the stables she followed, chasing him through a public house and out at the back. Having caught him, she refused to prosecute, but told the police, 'I only wanted his name, in the public interest.'

On another occasion Communists tried to howl her down while she was speaking at Glasgow. Undaunted, she started to sing *Keep the Home Fires Burning*, which silenced the crowd.

She had little respect for people or institutions. Meeting one of her own parliamentary leaders after she had opposed him in the House, she remarked, 'I have been defending you against the Labour Members. They say you are not fit to feed with pigs. I say you are.'

'You need not call it the League of Nations,' she once said. 'Give it a new name every week, but give it a chance.'

It was not until 1921 that other women joined her; the number of women Members remained very small until the thirties. When, against considerable opposition, a law was passed in 1928 enfranchising all women of twenty-one on equal terms with men, over five million women voters were suddenly added to the national registers. Women had at last achieved equality with men, although they were usually still paid less for doing the same job.

What were the young women of the twenties really like? It would be quite wrong to believe that many of them fulfilled the picture presented by a contemporary writer:

Mother's advice, and Father's fears
Alike are voted—just a bore
There's negro music in our ears,
The world is one huge dancing floor.
We mean to tread the Primrose Path,
In spite of Mr. Joynson-Hicks.
We're People of the Aftermath
We're girls of 1926.

In greedy haste, on pleasure bent,
We have no time to think, or feel,
What need is there for sentiment,
Now we've invented Sex-Appeal?
We've silken legs and scarlet lips,
We're young and hungry, wild and free,
Our waists are round about the hips,
Our skirts are well above the knee.

We've boyish busts and Eton crops,
We quiver to the saxophone.
Come, dance before the music stops,
And who can bear to be alone?
Come drink your gin, or sniff your 'snow,'
Since Youth is brief, and Love has wings,
And time will tarnish, ere we know
The brightness of the Bright Young Things.

True? No, this was an exaggerated picture of a very small section of the community. Most women were too busy looking after husbands and families to join the much-publicized minority who 'drank, and drugged, and stole each other's men.'

Commences Monday next, and continues for 4 weeks.

50 UNBRUSHED WOOL CARDIGANS (as sketch), made from superior quality yarn, on well-fitting lines. In almond, putty, silver, black, saxe, brown/white, black/white, etc.
Usual price 35/6
Sale Price 21/-

(15 only) ORIGINAL MODEL FUR COATS, of which one sketched is a typical example in fine quality seal dyed musquash, with edges to collar and flounce of Sable dyed Kolinsky, lined rich French Brocade.
Original prices 135/198 Gns.
Sale Price 98 Gns.

50 TEAGOWNS to clear, of which sketch in rich metal brocade, is a typical example, in several colours, also black.
Price 10½ to 15½ Gns.
Sale Price 8½ Gns.

25 MODEL COATS in various good quality materials and designs, of which sketch in novelty rep embroidered and finished with accordion pleated frills, is an example.
Usual prices 14½ to 18½ Gns.
Sale Price 10½ Gns.

DISTINCTIVE TUNIC made in heavy crêpe-de-Chine, a band of fine tucking forms the low waistline and trims the sleeves. In ivory, sandalwood, grey, beige.
Sale Price 39/6

Brogue Shoes in black Box Calf and Tan Willow.
Usual Price 39/6.
Sale price 21/9

REMNANT DAYS THURSDAYS.

Sale Catalogue post free.

Goods cannot be sent on approval during the Sale.

MARSHALL & SNELGROVE,
(Debenhams, Ltd.),
VERE ST. and OXFORD ST., LONDON, W.1.

Patent and black suède tan calf front and back fawn suède, one bar shoe, open side. L.XV. (as sketch).
Sale Price 42/-

CHAPTER THIRTEEN

Motoring

I

IN 1911 THERE had been some 47,000 private cars in Britain, and the number was rising by ten to twelve thousand a year. British manufacturers were concentrating on the luxury car. A 50 horse-power six-cylinder Austin cost £650, but this price covered only the chassis, with tyres. A Vauxhall chassis cost from £395 to £495, an Armstrong-Whitworth chassis from £375 to £850. Most bodies were coach-built, and there were few cheap cars. An exception was the two-seater N.A.G. (at £350 complete) and the B.S.A. two-seater coupé, but motoring was still for the wealthy, and there were few models of less than 20 horse-power. And because these cars were expensive to run, large numbers of cheaper American models found a ready market in England, especially the Ford. At the price, the Ford could beat all its rivals for power, hill-climbing and low petrol consumption.

Britain's chief motor manufacturer during the post-war period, competing favourably with his American rivals, was W. R. Morris, later to be knighted, and then to become Lord Nuffield. When he was 16 he had worked for a bicycle maker, and after only nine months, with less than £5 capital, he had set up business on his own, and produced a bicycle which was so good and cheap that models were soon much in demand around Oxford, where he lived. Young Morris then designed a motor cycle with a vertical engine and a countershaft drive, two innovations in advance of anything else on the road.

This success led him to experiment in designing a car, for he considered that there was a demand for a cheap, light model which could carry four people, a motor for family use which would be cheaper to buy and run than the big high-powered models then on the market. In 1912, backed by the success of his bicycles and his motor cycles, he bought a small factory at Cowley and started to work, thirty hours at a stretch, on his plan. He was still only 20, and he had taught himself all he knew about engineering. What is more, there were several rival factories with more capital already producing cars intended to appeal to the public which he wanted to capture. What he had to do, if he was going to succeed, was to turn out a car which was cheaper and more reliable than those of his rivals.

In 1912 a 20 horse-power car from America cost about £200, but an English or continental car of 12 horse-power cost at least £300. The N.A.G. went about 25 miles to the gallon, or on bad roads (and many side roads were bad) or in town, 20 miles to the gallon. Petrol cost 1s. 6d. a gallon in 1912, and the average small car used about 210 gallons a year, bringing the fuel bill to £15 15s. Little enough by modern standards, but in 1912 a year's motoring bill for a small car worked out like this:

Petrol at 1s. 6d. a gallon	15	15	0
Oil at 3s. 6d. a gallon	3	12	6
4 tyres, lasting a year	25	0	0
Garaging, incidentals	10	0	0
Driving licence		5	0
Post Office tax	4	4	0
Insurance	10	0	0
	68	16	6

The second year's running was estimated to cost slightly more. After about 5,000 miles there would be an accumulation of carbon to be cleaned from the pistons with oxygen, new tyres would be needed, and the bill would reach £100. After five years the second-hand value of the car would be about £150. It was, by pre-war standards, an expensive luxury.

The bigger cars, the Rolls-Royces, Napiers, Daimlers, Straker-Squires, Connaughts, Sheffields, Wolseleys and Adlers with Morgan cabrio-landaulette bodies, these were the large saloons and heavy tourers which had replaced the four-in-hands and the private carriages of the influential upper-classes. Their owners were slightly surprised to see the first Morris-Oxford on the road in 1913. It was exactly what the middle classes were seeking for family use, and as late as 1928 some of the first Morris cars were still running, in regular commission.

The first 400 Morris cars were built in a factory converted from the military college buildings which had been added to a grammar school in which Morris's grandfather had been educated. In 1914, when war was declared, private motoring was seriously affected, and the number of cars fell from 92,000 to 50,000. The little Morris factory was soon engaged on war work, including the making of some 50,000 mine sinkers for the North Sea minefields. Morris himself was tremendously patriotic, and during the twenties he had a large Union Jack flown above the factory at Cowley, floodlit at night. He used the slogan 'Buy British and be proud of it,' and later added another, 'Even if you don't buy a Morris, at least buy a car made in the United Kingdom.'

As early as 1915 he began to plan his post-war model, realizing that there would be a spending boom. When peace came he was 41, and Ford already had a big assembly plant in Manchester where thousands of new T-models were being put together. The price of components had risen two or three times compared with pre-war figures, and wages were soaring, so that the post-war Morris cars were not as cheap as their creator had hoped. The Morris-Cowley cost £315, and the Morris-Oxford (with an electric starter) cost £360 for the two-seater, £390 for the four-seater and £450 for the coupé. Even at £315, however, the Cowley cost considerably less than most of its rivals, although the 10 horse-power A.B.C. was selling for only £195 and the two-cylinder Palladium was sold at 265 guineas.

A feature of the 1919 cars was their association with the war, which still occupied the thoughts of the average citizen. The H.G.F. was described as 'made like an aeroplane' and the Crossley as 'the car that's served the R.F.C. in every battle area.' Many cars were fitted with the Gabriel bugle, a tiny four-pipe organ hooter which worked from the exhaust.

By 1921 many of the manufacturers realized that they were making losses, and were unlikely to be able to compete profitably with the Americans. Morris had thousands of models in showrooms all over Britain, and he could not sell them fast enough. The slump had set in, and small car companies were going bankrupt every month. The surviving manufacturers therefore met to discuss how they could raise their prices to meet the new wage demands, and how high they should fix the prices. Morris, however, decided to reduce his prices, and chose the week just before the 1921 Olympia Motor Show to announce his price cuts. His decision made him very unpopular with the motor trade, but eventually the surviving companies were brought into line, out of necessity. The *Autocar* of February 12, 1921, carried the announcement:

Morris-Cowley 4-seater	down	£100 to £425
Morris-Cowley 2-seater	down	£ 90 to £375
Morris-Cowley chassis	down	£ 65 to £325
Morris-Oxford 4-seater	down	£ 25 to £565
Morris-Oxford 2-seater	down	£ 25 to £510
Morris-Oxford coupé	down	£ 80 to £595

These reductions, said Morris, were an attempt to cheapen the price of a very sound type of British car by increasing the demand. The attempt was a great success. British car sales suddenly soared from 122,000 in 1920 to a quarter of a million in late 1921. Soon Morris cars were coming out of the factory at the rate of 56,000 a year, and the demand was exceeding the supply. Customers had to wait for delivery. Other car prices fell; the 10 horse-power four-seater Citroen was reduced from £495 to £395; Hillman's guaranteed the cost of car hire up to £30 if their owners had to have their cars repaired. And in October 1922 Morris again cut his prices, making the two-seater Morris-Cowley only £225.

In 1919 only 337 cars had come out of the Oxford factory, in 1922 there were 5,166, but in 1923 the turnover was £6,000,000 and a year later it was nearly double. Between 1922 and 1923 there were 15,987 Morris cars sold, and by 1925 the figure had risen to nearly 50,000.

During the nineteen-twenties other companies were absorbed, to form the Morris group. In 1923 the Hotchkiss concern in Coventry was bought, then a Coventry coach-building firm was taken over, and in 1927 the famous Wolseley company was bought for £730,000. It had lost £97,000 in 1921, just when Morris was lowering his prices, and £364,000 in 1924.

In 1928 Morris announced that he would produce a new 'baby' car, in competition with the now famous 'baby' Austin, which had become one of the most popular cars on the road. This new model was the Morris 'Minor,' selling at £125 for the touring car and £135 for the fabric saloon, with £2 extra for a windscreen made of safety glass and £6 10s. if all the windows were fitted with safety glass. By 1930 the price was reduced to £100, for which one could buy a two-seater capable of travelling at 40 miles to the gallon. Two people could drive from London to Brighton and back for 3s.

As the demand for Morris cars grew, so new factories were built, dwarfing the original buildings. In 1923 Morris Commercial Cars Limited was formed, making trucks, vans and lorries. In 1925 came the first M.G. sports models. By

1951 the 214-acre assembly plant at Cowley could produce 15,000 models a year, 3,000 cars in a single week. The vast Nuffield organization, working in fourteen factories, employed over 25,000 workers.

'When things are difficult, do not moan, but set to and get business. It will not always come to you.' This was one of Lord Nuffield's favourite maxims. 'I began with nothing,' he said in 1926. 'I hadn't even a five-pound note. But although I was only seventeen I felt that W. R. Morris would pay me a higher salary than anybody else. So I started to work for W. R.'

In 1943 this remarkable man formed the Nuffield Foundation, valued at £10,000,000, 'the largest and most notable gift in the history of the nation.' At one time, in the late nineteen-thirties, he was giving money away at the rate of £8 a minute. On Armistice Day 1939 he dropped a cheque for £100,000 into the box of a poppy-seller. Altogether he has given away well over £26,000,000. But the turning point of his career and of the vast organization which he built up was decided on that day in 1921 when, a week before the Olympia Motor Show, he made up his mind to reduce his prices.

Morris and Austin were the cars for the middle classes, and Rolls-Royce was the motor for the rich. With the Daimler, the car favoured by the royal family, the Rolls-Royce represented all that was best in English manufacturing perfection. By 1921 the cars, which had been made only in England during the last seventeen years, were also being made in Springfield, Massachusetts, under the supervision of experts from the Derby works. The chassis sold for 11,750 dollars, and the bodywork was designed according to the customer's wishes. But the Rolls-Royce remained beyond the reach of most people, and was something elegant, to be admired gliding down the new Regent Street. The average motorist was more concerned with the mysteries of double-declutching and changing gear, and the Daimler Company issued hints, in their advertisements, to the thousands of learners who were starting to drive:

> The secret of confidence is practice. Do not wait for a hill. Learn on the level by half-an-hour's continuous changing up and down. Choose a flat clear road, and run the car at about twenty miles an hour in top gear. To practice changing down, press firmly on the gear lever and suddenly raise your foot from the accelerator. The lever will move at once into neutral without declutching, but if you forget to press on it first it will often stick even when you do declutch.

Simple? The lanes of Britain were full of motorists learning how to drive. On the wireless Grandma Buggins 'went for a spin' with the family, and became, like so many members of other families, a back-seat driver who knew all about everything. And on the stage, Harry Tate was still getting roars of laughter from audiences with his popular sketch, *Motoring*.

It was a wonderful way of getting out of town at week-ends. A Wolseley 'ten' two-seater carrying five fair bathers direct from their home to the beach at Hove, Sussex, was described in the *Illustrated London News* as a 'motor car eliminating the bathing machine.' Couples in little open cars sat out at night on Surrey commons, and planned the future. The coming of cheap cars had made it possible for whole families to move out of industrial areas. But in London the traffic problem was growing acute, and in 1924 Sir Alfred Yarrow, the Clyde engineer and shipbuilder, designed a scheme for building bridges at intersecting points of important roads. He offered to build such a bridge at his own cost, providing that he should be reimbursed if it remained permanent after two years, and that if it proved unsuccessful he would pay to have it removed. This, he claimed, would solve London's future traffic problems. Oxford Circus was the point suggested for the test bridge, and other points mentioned were the junctions of Kingsway and Holborn, and of Oxford Street and Tottenham Court

Road. His offer, however, was not accepted and the Yarrow plan, which might have helped to solve the problem of London's present traffic congestion, was filed away and forgotten.

American cars continued to offer considerable competition to the English models. It was only with our light cars that the American makers could not compete. As the motoring correspondent of the *Illustrated London News* asked in May 1924:

> Where from abroad do we get cars like the Hillman, the Riley, the Lea-Francis, the Swift, the Triumph, the Bean? One light car I have left until last, because it deserves a mention all to itself. I refer to the Morris, which is beyond doubt the most popular car of the day. Here is an all-British car, excellently designed and conscientiously constructed, equipped with starter, electric lighting, and all the rest which the present-day motorist requires, and which can be purchased for under £200—actually less by a substantial amount than a similar car would have cost before the war. Truly, the British industry is a long way from its decease.

The popular 'baby' Austin seven was now well established. It sold at £165 and was bought by families who had never before owned a car, or expected to possess one. Even cheaper, at £125, was the solid-tyre Trojan, with the engine at the back. 'Before we offer you a second-hand Trojan,' advertised the Lewes Motor Works, 'we spend from £10 to £15 on overhauling it.'

By 1926, when Mr. Ford had made his fifteen millionth 'T' model, the motor industry employed over a million people. 'If only our roads and our traffic control can be put on a sound and efficient basis,' complained *Country Life*, 'the number can be immensely increased.' In May 1925 there had been a two-hour traffic block in the Strand. Many of the roads of England were too narrow for the double rows of cars, and towns had to be bypassed. The ever-increasing number of women motorists revolutionized feminine fashions. When motoring had first become popular there had been a great fuss about the special clothes which had to be worn and horrible cloth hats were designed, to be worn with a 'motoring veil' tied round in a bow under the chin, but the wearer usually ended the journey looking dishevelled. Then came small hats with yards of flowing chiffon which trailed in the breeze. Now women found that to use their cars in a practical manner they had to wear ordinary, simple clothes.

The manufacturers were also catering for women with their new light cars, which were easy to run. Among the 1925 models was a 14 horse-power saloon containing silver flower-vases, and a compartment for a shopping diary. Ash trays and a floor rug were provided, and there was a silk blind in the back window.

There were so many different makes from which to choose, if one wanted to buy a car. In 1925 the 7 horse-power Jowett was selling for £160, the two-seater at £150 and the four-seater at £170. A second-hand Morgan de Luxe (with three wheels) cost £95, and a 1919 model only £49. One could still buy a second-hand 1912 38 horse-power Minerva Landaulette for £75, and a second-hand 1921 five-seater Ruston-Hornsby tourer cost £72 10s.

The G.W.K., made at Cordwalles Works, Maidenhead, was advertised as being 'so easy to manipulate that one of our travellers who lost one leg and one arm in the war is *one of our best drivers*.' A two-seater sold at £295.

The Aster, made at Wembley, was comparatively expensive, ranging from £570 to £935. The Lagonda, made at Staines, cost a minimum of £295. But the Bentley was the sports car for the serious motoring enthusiast, and an early model is still regarded as being unsurpassable in its special class.

The relative popularity of the various makes of cars in 1925 might be judged from a list made during a drive from Worthing, Sussex, through Chichester, Billingshurst, and back to Worthing, in May of that year. The census was as follows:

26 Morris
15 Ford
12 Standard
11 Citroen, A.C.
10 Austin, Buick
9 Singer, Rover
8 Essex, Wolseley, Bean
7 Vauxhall
6 Talbot, Humber, Swift, Armstrong
5 De Dion, Overland, Horstman, Daimler
4 Morgan
3 A.B.C., G.W.K., Rhode, Sunbeam, Hillman, Arrol-Johnston, Darracq, Fiat, Calcott, Chevrolet, Crossley, Maxwell, Studebaker
2 Minerva, Dodge, Hudson
1 Rolls-Royce, D.F.P., Bentley, Napier, Paige, Unic, Phoenix, Trojan, Aster, Chrysler, Lagonda.

The *Autocar* of that week contained the names of 230 different makes of cars, new and second-hand, which were offered for sale. By the end of the twenties, many of these companies were out of business, but while they lasted, and while their cars continued to run along the roads, small boys who delighted in 'spotting' the various makes, or collected cigarette cards issued by Lambert and Butler, had a busy time:

A.B.C., A.C., Adler, Albert, Alfa, Alvis, Angus-Sanderson, Ansaldo, Argyll, Ariel, Armstrong-Siddeley, Armstrong-Whitworth, Arrol-Johnstone, Aster, Aston-Martin, Aurea, Austin, Austro-Daimler, Autocrat, Ballot, Bayliss-Thomas, Bean, Beardmore, Belsize, Belsize-Bradshaw, Bentley, Benz, Berliet, Bianchi, Bignan, Bleriot-Whippet, Bond, Brasier, Briton, B.S.A., Bugatti, Buick

and so on, through

Clement-Talbot, Clyno, Coventry Premier to Cubitt, Deemster, Elgin, Eric Campbell, Galloway, Gwynne and Spyker, down to Windsor and Wolseley at the end of the list of 230 cars.

The 'baby' family car, suited to the pocket of the average wage-earner and the traffic conditions of the towns, had come to stay. *Punch* remarked, 'Owing to the small size of the latest fashionable dog, many large kennels would be absolutely useless if it wasn't for these two-seater cars.'

ROVER

LIGHT CAR PRICES REDUCED

The following prices are now effective:

8 h.p. STANDARD MODEL 2 or 4 SEATER **£139**

Or with Self-Starter, £149 10s.

Horizontally opposed twin-cylinder engine, three speeds and reverse, equipped with electric lighting, horn, spare wheel and tyre, all-weather side curtains, etc., finished in Nile blue or red.

9/20 h.p. STANDARD MODEL 2 or 4 SEATER **£175**

WITH SELF-STARTER

Four-cylinder, water-cooled, overhead valve engine, three speeds and reverse, equipped with electric starting and lighting, horn, spare wheel and tyre, all-weather side curtains, etc., finished olive brown.

9/20 h.p. DE LUXE MODEL 2 or 4 SEATER **£185**

De Luxe models have following equipment additional to standard models: two large headlamps, 8-day clock, speedometer, and choice of body colour.

9/20 h.p. LONG WHEEL BASE 3-DOOR 4-SEATER **£200**

Wheelbase is five inches longer, body very roomy and fitted with three doors. This model has De Luxe equipment specified above with following additions: electric horn, screen wiper, driving mirror, spare petrol can and tin of oil, spring gaiters, grease gun equipment and tyre pressure gauge.

9/20 H.P. L.W.B. 3-DOOR WEYMANN TYPE SALOON, £275

THE ROVER COMPANY LTD., COVENTRY
61, New Bond St., W.1 Lord Edward Street, Dublin

CHAPTER FOURTEEN

The Bright Young Things

I

CABARET HAD BEEN popular for many years on the Continent and in America, but in London it was not firmly established until 1924, when 'floor shows' were presented at many restaurants and ballrooms, and also in night clubs. The pioneers of cabaret were one or two more or less exclusive night clubs whose social position was dictated by their patrons' spending power.

The Hotel Metropole, with its 'Midnight Follies,' was probably the first; Sir Francis Towle was perhaps the pioneer of 'supper entertainment,' assisted by George Grossmith, J. A. E. Malone and André Charlot. At first the L.C.C. would allow only six performers at the Metropole, and all had to wear conventional evening dress. When concessions were made, the management were soon ordered to revert to the original rule. Only after a considerable fight was the L.C.C. persuaded to allow more performers, according to the dressing-room accommodation. But even as late as 1925 no scenery was permitted, only 'scenic effects,' and in that year the company at the Metropole included thirty-one artists, irrespective of stars, nine stage hands, four electricians and an orchestra of nine. Stars from leading theatres and music-halls were engaged for a month at a time, and the average cost of the cabaret was £1,000 a week.

Under Clifford Whitney's management in 1924 the artists included, in turn, the Trix Sisters, Jack Buchanan,

Beatrice Lillie, Jack Hulbert and Cicely Courtneidge, Sophie Tucker, Trini, June, and Yvonne George. The producer of the original Metropole floor show was Jack Haskell, and the show started at midnight and lasted an hour. On Sundays a separate entertainment was given, described as 'Diners Fleuris.'

The largest cabaret show during the years 1924-25 was presented at the Princes Restaurant by a company of thirty-five, including five electricians, five stage-hands and four dressers. There were also four dance bands. Percy Athos, the producer, estimated that each show, running for about six months, cost from £3,000 to £4,000. A feature of the Princes was an ebony dance floor covered by an ordinary wooden floor when the cabaret was on.

The 'Picadilly Revels' at the Picadilly Hotel consisted of two separate shows, one during dinner and the other during supper. Starting with a chorus-ballet of eight, the number was later increased to twelve. Dinner or supper here, exclusive of wines but including dancing and the floor show, cost a guinea. Jack Hylton's band was the chief attraction, supported by well-known variety acts.

Another popular cabaret centre was the Trocadero, which for a time engaged Charles B. Cochran to provide the floor show. It catered for a public which generally preferred light classical music to 'jazz,' and the stars here included Alice Delysia, Grock, Lee White and Clay Smith. Cochran also presented his 'ballet with supper,' his company including Lena King, George Kyasht and Sophia Ilinski, with a ballet of fourteen and an orchestra of twenty in a sunken pit. Ballet, however, was not allowed on Sundays.

The '1.30 a.m. Follies' at the Cabaret Club, the 'London Cabaret' at the London Club, the show at the Criterion and the cabaret at Moody's were also popular. At the Queen's Hotel, Leicester Square, one could have dinner, dance to a ladies' Russian orchestra, and see the 'Queen's Own Peaches' cabaret for half a guinea. At the Metropole guests were encouraged to save themselves the fatigue of applauding by banging on small gongs with little hammers.

These were the sedate and orderly places for midnight entertainment, but there were others to be found in the back-streets of London's West End which were less respectable; dirty little clubs in dingy alleys which offered drinks after licensing hours to hastily-enrolled 'members' who could afford to pay high prices; basements where the daylight seldom penetrated, where tired, blowsy, badly made-up women acted as 'hostesses'; one-room clubs, two-room clubs, clubs that constantly changed names and owners; places where the air was thick with tobacco smoke and heavy with the smell of drink and cheap scent.

But they were not all like this. Ye Olde Ham Bone, in Ham Yard, was the respectable haunt of artists, writers, stage folk and business men. Entry was by way of a bare, dingy staircase, under the watchful eye of an ex-police sergeant who guarded hats and coats. Once inside, past the cloakroom notice announcing 'Boiled Shirts Not Recommended,' the club revealed itself to be clean, if slightly bohemian in decoration. Near the bar hung the notice, 'Work is the ruin of the Drinking Classes.'

The Ham Bone was started in 1921 with £100 borrowed from a waiter at the Café Royal. Lunch cost 2s. and a four-course dinner half-a-crown. At first the bohemian members paid a subscription of a guinea a year, and business men paid two or three, but later the terms rose. Among the many distinguished members was Jacob Epstein, who had established himself as a rebel. In 1925 his 'Rima' memorial in Hyde Park created a stir, and during the twenties there was seldom a time when some Epstein scuplture was not being criticized by puritans. His fellow-members included Sir Thomas Beecham, Herman Darewski, Melville Gideon, Leslie Henson, Billy Bennett, Santos Casani, Ella Shields, Marie Burke, Elsie and Doris Waters, the Western Brothers, William le Queux, Sax Rohmer, J. B. Morton, Ethel

Mannin, Charles Graves, Hannen Swaffer and Gilbert Frankau.

This was not the type of club which led, in 1922, to a movement to 'purify the night life of London.' The Vigilance Committee of Whitefield's Central Mission, Tottenham Court Road, started the campaign in order to draw attention to the 'growing scandals' of London night life, and to suppress 'shady night clubs.' Inspector Fife, of the Women's Auxiliary Service, publicly protested against the so-called 'dance clubs.'

Many of these night clubs were frequented by the new post-war generation, the people who in the middle and late twenties became known as the 'Bright Young Things.' By May 1925 the fashion of wearing baggy trousers, inaugurated at Oxford, had spread farther abroad, and many young men were sporting voluminous trousers measuring as much as 32 inches round the turn-up. With these, smart young bucks wore Fair Isle pullovers, and sometimes a felt hat with a flat three-cornered dent and the brim turned up in front and down at the back. Oxford 'bags,' as the trousers were called, could be obtained in various shades, such as blue, mauve, sage-green, 'toffee' and 'Indian skin,' after a type of silk stocking. Mauve and fuchsia were the predominant colours in most suburban homes at that time.

This new generation of youngsters, most of whom were too young to have served in the war, had inherited the frivolity, or as Sir William Joynson-Hicks, the Home Secretary, suggested, the immorality, of the war period. One had only to look at the increase of dancing clubs, he said, and the decrease of dancing *clothes* to realize the extent of this spirit.

Not everyone was happy and gay in post-war England.

In his book, *Yesterday and To-day*, Ralph Nevill criticized the country as he found it in 1922. These are some of the things he said:

> Last year ex-Councillor Clark very kindly undertook to supervise the bathing at various watering-places, while more recently an explosive

t, Councillor Grimes, the representative of Staines, expressed himself 'scandalized by the disgraceful river scenes and abandoned river-goers who sully the fair Thames from Staines to Maidenhead.'

Bathing at Eastbourne on Sunday is prohibited after noon. Formerly you might not bathe after nine! The most riotous form of recreation permitted on the seventh day is a walk or drive up to Beachy Head—this, I believe, has not yet been decreed to constitute a Sabbath desecration.

The average Englishman, except in very rare cases, can no more forget his respectability than he can get rid of his shadow. The word 'improper' is the badge of slavery . . . the West End indeed seems to have entered upon a permanent phase of dullness . . . notwithstanding that the streets are once more well lit, London is sadder by night than it was in the days when the old hansom cabs plied for hire . . . for some inexplicable reason early hours are more or less imposed upon the Londoner whether he likes them or not . . . what should be the work of the priest has become that of the policemen.

In some ways our puritans could not more effectually have increased vice had they deliberately set out to do so; the petty and harassing restrictions dear to social reformers have produced a great number of more or less secret resorts run by undesirables for undesirables. . . you can restrict the hours of public drinking, suppress suppers, and harry all outward manifestations of illicit love, but there is one thing you cannot suppress, and that is human nature, eternally impatient of restraint.

The 'Bright Young Things' rebelled against the spirit of intolerance and the restrictions of D.O.R.A. (the Defence of the Realm Act). They cannot, however, be pigeon-holed as people who frequented the night clubs. In fact, many of them did not. But for the richer young people and the Bohemians, whose numbers seemed to increase every year, there were always parties . . . endless parties, from dusk until dawn. According to Evelyn Waugh's *Vile Bodies* there were 'Masked parties, Savage parties, Victorian parties, Greek parties, Wild West parties, Russian parties, Circus parties, parties where one had to dress as somebody else, almost naked parties in St. John's Wood, parties in flats and studios and houses and ships and hotels and night clubs, in windmills and swimming baths . . .'

MAY 13, 1925.] PUNCH, OR THE LONDON CHARIVARI.

FLOWERS OF SPEECH.

Young Woman (greeting fiancé). "GOSH, JIMMY! SOME JEMIMA-BAGS!"

There were also bottle parties, which allowed people to entertain when they could not afford to do so properly, there were baby parties where everyone wore infant's clothes, circus parties complete with ring-master and clown, and up and down the country, except in the industrial areas (where people were too busy to bother about parties or were on the dole and could not afford them) there were 'treasure hunts' in which competitors set out in open cars to collect objects described on a list, or find clues which led from place to place.

A typical 'treasure hunt' list of November 1926 included the following items:

A war-time ration card
A Player's cigarette card numbered 3
A theatre programme
A large lump of coal
A baby's bottle
A copy of yesterday's *Daily Mirror*
A spider in a matchbox
An envelope with a Kent post-mark

In this case the competitors were required to arrive at their destination with all these objects. Variation of the game might require them to travel from place to place following rhyming or cryptic clues.

There were also cocktail parties, for this was the beginning of the cocktail age. 'Cocktails,' said X. Marcel Boulestin, the famous restaurateur, 'are the most romantic expression of modern life, of post-war civilization. But the cocktail habit as practised in England now is a *vice*, unless it is a mortification.' Martinis, Manhattens, Bronxes, White Ladies and hundreds of other concoctions were blinding the eyes of the nation to the beauties of wine. But the cocktail parties increased every year, friends 'dropped in for a cocktail' before lunch or dinner, little bits of food and tiny sausages arrived, and—worst of all—a hideous piece of furniture known as a 'cocktail cabinet' appeared. A Bond-street shop sold cocktail shakers shaped like dumb-bells.

'I'd rather scrub a floor than give a party,' said Lady Astor, just before welcoming guests who included the Queen of Rumania, Prince Arthur of Connaught, the Infante Alfonso and the Infanta Beatrice of Spain.

No one seemed able to sit still for long; perhaps the war or the tempo of the new dance tunes had made people restless. At a week-end party held in May 1921 at Knepp Castle by Sir Merrick and Lady Burrell, the guests included Mrs. Claude Beddington, Mrs. Patrick Campbell, Lady Churston, Peter Gawthorne and Cyril Maude. After dinner Mrs. Claude Beddington gazed at the talented company and, jumping up, exclaimed loudly, '*What* material for charades!' Mrs. Pat Campbell then chose the word *Lavatory* for them to act, but the audience was too polite to say the word after it had been acted and correctly guessed.

The younger 'Bright Young Things' were, in the opinion of their elders, always gallivanting about, staying up too late, smoking too much, and drinking to excess. The freedom of shorter skirts was strongly opposed in many quarters. Councillor Clark of Tonbridge protested, 'I will lift up my voice against the *barbaric* licence of women's dress and the vulgarity of their bathing costumes.'

In London the mysteries of the Charleston were introduced in July 1925 to some fifty or sixty prominent ballroom teachers at a special Tea Dance arranged by the *Dancing Times* at the Carnival Club, Dean Street. It was demonstrated, in evening dress, by Miss Annette Mills and Mr. Robert Sielle, who danced to a three-piece orchestra and posed for photographs, giving a preview of the new craze which had captured America and was soon to sweep England.

At first the dance was condemned as 'vulgar,' but it gained distinction when the Prince of Wales danced it. The Vicar of St. Aidan's, Bristol, attacked it violently: 'Any lover of the beautiful will die rather than be associated with the *Charleston*.

It is neurotic! It is rotten! It stinks! Phew, open the windows!' But the Bishop of Coventry liked it. 'It is a very nice dance,' he announced.

The period 1926–29 was the hey-day of the 'Bright Young Things,' but their activities spread on into the thirties. The inhibitions which they flung aside brought into the open tendencies in human behaviour which had previously been politely ignored, particularly problems of sex. Thus, although there was no evidence to show that homosexuality had increased, it was now openly discussed, and even paraded.

In 1918 London had been shocked by the Billie Carleton case. Billie Carleton, whose real name was Florence Stewart, was an actress. When she was found dead, killed by an overdose of drugs, the police discovered that she was associated with a young dressmaker named Reggie de Veuille, whose dressmaking business had brought him into touch with drug addicts. His rooms in Clarges Street were heavy with scent and incense, and the bed-linen and carpet were black. When proceedings were brought against him, many newspapers reported the case in detail, and readers were shocked. But in the later twenties many similar cases were reported, and fewer readers were shocked; it was all too familiar. 'Odd' behaviour was now accepted, even if it was regarded as 'not quite nice.'

Many of the 'Bright Young Things' made a point of 'gatecrashing' parties to which they had not been invited. It was soon necessary to take invitation cards in order to get past the door. One young man, who was invited to several parties before his trick was discovered, had perfected a neat way of making money. At the back of his host's house he would leave a car and an accomplice. When the party was in full swing he would pass bottles of champagne or spirits out of the house, into the car. The host or hostess would soon discover that the drink was running out, or had been finished, and would wonder where—at such a late hour—some more could be obtained. At this point the young man would come to the

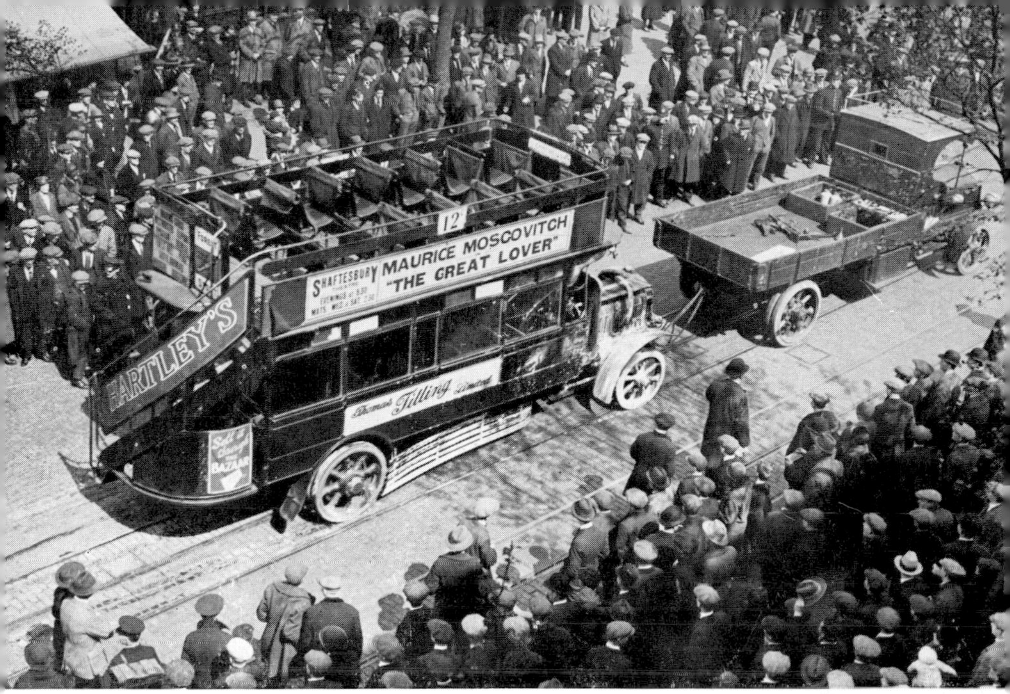

VIII. *A damaged London omnibus is towed away in the General Strike, 1926.*

In the garden at 10 Downing Street in 1929: Mr. Ramsay MacDonald with Miss Margaret Bondfield, first woman Cabinet Minister.

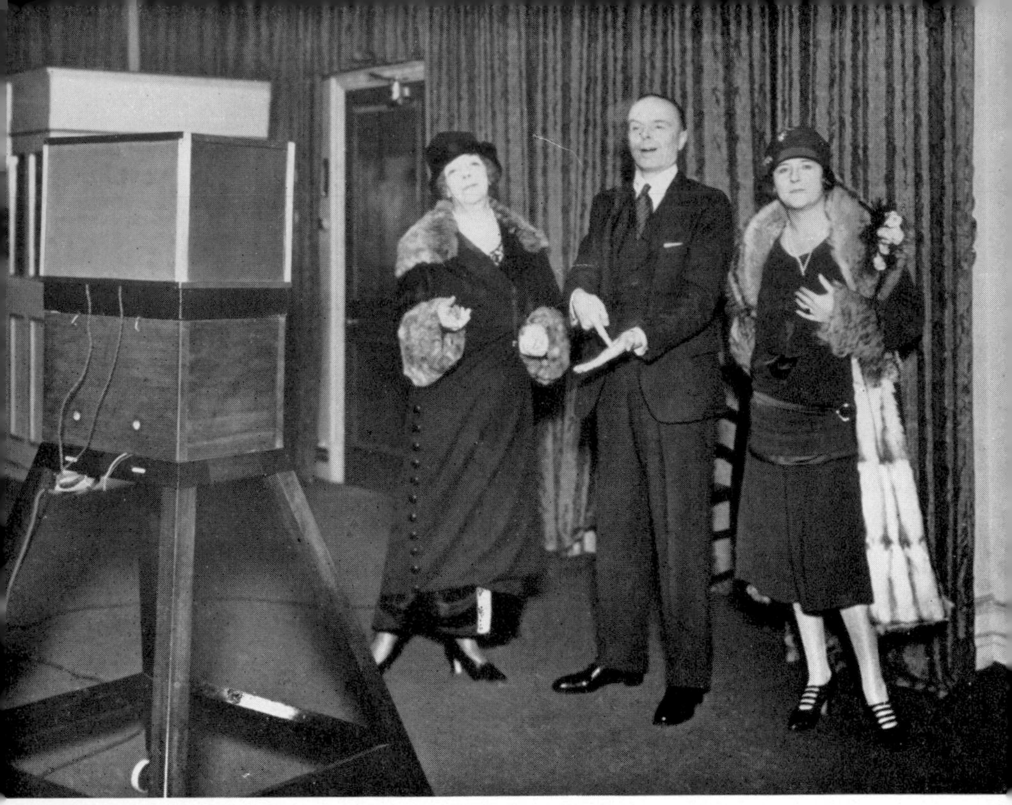

IX. *Lady Tree, George Grossmith and Alice Delysia face the box microphone at Savoy Hill, London, November 1926.*

John Gielgud in Hamlet *at the Old Vic; the promise of greatness to come.*

rescue, claiming that he knew where to get some more drink—'from a friend.' But this drink, he would explain, was slightly more expensive than usual, being obtained after closing-time. A telephone call would then bring the car to the house, and the host or hostess would gladly hand over a cheque, not realizing that it was buying back familiar bottles.

In 1925 *Punch* described closing-time as the hour at which Britons, who could never, never be slaves, saw public-house doors bang in their faces. 'We may now refresh ourselves,' wrote E. V. Lucas, 'not at our own need but when the Government permits. In most cities the closing-times are fixed, but London is large enough to have different closing-times on each side of Oxford Street, so that, being turned out at 10.30 on one side, you may cross the road and continue until 11 on the other!'

In his novel *Kept* (1925) Alec Waugh described the night clubs where people went to escape from the absurdities of licensing hours as 'second-rate places for third-rate people.' The average club, he said, was less a dance club than a drinking club. It was a place to which people went when they could get a drink nowhere else; a protest by free people against the restraint of drinking regulations. It was not the drink which was the attraction, but the tactics which had to be employed to get in. First there was the argument with the porter, the bargaining with the management; then there was the offer of some dissipated shareholder to introduce the party as guests. Finally, one was inside. But in January 1925 the *Daily News* called London's night clubs the 'dullest places on earth.' The premises of one visited by a reporter had been a garage. The store rooms were now cloak rooms, and the old car lift had been walled round to form an open dome through which came a smell of fetid air and the sound of a band.

'At one or two tables sat men alone,' reported the journalist. 'They had the empty, expressionless faces of those utterly alone in a big city. At another were some Americans. A party of three girls were chuckling over a joke in a corner, there were a few parties of four 'up from the suburbs' . . . a more uninteresting crowd one could not have seen anywhere—no 'dope fiends,' no obvious 'sharks,' not even any over-painted faces, but just dull, stodgy people.'

The correspondent paid 5s. 6d. for a glass of orangeade and a packet of ten cigarettes and 3s. 6d. for a nip of 'rank whisky of the vilest kind.'

'In every one of these haunts one visits there is the same squalid dullness and lifelessness,' he reported. 'Not one in ten thousand Londoners has ever entered their guarded doors.'

But many thousands of people went every year to one or other of Kate Meyrick's notorious underground clubs, where the licensing laws were completely disregarded. The most famous of these was the '43', at 43 Gerrard Street, a damp, ill-lit basement filled every night with nobility, the rich, the folks who did not want to go home, the seekers after illusive excitement.

A feature of these establishments was Mrs. Meyrick's 'girls,' or 'dance instructresses,' sometimes quite attractive youngsters, who persuaded customers to spend money. They were each paid £3 a week and commission. There were also four attractive Meyrick daughters, who married into the nobility.

Kate, or 'Ma' Meyrick, as she was called, was the daughter of a Dublin doctor who had married a young medical student and moved to England. At Sylvan Hall, Brighton, two sons and four daughters were born. The girls went to Roedean, the boys to Harrow. But in 1919 the Meyricks separated, and Mrs. Meyrick was left with only about £50 on which to support her large family. She therefore decided to work for her children, and invested her money with a Mr. Murray Dalton, who ran Dalton's Club, next to the Alhambra Theatre, Leicester Square. Here tea-dances were held, for this was a typical 'dance club' of the period, but it was soon raided by the police, and a number of undesirable girls were arrested. Mrs. Meyrick, protesting strongly, was fined £25 and heard her 'innocent venture' described as 'a sink of iniquity.'

Soon after this she started Brett's Club in the Charing Cross Road, which she sold for £1,000. Then, in 1921, came the famous '43,' which was raided only two months after the opening night. 'Ma' Meyrick was fined £300 and costs for selling drinks after closing hours, but the name of the club was immediately changed to Proctor's, and business went on as usual. Other clubs followed, the New Follies, the Manhattan, the Little Club, the Silver Slipper . . . many others. To some of these, especially to the '43,' went such prominent people as King Carol of Rumania, the Crown Prince of Sweden, Rudolph Valentino, Tallulah Bankhead, Steve Donoghue, and some of the peers and millionaires of England.

The Meyrick clubs flourished until the late twenties, when London's night club queen was sentenced to fifteen months' hard labour for bribing a police official. The officer was Station-Sergeant George Goddard of the C.I.D., who was in charge of the vice squad which reported on night life, clubs and brothels. He had been commended ninety-one times for his devotion to duty, but for several years he had been accepting bribes from night club owners. Mrs. Meyrick openly boasted that Goddard was paid to protect and warn her. He was charged at the Central Criminal Court with 'corruptly accepting or obtaining as an inducement for doing or forbearing to do certain acts' large sums of money from two night club owners, Mrs. Meyrick and Luigi Ribuffi, who ran a club known as 'Uncle's' in Albemarle Street.

The trial, before Mr. Justice Avory, lasted for eight days. Goddard's pay had been £6 a week, but £12,000 in cash, including several £100 notes, had been found in a safe deposit in his name. Several notes had been traced to Mrs. Meyrick and Ribuffi.

Goddard had been exposed by an anonymous letter stating that he owned a freehold house at Streatham, a car and two safe accounts stuffed with notes. All these statements were true, and it was soon proved that he had not only protected Mrs. Meyrick, but had warned her of raids. He was sentenced to eighteen months' imprisonment with hard labour, fined £2,000, and ordered to pay the cost of the prosecution. Mrs. Meyrick and Ribuffi were each sentenced to fifteen months' imprisonment with hard labour.

Almost immediately there was a sequel when it was revealed that seven years previously a Sergeant Josling had been called upon to resign his position on being found guilty of bringing a false charge of corruption against Goddard. Now it was proved that Josling had been right, and he was awarded £1,500 compensation.

When the famous 'night club queen' was released, London's 'Bright Young Things' sang:

> Come all you birds
> And sing a roundelay,
> Now Mrs. Meyrick's
> Out of Holloway.

Twice more she went to jail, but in 1932 a benevolent magistrate said that as prison was obviously no deterrent he proposed to make her give 'an honourable undertaking to have no more to do with night clubs.' When she died a year later it was estimated that at least half a million pounds had passed through her hands. She left £58, and no successor, but by then night-clubs had become bottle-parties, where one could become a member and keep wines and spirits. It was then possible to drink at any hour, legally.

2

The enemy of everything wicked and sinful, a teetotaller of the old-fashioned ardent type, and a strict anti-gambler, was the Home Secretary, Sir William Joynson-Hicks. Nicknamed 'Jix,' he was dapper, frock-coated, debonair, cheerful and self-complacent.

'I still wear the reactionary frock-coat of the Victorian Tories,' he said proudly. He once appeared on the platform at the Queen's Hall with Mrs. Bramwell Booth to denounce the evils of smoking among women, and condemned mothers who blew tobacco fumes over the innocent faces of their children. When he became Home Secretary he expressed his anxiety to clean out what he called the 'social sewers' of London. He tried to make it difficult to buy a drink, and he made efforts to close night clubs, to keep the stage pure, and to prevent the publication of 'indecent books.'

Night clubs had been raided long before 'Jix' entered the Home Office, and their owners had been fined. The night club business was often so profitable that a fine could be written off as an incidental expense, while disqualification of the premises for a year meant that the owner moved, and opened another club with the same patrons next day.

Under these circumstances, 'Jix' waged a relentless war. Towards the end of 1928 some sixty-five clubs had been prosecuted since 1924, and sixty-two had been struck off the register. One proprietor, who had been forced to leave the country, wrote to Sir William:

> May I take this opportunity of wishing you a very happy and prosperous 1929. I will be honoured if, when in Paris, you will give me the pleasure of visiting my new *Chez Victor*.

The Home Secretary courteously replied that he would certainly accept, but it is doubtful if he went. As P. R. Stephenson and Beresford Egan observed in their *Policeman of the Lord: A Political Satire:*

> In 1865,
> When Little Jix was born, or came alive,
> The Great Queen ruled, and everyone was good.
> Since then the times have changed, the clock has clicked . . .
> Jix does not think so, Jix was brought up strict.

The publication of this political lampoon was provoked by the spectacle of the Home Secretary suppressing books which he considered obscene—or, to be more accurate, taking action to ensure that they were suppressed.

'I am not a literary censor,' he announced. 'I have no qualifications for the post. My duty is to see that the law is carried out, and when the law says definitely that obscenities and indecencies are not permitted in the land, it is my duty to carry out the law and call the attention of the Director of Public Prosecutions to the publication of indecent matter.'

But what was an 'indecent' book, and how could the Home Secretary decide? When a number of poems in typescript, written by D. H. Lawrence, were sent from abroad in open covers at the cheap postal rate, the postal authorities decided that they were of such a nature that they must be sent to Sir William. From the Home Office they went straight to the Director of Public Prosecutions. Lawrence's many admirers angrily protested when 'Jix' zealously told the House of Commons that 'there was no possible doubt that they contained indecent matter.'

'Jix' led the attack, but there were many other virtuous and outraged citizens who found the new order unacceptable. The police took action against Radclyffe Hall's novel *The Well of Loneliness*, and the Warren Gallery was taken to court for exhibiting D. H. Lawrence's paintings. They also seized a French translation of *The Hunting of the Snark*, and some drawings by William Blake, presumably supposing them to be 'indecent.' James Douglas denounced the 'blasphemy' of Aldous Huxley's *Antic Hay*, and other novels, and so increased their sales. And meanwhile the parties went on, cocktail parties, literary parties, parties given by stage folk and gay Bohemians in Bloomsbury and Chelsea, at some of which it was often difficult at a first glance to determine the sex of the guests, even in everyday clothes. In March 1925 *Punch* published a George Belcher cartoon showing a 'man-woman' wearing a pork-pie hat, collar and tie, monocle, spats and tweed coat and skirt, saying, '*In the old days I never paid more than sixpence for a hair-cut; now they call it a shingle-trim and charge me three-and-six!*' Another person of uncertain sex was shown being peered at by a short-sighted old lady who inquired, '*Excuse me, but did you say you were going up to Trinity or Girton next term?*'

Seven months later the latest fashion provided a joke in which another short-sighted lady mistook Russian boots for stockings which had fallen down. And in July 1925 Mr. Belcher reflected the hostility of the public for Epstein's work by showing a woman in the dock accused of hitting another woman:

Magistrate: Why did you assault the plaintiff?
Defendant: She called me a *Epstein Female*, yer worship.
(Discharged)

The last hectic party of the twenties, the party to end all parties, surpassing even the Wild West party and the Court party, the final fling of the 'Bright Young Things,' started at eleven o'clock on the evening of November 21, 1931, in the house of the dancer, Maud Allan, although it was not her party.

The invitation cards had been sent out a fortnight earlier, and were much in demand. Many were stolen from chimney pieces and were later presented by uninvited, unwanted guests. The wording on each card, engraved in white on a brilliant scarlet background, requested guests to confine their costumes and clothes to the colours red and white. It was to be a red and white party, a 'monster ball,' as the young men of the West End called it.

Some 250 cards were sent out, but nearly four hundred guests arrived. Their host greeted them in the hall, wearing a modified sailor suit of white angel-skin with red trimmings, elbow-length white kid gloves loaded with diamonds and rubies, two diamond clips and a spray of white star orchids costing about £2 a bloom. He posed for photographs holding a muff made of white narcissi, which newspapers reported had been flown from North Africa, but which had been bought that afternoon in Chelsea. A pair of red leather shoes completed the ensemble.

The food at the party was entirely red and white—red caviare, lobsters, salmon, ham, apples (but no pears), tomatoes (but no lettuce), pink and red blancmanges, trifles and jellies. Everything was of the best, and cigarettes were contained in red and white boxes.

The upstairs rooms of the house were empty, and a rope across the foot of the stairs indicated that guests were not expected to leave the ground floor. However, this did not prevent many people from disappearing upstairs, to descend, later, covered in dust.

Guests arriving at the house found the entrance guarded by uniformed Metropolitan policemen, who solemnly examined all invitation cards but let everyone in whether they had cards or not. In those days 'off duty' policemen could be hired for private parties. Inside, after being greeted by their host, guests walked over a long red carpet through a vast hall towards three large rooms, *en suite*, with big double-doors leading from one to the other. The centre and largest room was hung with broad strips of scarlet and white bunting. Banquettes were covered with red velvet. Dancing took place here to a negro orchestra—a *sine qua non* in those days—each musician wearing white tails with scarlet facings. The two slightly smaller rooms were hung respectively with white and red bunting, the white room being a vast bar. The red room, furnished with red-covered mattresses, was for sitting-out.

What began as a reasonably formal, although distinctly eccentric, gathering soon developed into a noisy and hilarious free-for-all. Hired servants, dressed in scarlet double-breasted coats with large white buttons, struggled among the seething, jostling, swaying, shrieking mass of dancers and drinkers. The orchestra, overwhelmed by the noise, played louder and louder; the rooms became thick with smoke and the smell of scent.

No whisky was available, only champagne, white or red wine, and gin. There were plenty of bottles for everyone. The kitchen was stacked high with crates of liquor and boxes of hired glasses. Some guests mixed the drinks and gulped them down; then mixed their dancing partners. The huge room became a medley of red and white sailor suits, white dresses and sashes, red wigs, long white kid gloves, pink hats, and even false red noses. Red and white 'nuns' danced with men dressed as exotic birds with highly elaborate feather head-dresses, men danced stripped to the waist, wearing red sailors' bell-bottom trousers; a man dressed as Queen Elizabeth, in a red wig, sat in the hall solemnly playing *Abide with Me* on an organ.

At about one o'clock a girl had to be prevented from pulling the hair of another woman who was attempting to get herself a drink. Half-full glasses and bottles stood all around, under chairs, behind curtains, under tables. The girl was wearing only a choker of pearls and a large red and white spotted handkerchief fixed around her middle by a thin white belt. People wearing more clothes found it almost unbearably hot.

The party finished with the dawn, long after the last policeman had finished guarding the doors and had gone home. It was afterwards estimated that the evening had cost about £500. *The Bystander* suggested that the money, a considerable amount to spend on a party, might perhaps have been spent more usefully, particularly at a time when unemployment was heavy. But the merits or demerits of this and the other abandoned, carefree revelries of the twenties indicated that even in the middle of the depression there was no room for what Noël Coward later called those 'Twentieth Century Blues.' Maybe it was true to sing, with Coward:

> Someday soon you'll know
> The years you are tasting
> Are years you are wasting
> Life is a bitter foe;

With fate it's no use competing
Youth is so terribly fleeting;
By dancing much faster
You're chancing disaster,
Time alone will show.

Youth is so terribly fleeting sang Mr. Coward. Perhaps that is why the 'Bright Young Things' danced so hard. They certainly enjoyed themselves. One day older, wiser men and women might look back at the famous Red and White Party and wonder . . . but there would be few regrets. Such carefree, extravagant, ridiculous evenings would not come again. Did the lights seem brighter then? You dressed up, you went out in search of elusive excitement, and you probably got drunk. Perhaps you played at being a Bohemian, just for a little while, living in a strange world of pseudo-intellectuals, semi-sophisticates, among divans, orange lamp-shades and bottles, hundreds of bottles. Whatever you were, you probably enjoyed yourself if you were young, and were lucky enough not to be born into a working-class family in one of the industrial areas. Perhaps some of the 'Bright Young Things' were not too young and not too bright; perhaps most of their parties were stupid, and a waste of money. But they never went to the extremes of their opposite numbers in Germany, and they represented only a small part of the population, and had little influence on the country.

It was true that *some* people danced all night and almost all day, but very few had the time, the money or the inclination. Only when the newspapers discovered a Baby Party (at which men and women appeared as infants) or a party at Paddington Baths (which shocked readers) did the majority of English men and women learn about the hectic minority which was, in later years, to serve novelists so well.

Compared with the rich and pleasure-loving young aristocrats of the Victorian and Edwardian ages, the 'Bright Young Things' were remarkably pale; they hardly affected the normal life of the country, and there were few public scandals.

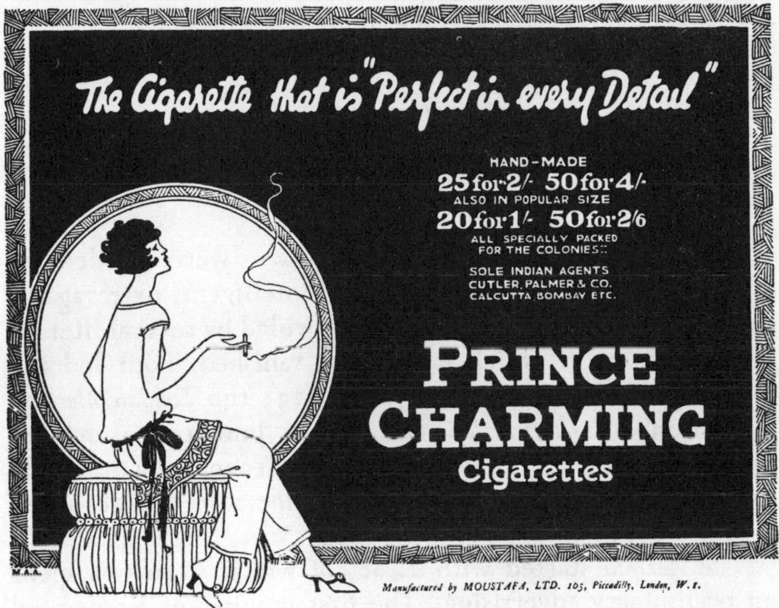

CHAPTER FIFTEEN

Literature

I

'THE TWENTIES,' says Rose Macaulay, 'were, as decades go, a good decade; gay, decorative, intelligent, extravagant, cultured.' Culture in reading was provided by several literary journals, most of which have since vanished. Four led the way—the *Adelphi* started in June 1923; the *London Mercury* in November 1919; *Life and Letters* in June 1928; and the *Bermondsey Book* in December 1923. In 1920 Lady Rhondda founded *Time and Tide*; in 1921 *The Athenaeum* was absorbed by *The Nation*.

The *Adelphi* started with £400, of which £250 was spent on preliminary advertising. The first number was reprinted five times, 18,000 copies being sold, although only 4,000 had been planned. The distinguished contributors to this or subsequent editions included D. H. Lawrence, Edmund Blunden, H. M. Tomlinson, Frank Swinnerton, J. Middleton Murry, H. G. Wells, Harold Laski, J. W. N. Sullivan and Edward Garnett. Among those who wrote for *Life and Letters* were Max Beerbohm, E. M. Forster, George Santayana, Hilaire Belloc, Virginia Woolf, Augustine Birrell, Lytton Strachey and Harry Graham.

Eventually most of the journals disappeared, usually after a life of three or four years, owing to the lack of firm orders and a failure to appreciate that advertisements make a magazine or newspaper pay.

Intelligent readers subscribed regularly, and did not fail to read their weekly copy of *The Times Literary Supplement* or

J. C. Squire's *London Mercury*, which had been founded in the first year of peace, and to which Hardy, Yeats, Belloc, Kipling and Robert Bridges contributed. Later they read the *Criterion*, edited by T. S. Eliot.

The outstanding authors of the period were James Joyce, Aldous Huxley and George Bernard Shaw. Huxley had been born in 1894, the third son of Leonard Huxley, the editor of the *Cornhill*. Educated at Eton and Oxford, he worked for several years as a journalist and dramatic critic in London and then devoted himself to writing novels. He first attracted attention in 1920 with a volume of short stories called *Limbo*, and followed this a year later with his first novel, *Chrome Yellow*. In 1923 came *Antic Hay*, and in 1925 *Those Barren Leaves*. Three years later he completed *Point Counter Point*, and in 1932 *Brave New World*. Later came *Eyeless in Gaza*, *After Many a Summer*, and *The Art of Seeing*. His travel books included *Jesting Pilate* (1926) and among his collections of essays were *Proper Studies* (1927) and *Do What You Will* (1929).

Probably the most representative writer of his time, Huxley enjoyed great popularity. *Antic Hay*, a satirical masterpiece taking its title from one of Marlowe's couplets, was set in post-war London in the years of disillusionment and excess in which the old values were submerged in a tidal wave of cynicism. The characters were portrayed as living a crazy life, artists adrift, intellectuals who had lost their way, women trying to forget their griefs in the pursuit of pleasure. Huxley's rakes and escapists were drawn with such precision and colour that many of his readers thought he approved of their attitude to life.

In *Antic Hay*, Theodore Gumbril, Jnr., B.A. Oxon, a young master in a boys' preparatory school, finding his seat in chapel uncomfortable, invents a pair of air-inflated trousers which bring him wealth and take him to London. Here he grows a beard as a symbol of virility. At the end of the story Gumbril and his friend, Mrs. Viveash, seeking pleasure, drive around the West End of London in a taxi. Journeying from dinner to a Royal Albert Hall concert, they visit night club after night club. Finally they arrive at a laboratory to watch the physiologist Shearwater sitting on a stationary bicycle, pedalling unceasingly like a man in a nightmare in a glass cubicle to find out how much sweat the human frame can produce. On the last page of the novel Mr. Huxley's characters lean on the window-sill and look out at the lights of London Bridge.

'Tomorrow,' says Gumbril at last, meditatively.

'Tomorrow,' Mrs. Viveash interrupts him, 'will be as awful as today.'

2

According to James Bridie, Shaw entered into his kingdom early in 1928, when Thomas Hardy died, and Britain again needed a sage. He had been born in 1856, and when fifteen had become a clerk to a land agent in Dublin. Five years later he was in London, employed by the Edison Telephone Company, with whom he stayed until he was twenty-three. He spent most of his spare time in libraries, museums, lecture halls, concert halls and art galleries, and wrote novels. At first he could not live by his writing, but this was hardly surprising because his first novels were sold as love stories.

Most of Shaw's earliest associates were Radicals: R. B. Cunninghame Graham, William Morris, Hubert Bland, A. B. Walkley, Annie Besant, Sydney Olivier and Sidney Webb. In 1883 he gave up novels to write pamphlets, and five years later became art critic of *The World*, literary critic of *Truth*, and musical critic of *The Star*. It was not until 1925 that he became a dramatic critic, by which time his many plays had achieved world-wide recognition, and he had become a well-known figure. Mr. Bridie said that Shaw was 'a deeply religious man . . . if the description seems odd to the old lady who recently tore her copy of *The Black Girl in Search of God* to pieces before her bookseller's eyes, or the people who recall with horror how Mr. Shaw once took out his watch on a platform and challenged the Almighty to strike him dead within two minutes, I cannot help it. His religious sense is to be compared with that of Bunyan, his literary hero. He believes man to be endowed and moved by the spirit of God working within him.'

Of his purpose as a playwright, Shaw said, 'I am no ordinary playwright. I am a specialist in immoral and heretical plays. My reputation was gained by my persistent struggle to force the public to reconsider its morals.' He wrote plays, he insisted, with the deliberate object of converting the nation to his opinion on sexual and social matters. In 1925 he declared, 'I don't go to theatres to understand plays; I go to enjoy them. I hate plays that I can understand, because they are not like life, which nobody understands.'

The outstanding social prophet of his time, in the opinion of V. S. Pritchett, was H. G. Wells. The minds of a generation were formed, swayed and provoked by his teaching; like Shaw he made people revise their ideas of religion, politics, social life, and love. Many of his prophecies were depressing:

> This world is at the end of its tether. The end of everything we call life is close at hand and cannot be avoided. . .

Philip Guedalla summed Wells up as 'a pair of bright eyes watching the world alertly, and not without malice.' Wells had been born in 1866, the son of a cricket professional. He went to Midhurst Grammar School, and later took his B.Sc. with first-class honours in zoology at the Royal College of Science. In *The Dream*, published in 1924, he described and discussed the social conditions of the twenties as seen through the eyes of a man living 2,000 years later.

'We are witnessing a remarkable revival of taste,' wrote Edmund Gosse in the *Sunday Times* on February 20, 1927.

'The despised and defeated Victorian authors, of whom proud Georgian youth said that it could not read a page, have made a great rally and are now bearing down upon us

> like lions after slumber
> in unvanquishable number.

'One after another the writers who were understood to be consigned for ever to the waste-paper basket have been popping up in recovered popularity. Where is it to stop? Trollope yesterday and George Eliot today!'

Sir James Barrie thought that there was nothing wrong with the new writers. 'These young authors!' he said in November 1924. 'Happy they! Multitudinous seas incarnadine boil in their veins. They hear the thousand nightingales which we once thought we heard. They have a short way with the old hands, but in our pride in them we forgive them for that. Perhaps they sometimes go a little to excess, treating even God as if he were, shall we say, the greatest of the Victorians.'

The impact of D. H. Lawrence was now being fully experienced. It was so strange, so violent, that controversy and partisanship at first obscured judgment. Much of his writing was uneven, but at his best he was a master of descriptive prose. Very little escaped his appreciative notice, and his work was often poignant and moving. His tone was completely natural and unaffected. Born in 1885, the son of a Nottinghamshire miner, he had been brought up in poor surroundings; the only love which satisfied him was his mother's. Throughout his life he was obsessed by this love for his mother, and this was apparent in his work; haunted by tuberculosis, disliking society, and abnormally sensitive, he was almost pathologically affected by it. His first two literary efforts were history books, written under the name of Lawrence H. Davidson. *The Rainbow*, written in 1915 and suppressed by the police, turned his growing fame into notoriety. A visit to Mexico resulted in his novel, *The*

Plumed Serpent, which was influenced by the remains of the Aztec civilization.

Towards the end of his life Lawrence held an exhibition of his paintings in London, for which he published a catalogue and wrote an introduction. The pictures were described by one critic as 'sex-ridden obsessions in paint, with (as he was an entirely untrained artist) revolting results.' A series of large canvases included representations of the artist in association with extremely gross nude women. One picture used the Cruxifixion as its motif, and was a crude caricature of the red-bearded Lawrence nailed to the cross with a nude woman on either side. The exhibition was closed by the police.

Lawrence's principal works during the twenties were *Women in Love* (1920), *Fantasia of the Unconscious* (1922), *The Ladybird* (1923), *Sea and Sardinia?* (1921), *St. Mawr* (1925), and *Lady Chatterley's Lover*, published in Florence in 1928 and banned in England. Robert Graves and Alan Hodge later considered Lawrence 'not only unhealthy but spiritually blind, and trying to overawe the best in others by vulgar menaces.' After his death in 1930 a number of pseudo-scientific works were written about him, explaining his 'message,' his complexes and his mythical sex-life.

Of the poets the most dominating was T. S. Eliot, who had been born in 1888 in St. Louis, Missouri, and was educated at Harvard, the Sorbonne, and Merton College, Oxford. In 1922 his poem *The Waste Land* revealed the spirit of disillusionment felt by many of the younger generation:

> What are the roots that clutch,
> What branches grow
> Out of this stormy rubbish?

Among the most widely-read poets were Edmund Blunden, Hilaire Belloc, Harold Monro, Victoria Sackville-West, T. W. Earp, the Sitwells and Siegfried Sassoon, whose semi-autobiographical *Memoirs of a Foxhunting Man* was published anonymously in 1928.

Although increased facilities for education had more than doubled the number of book readers, this did not mean that the new reading public showed discrimination The subscribers to the popular libraries rejected Joyce, D. H. Lawrence, and all other authors whom they found difficult to understand, in favour of their favourite novelists, Hugh Walpole, Warwick Deeping, P. G. Wodehouse and Dornford Yates, writers who hardly expressed the spirit of the times, but told a good story. The best-selling novel of 1922 was *If Winter Comes* by A. S. M. Hutchinson, published in Britain by Hodder and Stoughton and in America by Little, Brown & Co. Over 175,000 copies were sold in Britain between August 1921 and October 1922.

'The mouthpiece of the decade,' says Alec Waugh, 'was William Somerset Maugham,' whose first novel, *Liza of Lambeth*, had earned him only £20 in royalties during its first year, but had encouraged him to abandon medicine for writing. Later his plays and novels brought him vast sums of money, and during the twenties the publication of *Cakes and Ale* established him as one of the most talented writers in English literature. In *The Moon and Sixpence*, *The Casuarina Tree* and *The Fall of Edward Barnard*, he faithfully and revealingly portrayed the outlook of the disillusioned 1920's.

By 1924 the novel *The Green Hat* was a best-seller on both sides of the Atlantic. Its author, an Armenian from Bulgaria named Dikran Kouyoumdjian, had adopted the name of Michael Arlen, and was welcomed as a writer of mordant wit 'skipping from impudence to impudence like a mischievous elf.' His novel was set in Mayfair, in a world of fast, sleek cars, expensive night clubs and well-dressed men, and it championed the spirit of independence in the rising generation. Its heroine, Iris Storm, demanded the right to live her own life in her own carefree way.

D. H. Lawrence thought Michael Arlen a romantic. Soon

he became not only a popular writer but a vogue, with his regular table at the Embassy Club each night, and a familiar long yellow Rolls-Royce waiting outside. Years later he confessed that he was a 'flash in the pan' in the twenties, but that by the grace of God there had been gold dust in the pan. He dramatized *The Green Hat* and *These Charming People*, and both were filmed. By 1939 he had made enough money, at a time when income tax was not excessively high, to retire.

The *enfant terrible* of the late twenties was Evelyn Waugh, who has remained firmly attached, at least in the public mind, to the period in which he started to write. Born in Hampstead in 1903, he was the second son of the distinguished publisher Arthur Waugh. After leaving Oxford, where he read modern history, he studied at an art school and spent a brief period as a schoolmaster. His experiences gave him the setting for his first novel, *Decline and Fall* (1928) which was an immediate success and was hailed as one of the most amusing novels to be published for many years.

Nine years spent in Europe, the Near East, the Arctic and tropical America brought several travel books and extravagantly witty novels. Through the whirl of gay parties and strange happenings in *Vile Bodies* (1929) runs the love story of Adam Fenwick-Symes, an impecunious young writer, and Nina Blount, the daughter of a slightly mad aristocrat. Other characters in this hilarious adventure include last week's Prime Minister, Mr. Outrage, Mrs. Ape the American lady evangelist, Lord Simon Balcairn the gossip-writer, Lady Circumference, Mrs. Throbbing, Lord Chasm and a drunken major who wins £35,000 pounds for Adam Fenwick-Symes at the races, but keeps disappearing just before he pays it.

Evelyn Waugh, who laid bare the heathen idol of British sportsmanship, the cultured perfection of Oxford, and the inviolability of love as practised by gentlemen, was in the estimation of Alexander Woollcott 'as near to being a genius as any member of the post-war generation now writing in England.' Edmund Wilson hailed him as 'the only first-rate comic genius who has appeared in England since Bernard Shaw.'

In 1932 Dr. C. E. M. Joad looked back at the twenties and considered that the stars who had risen in the literary firmament since the war did not shine with such brilliance as the older gods of the pre-war era, Shaw and Wells and Bennett. But to some of the new authors, J. B. Priestley, Sinclair Lewis, Virginia Woolf and Aldous Huxley, he offered his unstinted admiration. Joad thought that too many writers were reflecting the spirit of the age, which was one of little faith.

'We are lukewarm in religion,' he said, 'unimpressed by authority, distrustful of moral codes, and impatient of moral restraints.' The cult of unreason, he thought, had a prejudicial effect on art and literature. D. H. Lawrence, and a number of other writers, were preoccupied with sex; it was the distressing amount of sexual maladjustment that accounted for the vogue of the biting, scratching, cursing, hating and ferociously loving men and women of these novels.

J. B. Priestley was one of the new writers whom Joad admired, as did the reading public. He had been born in Bradford in 1894, the son of a schoolmaster, and he had seen active service during the war before starting his literary career with *Papers from Lilliput* and *I for One*. In 1922 *Brief Diversions* and in 1925 his *English Comic Characters* added to his growing reputation as an essayist, but it was with the publication of his picaresque novel *The Good Companions* (1929) that he attracted widespread recognition and popularity. This story, in the tradition of Fielding and Dickens, was immensely successful, dealing sympathetically and realistically with the homely aspects of English life as lived by real people. Established as a popular novelist, Priestley showed himself during the thirties to be a brilliant playwright, particularly with *Dangerous Corner* and *Eden End*. Before writing *The Good Companions* he wrote *Adam in Moonshine* (1927), *English Humour* (1928), and a brilliant study of *George Meredith* (1926). Later he wrote *Angel Pavement* (1930), *Wonder Hero* (1932), *English Journey* (1934) and a large number of other novels, plays and film scripts indicating that he was among the most prolific of English writers. During the Second World War his *Postscripts*, broadcast to the nation during a critical time in its history, were second in importance and appeal only to those delivered by Winston Churchill.

It was in the early autumn of 1922 that the young J. B. Priestley had first arrived in London, having taken his degree at Cambridge and got married. Determined to write, he found a seven-roomed flat on the ground floor of King Edward's Mansions, Walham Green, at a rent of about seventy-five pounds a year. For the first few months the Priestleys shared the flat with Edward Davison, the poet, who had come to London to edit a Liberal Church weekly called *The Challenge*. They shopped for odd bits of furniture along the Fulham Road, bought a Broadwood grand piano on hire purchase, and did their own decorating.

'In 1922,' says Mr. Priestley, 'Walham Green still seemed to belong to the London of Phil May. It was crowded and noisy with street stalls and barrows, fat women drinking stout at pub doors, young mothers shouting at wizened babies, chaps waiting to learn what won the two-thirty, greasy little eating-places; with the Granville Music-Hall and Stamford Bridge (where Davison and I cheered for Chelsea) representing the arts and athletics.'

At first he had to depend largely on reviewing, for which there was then ample space. Most daily papers carried at least one book page a week, and there were far more bookish weeklies and various monthly reviews open to young writers. The pay was low, especially for unsigned short notices, but often the bulky volumes of travel and memoirs were fairly expensive, and then the reviewer could sell the copies at half the published price.

'The old fellow who bought them had one touch of

genius; he always paid us in new pound notes, deliciously clean and crisp, and to be handed seven or eight of these was always an exhilarating experience, like being in a fairy tale for a few minutes. We used to hurry out of that shop, all Fleet Street ours, like Ali Baba out of the robbers' cave. It is, I think, the only money I have ever had that brought with it every possible good sensation of wealth.'

During his first year young Priestley did regular reviewing, mostly signed, for the *London Mercury*, the *Outlook*, the *Bookman*, the *Daily News*, the *Daily Chronicle*, and a little later he wrote long signed reviews for the *Spectator* and the *Saturday Review*. He was also paid £6 a week as a publisher's reader for John Lane.

'If I missed anything first-class,' recalls Mr. Priestley, 'successfully published elsewhere, I am unable to recall a single example. What I do know for certain is that I recommended—and without difficulty, because there was much new talent about in those years—an impressive list of first books and new authors, headed by Graham Greene and C. S. Forester.'

Food, drink and service were still comparatively cheap in those days. In Soho it was possible to buy a dinner for 2s., and for 10s. you could add a bottle of wine, a brandy or two, and a cigar with your coffee. Mr. Priestley's favourite restaurant was the one-roomed *Escargot* in Greek Street, Soho, where there were only about four tables, but where the food was excellent. Another of his haunts was the long bar in Poppins Court, underneath the offices of the *London Mercury*. Here, every week-day between twelve-thirty and two, gathered the Editor, J. C. Squire, and many of his contributors, Robert Lynd, James Bone, George Mair, Hilaire Belloc, J. B. Morton, Bohun Lynch and other good talkers.

Mr. Priestley recalls, 'I was never out of London very long throughout the twenties, and probably would never have left it at all if I had not had a young family, for I soon came to feel an affection for the sprawling monster. Even its shocking extremes of wealth and poverty I disliked more in theory than in actuality, I was fond of wandering about in it and taking buses and trams to its remote suburbs, and must have written scores of essays—I wrote at least one essay a week for many years—that had a London background, as well as one long novel, *Angel Pavement*. Its life then had many blots that have now been sponged out. There is now far less truly appalling misery. But most other changes have been for the worse. There is now far more cheap spivvery, even in the West End. The kind of subhuman faces you see in the neon lighting of Coventry Street any night now, passing like an unending parade of the seven deadly sins, I do not remember seeing when I was first in London.'

3

The popular women novelists of the period included Ethel M. Dell, whose strong silent heroes carried their heavy heroines over mountain ranges to remote castles, or made love to them in tents in the tradition of Elinor Glyn. In 1922, when Miss Dell married, she was the most successful woman writer of the time. For ten years she had reigned supreme. Although she refused to be interviewed or photographed, and shunned publicity, her book sales were second only to those of H. G. Wells and Arnold Bennett. A quarter of a million copies were sold in six months. One type of hero predominated, the intensely virile man who was strong almost to the point of cruelty. Her genuine dislike of publicity led her to build a high brick wall around her house in the most secluded part of Guildford. Reporters were never admitted.

In 1925 *Punch* published a clerihew, in the style of E. C. Bentley:

> Mr. H. G. Wells
> Thought his novels were better than Miss E. M. Dell's
> (Or even than Ouida's)
> But it largely depends upon the taste of the readers.

Ruby M. Ayres, who up to the time of her death in 1955 wrote nearly two hundred novels, each being serialized in one or other of the many women's periodicals before book publication, succeeded Miss Dell. Early in her writing career she had been told by Lord Riddell to 'take her heroines as far as the bedroom door, and then leave them.' The advice was sound, and Miss Ayres took it. Born in 1883, she had started writing fairy tales as a child, and when about twenty-five began writing romantic stories. She claimed that she had been expelled from school for writing a love story which the head-mistress thought precocious and unsuitable. This convinced her that it must be good, and she determined to continue writing. Her first serial stories appeared in the *Daily Chronicle* and *Daily Mirror*, and soon there was hardly a popular magazine or newspaper which did not want to publish her work. Three of her books were filmed, and in 1921 the Gaumont Company were involved in a law-suit over one, *Castles in Spain*, when the producer sought to recover £1,597, which he claimed was owing to him by Gaumont for the making of the picture.

The main defence was that the cost of the feature film was not to exceed £4,000, and further that it was to be a first-class production, which Gaumont thought it was not. They therefore sought to pay the producer out of the profits. After a four-day hearing the Judge said that he had the greatest difficulty in arriving at what was a first-class film. He felt that there had been some extravagance in the making of the picture (£40 for a bulldog, and £211 for the hiring of an hotel for a few weeks) and he found that the plaintiff was entitled to judgment for £427, and also for £697 as indemnity for expenses incurred in advertising. Meanwhile Miss Ayres could claim to have the longest queues at the lending libraries, and her name was known to people who had never even heard of Aldous Huxley, D. H. Lawrence and the Sitwells.

Other popular women novelists were May Christie, Margaret Pedler and Berta Ruck, whose titles included *The*

Youngest Venus and *Kneel to the Prettiest*. Concordia Merrel, one of the most successful of Hodder and Stoughton's romantic novelists, found an enormous public ready to read her *Heart's Journey*, *The Miracle Merchant*, *Love and Diana*, *Ordeal by Marriage* and many other stories. Like her rivals, she relied on the language of the time and placed her heroes and heroines in situations with which her readers immediately identified themselves. There was considerable art in doing this, and it could not be achieved without sincerity. Her readers demanded not only strong romance, but also action and a constantly changing scene, and to provide this the writer needed powers of observation and description, and a considerable knowledge of human nature. In her highly successful story *The House of Yesterday*, Miss Merrel described a romantic meeting:

> The sound of footsteps made her look up, startled, and there was Tommy, materializing out of the gloom of the avenue. Tommy, in red-brown tweed, the plus-fours cut wide and handsome on the nursery-romper pattern, swinging along towards her in his loose-limbed way; grinning as broadly as ever; waving a hand showing no single symptom of a sense of guilt. And certainly not looking in the least like a young man about to pour forth floods of apology.
>
> 'Hallo, Moon of my delight!' he sang out. . .
>
> 'Tommy, you are a darn fool! What do you want to come messing around here for when I'm busy?' she cried, the laugh quite out of keeping with the wrathful words.
>
> 'This,' he said, and leaning forward he kissed her, looked up, said into the air:
>
> 'Sugar and spice and everything nice,' and bent down and kissed her again.
>
> And now her lips were eager and clinging beneath his, and all her crossness melted away.

It was perhaps not surprising that hundreds of thousands of women, many of whose husbands were 'on the dole,' living in dismal back-streets in industrial smoke-laden cities, found romance and excitement in these stories. It was better than going to the pictures, because more things happened.

For ninepence Miss Ayres and Miss Merrel brought happiness into millions of homes.

On a more sophisticated level there were E. M. Delafield, Margaret Kennedy, Clemence Dane, Storm Jameson, Stella Benson, May Sinclair, Dorothy Sayers, Virginia Woolf, Eleanor Scott and Rosamund Langridge. There was also Miss Rosita Forbes, who travelled to most places in Africa and the Near East, but not quite to Mecca, and told how she had visited Kufara, the secret city of the Sahara, and Jizan in Asir, where she claimed no white woman had ever been before.

Some novels were even more sensational. *The Well of Loneliness*, published in 1928, aroused a storm of indignation, and was hotly defended. Its theme, the world's misunderstanding of Lesbian love, had been well presented by the author, the mannish Radclyffe Hall. James Douglas, writing in the *Sunday Express*, protested, 'I would rather give a healthy boy or girl a phial of prussic acid than this novel.' When the book was banned it was immediately published in Paris, with great success; but it did not appear in England for several years.

At this time, Compton Mackenzie was adding to his reputation with *Guy and Pauline*, and Hugh Walpole was writing his *Jeremy* novels, while Robert Keeble shocked readers with *Simon Called Peter*, the story of a clergyman who renounced his orders and went downhill to ruin.

Hugh Walpole was one of the most prolific authors of his day. The son of the Bishop of Edinburgh, he had first found fame in 1911 with *Mr. Perrin and Mr. Traill*, a study of a schoolmaster's life. In 1919 he began a trilogy of tales about children and schooldays, *Jeremy* (1919), *Jeremy and Hamlet* (1923) and *Jeremy at Crale* (1927). In 1920 came *The Captives*, one of his best works, and in the same year *The Cathedral*, which was later dramatized. This was the first of a series of novels about the little Cornish town of Polchester, which was also the scene of *The Old Ladies* (1924) and *Harmer John*

(1926). In 1925 he wrote a macabre thriller, *Portrait of a Man with Red Hair*, and in 1929 he collaborated with J. B. Priestley to write *Farthing Hall*.

In 1928 Walpole helped to found the Book Society. Book Clubs were doing well in Germany and also in the fabulously prosperous United States, where the Book-of-the-Month Club had been started. With the help of Arthur Barker and Alan Bott, the Book Society came into being under a committee consisting of Walpole, Professor G. S. Gordon of Magdalen College, Oxford, J. B. Priestley, Clemence Dane and Sylvia Lynd. The headquarters were, first a cellar in Bloomsbury, then an attic in Grosvenor Gardens, and then a floor above the offices of *The Spectator* in Gower Street. By February 1929 the stage was set for the distribution to subscribers of the first Book Society 'choice,' but the book had not been chosen. The committee read hard, met, read some more, met again, and finally selected a novel by Helen Beauclerk entitled *The Love of a Foolish Angel*, which was posted to two thousand members together with the first issue of *The Book Society News* in April 1929. Its publishers, Sir Godfrey Collins and Mr. W. A. Collins, gave a dinner at the Savoy on publication day, and the Society had completed its first task. But in the week of publication there slipped into view a book, little-heralded, which the publishers had omitted to submit to the Book Society, and which the author, a retired Swedish doctor, had forgotten to mention to his friend Hugh Walpole. This was *The Story of San Michele*, which might well have been chosen had it been seen.

The membership doubled, trebled, quadrupled and continued to rise. The phrases 'Chosen by the Book Society' and 'Recommended by the Book Society' soon became known to readers. With time, Walpole, Priestley, Gordon and Clemence Dane resigned under pressure of their other work. Then Edmund Blunden, Margaret Kennedy, Julian Huxley, Cecil Day Lewis, Compton Mackenzie, V. S. Pritchett, Daniel George, Richard Church, C. V. Wedgwood,

Pamela Hansford-Johnson and Gerald Bullett replaced them or each other. These were the books chosen between April and December 1929:

Fiction

The Love of the Foolish Angel, by Helen Beauclerk
The Embezzlers, by Valentine Kataev
Nicky Son of Egg, by Gerald Bullett
A High Wind in Jamaica, by Richard Hughes
Whiteoaks, by Mazo de la Roche
The Lacquer Lady, by Tennyson Jesse

Biographical

The Adventures of Ralph Rashleigh, by Lord Birkenhead
Henry the Eighth, by Francis Hackett
Gallipoli Memories, by Compton Mackenzie

Among the books recommended were *Good-bye to All That*, by Robert Graves; *A Room of One's Own*, by Virginia Woolf; *All Quiet on the Western Front*, by Erich Maria Remarque; *The Man Within*, by Graham Greene; *Harriet Hume*, by Rebecca West; *The Simple Pass By*, by Joanna Cannan; *A Farewell to Arms*, by Ernest Hemingway; and *Carr*, by Phyllis Bentley. There had been no Book Society in 1922, when Ernest Raymond's *Tell England* was reprinted fourteen times.

One of the most successful short story writers was A. E. Coppard, who as a boy had been given the plays of Shakespeare to read, but much preferred Deadwood Dick, Calamity Jane and the penny 'bloods.' While a clerk at Oxford he wrote some tales, slowly, with infinite pains, spending many hours on revision. Meanwhile some of his poems appeared in *The Nation* and *The Westminster Gazette*. His first short story, *Piffincap*, appeared in 1918 in *Pearson's Magazine*, in a special holiday number edited by George Robey. Later that year Austin Harrison's *English Review* published another, *Dusky Ruth*, and others were accepted by the *Manchester Guardian* and the *Westminster Gazette*. On April 1, 1919, when he was forty-one, he gave up his job and became a teller of tales by profession.

L. A. G. Strong's first book of verse, *Dublin Days*, appeared in 1920. A year later he started to submit verses and short stories to editors, and made just over £30 in twelve months. Six years later he was still earning less than £100 a year from his writing, but he knew that his name and reputation were being established. *Doyle's Rock*, his first volume of stories, appeared in 1925. In 1929 came his first novel, *Dewer Rides*, which had taken two years to write. Novels, films and many short stories followed. That there was money to be made out of writing if one had ability and perseverance was obvious, but for all writers the first years were a hard struggle.

This was true even of Edgar Wallace, the most prolific writer of the twenties, who wrote so many books and stories that he did not remember their titles. In 1928 *Punch* depicted a bookstall salesman saying, 'Seen the mid-day Wallace, Sir?'

He had been born in London in 1875, of unknown parents, and was adopted nine years later by a Billingsgate porter. On leaving school he sold newspapers, served as a cabin boy, and enlisted in the Royal West Kent Regiment. He went with the Medical Staff Corps to South Africa in 1896 and began writing verse and political articles. On the outbreak of the Boer War he acted as correspondent for Reuters, and later for the *Daily Mail*. After the war he returned to London and joined the *Daily Mail*. His first successful work was *The Four Just Men*, which was followed by an enormous number of stories of crime, adventure and racing, as well as many plays and film stories. He wrote over 150 novels, some 15 plays, and innumerable articles and short stories. According to Sir Patrick Hastings he completed the play *Smoky Cell* so quickly that it was written, rehearsed and produced within three weeks. And it was a great success.

Another prolific writer was Nat Gould, a Manchester-born journalist who specialized in racing stories. He died in July 1919, but his books continued to sell for many years, and at the time of his death more copies had been sold than those of any other British or American author either before or during his period. He was the world's best seller, and by 1925 his sales had passed the twenty-five million mark. As a writer he was proud of the verdict once given by a clergyman, that his books 'could be put safely into the hands of any girl.'

4

In the field of popular journalism few success stories are more dramatic than those of the two Harmsworth brothers. Alfred C. Harmsworth began his writing career as a free-lance journalist when he was sixteen, and a year later became assistant editor of a boys' paper called *Youth*. His salary was 31s. 6d. a week. A year later, when the paper failed, he was free-lancing again and secured a position with a Coventry publisher in order to learn about printing. When he was twenty-five he returned to London and became part-owner of a business which produced cheap books such as *All About Railways*. Then, with the help of James Henderson, a publisher, he produced the first copy of *Answers to Correspondents* from a tiny room in Paternoster Square. The first issue contained an article on silk stockings, a piece entitled 'How to Live on Nothing a Year,' and readers were invited to send in questions.

The year was 1888, and *Answers* was an immediate success. The first issue was only 12,000 copies, and it was produced at a loss, sales being mainly confined to London, but every copy was sold. A prize of a guinea was offered for the best joke submitted on a post-card, a feature which became an essential part of the paper. In the second issue a more ambitious prize, a fortnight's holiday on the Continent, was offered. By hard work, Harmsworth began to create a demand for his paper in the provinces.

It was at this point that Harold Harmsworth, the future Lord Rothermere, gave up a civil service post to join his brother. He had left school with the reputation of being a good mathematician, and within a few months of his joining the firm the balance sheet showed a net profit of £2,000 a year.

When he was 35 Alfred Harmsworth was the world's greatest newspaper proprietor. No expense was spared to make his *Daily Mail* more popular every year, and all his long working hours were devoted to the task. He rose at six and worked until late every night. Illness was the penalty of overtaxing his strength.

With the rise of the *Daily Mail* old conventions and outworn methods of presenting the news were abandoned. By 1899 the circulation had reached a million a day. Four years later the Harmsworths bought the *Daily Mirror*, which after a shaky start succeeded as a halfpenny picture paper. Then the controlling interest in *The Times* was acquired, new printing presses and modern equipment were installed, and the price was reduced to a penny. Up went the circulation.

Harmsworth knew everyone working for him, and he expected them to work as hard as he. Always critical of Government bureaucracy, his reports of the Versailles Conference, in which he had hoped to participate, undoubtedly helped to undermine the prestige of Lloyd George.

Although his slogan 'Be bright, but dignified' was not always observed, Lord Northcliffe (as he now was) undoubtedly appealed to the great masses of middle and lower middle class readers with his bright and often sensational presentation of the news. During the war he helped to mould public opinion. When the *Daily Mail* declared that Lord Kitchener was starving the Army of shells there were demonstrations demanding Northcliffe's arrest as a traitor and the circulation fell by a hundred thousand copies. The *Daily Mail* was burned in the London Stock Exchange. But within a week Lloyd George, the new Minister of Munitions, told a Cardiff audience, 'We are short of shells.' And up went the circulation again.

In 1904 Harmsworth was made a baronet, in 1907 he became Lord Northcliffe, and shortly afterwards his brother Harold was created Lord Rothermere. When Northcliffe died, worn out, in August 1922, at the early age of 57, the *Manchester Guardian*, which had opposed his politics, summed up his career:

> As a material force there has been nothing in journalism to compare with him. . . He killed many shams in politics, and, in the Press, he scotched many abuses and made life more pleasant, as he made it more exciting, to the average man.

With his death a power had gone from Fleet Street, but his influence remained. Lord Rothermere, who had retired in 1912 to devote himself to other newspaper interests and had been Britain's first Secretary of State for Air, returned to control the *Daily Mail*. The circulation-raising days were over. Now began a series of crusades, and the first was for a stronger air force to defend Britain from attack.

In 1923, when most of its readers were thinking back to the war rather than forward to what the future held, the *Daily Mail* warned, 'Germany lost the war, but she is stealthily trying to win the peace!' Later it repeatedly drew attention to Germany's flagrant violation of the Versailles Treaty. In November 1933 Lord Rothermere himself wrote an article entitled 'We need 5,000 War Planes. When he died, in 1940, Winston Churchill wrote of him:

> He was one of the first Englishmen to realize the vital, or perhaps mortal significance of the two great facts which broke brutally upon the post-war world at the beginning of 1933—the power of the air, and the arrival of Hitler.

The Harmsworths had many competitors. In 1900 Arthur Pearson had launched the *Daily Express* to compete with the *Daily Mail*, printing news instead of advertisements on the front page to catch the eye. The Hulton Press empire included the London *Evening Standard*, the Manchester *Daily Chronicle*, the *Daily Sketch*, the *Sunday Chronicle*, the *Sporting Chronicle* and the *Athletic News*.

X. *Charles Chaplin in* The Gold Rush, *1925*.

Fred and Adele Astaire dancing on the roof of the Savoy Hotel, London, June 1923.

XI. *Malcolm Campbell at the wheel of his Napier Campbell racing car, November 1926.*

The perils of motoring—assistance from an A.A. patrol.

712 PUNCH, OR THE LONDON CHARIVARI. [JUNE 27, 1928.

OUR BETTERS.

Visitor. "NEW CAR?"
Hostess. "NO—NEW COOK."

To gain new readers the newspapers offered presents, paid for holidays, and insured families. The Liberal *Daily News*, owned by the Quaker Cadbury family, supported Lloyd George and offered life insurance to 'registered readers.' In 1922 it claimed to be 'the only paper that insures you and your home wherever you live.' It was also 'the only paper that insures your servants.' On January 5, 1922, it paid its third £250 fatality claim, to the headmistress of a Market Harborough school whose husband had been killed by a motor-cycle. The London *Star* at this time offered prizes of £5 notes to readers who best estimated how much money they had *saved* by shopping at stores which advertised in the paper—Selfridge's, Whiteley's, Gamage's, Meaker's, Thomas Wallis, and others. But most papers backed insurance as a circulation builder.

The war and Lord Northcliffe's influence had greatly altered the Press. Halfpenny newspapers vanished and could survive at the new price of a penny only when backed by large circulations. Although in 1900 there had been nine evening papers in London, including the influential *Westminster Gazette*, there were only three in 1924.

Northcliffe's career was equalled only by that of Max Aitken, the first Lord Beaverbrook. The son of a Canadian Presbyterian minister, he was reputed to have made himself a millionaire before he was thirty. Coming to Britain to seek fresh conquests, he entered politics and became Conservative member for Ashton-under-Lyne. In 1918 he bought the almost derelict *Daily Express*, which had failed to challenge the *Daily Mail* and had a small daily circulation of about 350,000 copies. Within a few weeks his remodelled and reorganized paper was seriously encroaching on the Northcliffe preserves. Soon it became the most popular newspaper in the country, encouraging Beaverbrook to found the *Sunday Express*, and in 1923 to buy the London *Evening Standard* from Hulton.

Lord Beaverbrook will be remembered in years to come

for his work in gearing the British war machine during the perilous early years of the Second World War. During the period from May to August 1940, through his drive and energy, the production of aircraft rose from nine hundred machines a month to one thousand and eight hundred. These were the aeroplanes in which 'the few' fought the decisive Battle of Britain above the English Channel and over the Weald of Kent and Sussex.

For the first thirty-eight years of his life he was plain Max Aitken, and at first he was a failure, unable to sell life insurance or sewing machines, or to pass a law examination. When he was 20 he had very little money; but in ten years, through hard work and speculation, he became a millionaire.

In its first year the new *Daily Express* lost £200,000, but it gained new readers every day. It supported Bonar Law, and after his tragic death, it backed Lloyd George; then came Beaverbrook's Empire Crusade, an imaginative attempt to keep the great brotherhood of nations strong and united and safe under the flag. An Imperialist, Beaverbrook believed that a strong Commonwealth was essential if there was to be peace and prosperity in the world. He hated apathy, and his newspapers were vigorous in their championing of the cause of Empire. Although the majority of the *Daily Express* readers were quite content to let the world drift by, the crusader never gave up his struggle or his beliefs. His loyalty to what he was sure were the best interests of the people was never in doubt. And in 1940, when his patriotism was proved, he might have reflected that for many years his newspaper had been trying to save Britain from the predicament in which she now found herself.

A rival to Beaverbrook and Northcliffe was provided by the Kemsley group, owned by the Berry brothers, William and Gomer, who later became Lord Camrose and Lord Kemsley. Starting with the *Sunday Times*, the *Financial Times* and the *Daily Graphic*, they bought the Manchester *Daily*

Dispatch and the *Evening Chronicle* in 1924, and began to build up a vast press empire which owned newspapers in Glasgow, Newcastle, Sheffield, Middlesbrough and many other centres. In 1926 they bought the *Daily Sketch* from Lord Rothermere, and acquired for £8,000,000 the immense Amalgamated Press group of periodicals which Northcliffe had started with *Answers*. Then they took over the *Daily Telegraph*. By the end of the twenties the Kemsley group consisted of seven morning papers, nine evenings and six weekly provincial journals.

The influence of all these newspapers, at a time when the wireless was still in its infancy, was enormous. The thoughts and habits and well-being of the nation were largely entrusted to the care of press lords and journalists. But the old tradition that the main duty of a newspaper was to give news had died; entertainment had become more important than enlightenment. Only the most influential newspapers, read by the minority, retained the old style; *The Times*, the *Manchester Guardian* and the *Morning Post*. After Northcliffe's death *The Times* passed to J. J. Astor, the younger son of the first Lord Astor. A body of trustees was then created to safeguard the future of the newspaper that could, and often did, dictate national policy.

An interesting development was the rise of the picture paper, of which the *Daily Mirror*, *Daily Sketch* and *Daily Graphic* were the leading examples. In the twenties the circulation of the *Daily Mirror* was a mere half-million. It was a ladies' paper, sedate, Conservative, modest, and one of its most popular features, enjoyed by thousands of middle-class children, was the daily Pip, Squeak and Wilfred strip cartoon. Pip the dog, Squeak the penguin and Wilfred the rabbit made their debut on May 12, 1919, introduced by Bertram J. Lamb, who became world-famous as Uncle Dick, and the artist Austin B. Payne. Actually Pip and Squeak appeared at first without Wilfred, who followed a little later. The success of the cartoon was phenomenal, and even in the middle of the 1926 General Strike the tiny one-page *Daily*

Mirror found space for a message for the children: 'Wilfred says goo-goo to his little friends.'

When the pets appeared in public at seaside towns immense crowds gathered to see them, although it was generally considered by adults that the transition from cartoon to life was not too successful. At Clacton, Pip was brought up before the magistrates for performing without a muzzle, and Uncle Dick was fined 50s. Later, Squeak bit a mayor on the nose, and then bit her keeper. But Queen Mary thought them 'sweet,' and they raised many thousands of pounds for charity through the Gugnuncs, a 'secret society' for children which had mysterious signs by which members could recognize one another, badges, and a form of recognition:

Challenge: Ick Ick Pah boo?
Reply: Goo Goo Pah Nunc!

There was also the Gugnuncs' Own Chortle, which youngsters proudly sang:

Gug, gug! Nunc, nunc!
To friends of all degree.
Give gugly hugs to nuncly gugs
Of the W.L.O.G.

Besides the three principal pets there were several other characters moving in and out of the cartoons—Popski and Wytzkoffski, the villainous Bolshevik dog and his master (usually carrying bombs), old Auntie, an aged penguin with a fish bag and a liking for herrings; Uncle Egbert who lived with her; the maid Angeline who married Tom Pippin and went to South Africa; Wilfred's mother; Pip's dog-friend Peter; a collection of penguin nephews of which the smallest was Stanley; two Scots terriers named Almost and Nearly; and a collection of moles. They all brought a great deal of happiness to a large number of people, long before the more revealing Jane, Garth, Belinda Blue Eyes, Buck Ryan, Jimpy and the other *Daily Mirror* cartoon characters appeared.

It was not until the thirties that the *Daily Mirror* began to fill its columns with photographs of women in bathing costumes and stories of marital relations and sexual aberrations. The more staid Kemsley *Daily Sketch* then met the challenge by announcing that it published only pictures and news 'fit to print.' This led even more readers to buy the *Daily Mirror*, which by 1939 was selling 1,700,000 copies a day. By 1945 the daily sales were well over two million, and in 1950 one quarter of the population of Britain preferred the *Daily Mirror's* lively presentation of news and views.

One of the highly successful features of the *Daily Mirror* was the syndicated column of 'Dorothy Dix,' an American journalist who claimed to have told a million girls how to get husbands. One of her first writing assignments had been to produce a feature article called 'Sunday Salad,' in which she advised women how to manage their emotions, their children and their husbands. When asked if she made up the letters which she answered she replied 'No!' very emphatically, and claimed that she received from a hundred to a thousand every day. These, she said, were amazingly human documents, a cross-section of life with nothing hidden. Sometimes she was asked incredible questions—whether it was bad luck to have a baby on a Friday, how to go to bed in a Pullman car, how to eat a stuffed tomato, and what to name a dog.

'Miss Dix,' wrote one correspondent, 'why am I not able to attract men? I have a medium-sized nose, full lips, and a college education.' Miss Dix did not reveal how she answered that question.

But the popular problems of the twenties were no more stupid than those of thirty years later. In 1955 a woman asked whether, if she had a child by a man with a wooden leg, the child would also be born with a wooden leg.

Until the *Daily Mirror* widened its appeal, the only daily newspaper which genuinely cared for the interests of the workers (and the workers alone) was the *Daily Herald*, edited until 1925 by George Lansbury, and later controlled by Julius Salter Elias, the first Lord Southwood. Under his guidance the newspaper prospered, and soon began to challenge the *Daily Express*. When it offered its readers a complete set of the works of Charles Dickens in sixteen volumes (worth 4 guineas) for only 11s., its rivals realized that the circulation war was on. At a meeting of the newspaper proprietors Mr. Elias surprised the company by explaining that the offer was not really a free gift of £3 13s. The *Daily Herald*, through Odhams Press, was able to produce each set of books for 11s. *and still make a profit.*

'The newspaper proprietors gazed at Mr. Elias in silence,' reported the London *Evening Standard*. 'Then Lord Beaverbrook broke the silence. He clapped on his little black hat and stamped out of the room. The meeting dispersed.'

The *Daily Mail*, *Daily Express* and *News Chronicle* now all placed orders for the works of Dickens. The *Daily Express* sold about 124,000 sets. The *News Chronicle's* set cost 10s. and claimed that it was 'in every way worthy of the great author who founded, and was the first Editor of, this newspaper.'

The *Daily Express* then offered Scott, Thackeray, George Eliot, Oliver Goldsmith, the Brontës and Jane Austen, all in a uniform set. The *Daily Herald* replied with 'twelve more *classical* classics, *all for 8s. 9d.*' This forced the *Daily Express* to reduce their sets to 7s. 6d.

The newspaper war continued.

CHAPTER SIXTEEN

The Royal Family

I

WITH HIS SUBJECTS the King had shared all the sorrows of the war. His son, the Prince of Wales, had gone early to the front, and had remained there. The King himself had visited the Army in France several times, the first British Sovereign to appear in the field since George II fought at Dettingen.

During the twenties the monarchy assumed a new importance, and became the sole link between the various self-governing states. The Dominions, no longer subject to rule by the British Parliament and the House of Commons, were now, in the words of Lord Balfour, united only by a 'common allegiance to the Crown, which is the symbol of their free association.' The King, the first Sovereign to have visited every Dominion and nearly every colony, became the father of the Commonwealth, and he and his family were regarded by his many millions of subjects first with respect, and then, as his personality became known through the medium of the wireless and his untiring devotion to his duty, with growing affection.

The reign was marked by changes which transformed all conditions of life. The aeroplane, which was a primitive contraption at the King's accession, had brought his farthest Dominion within three days' flight of London; he could now speak from his home in Sandringham to the people of the world, and touch their hearts with his 'God Bless You'; the long years of training in the Navy had taught him to be patient, understanding and sympathetic. And so there grew up between the King and his people a sentiment of mutual confidence which was strengthened with the years.

The King had no favourites, no inner circle of the privileged, as his father had enjoyed, but he had an enormous family of friends, and in evoking what was best in them, he led his people.

Certainly, no royal family worked harder than the family of King George V. When he ascended the throne he was 44, and was not a familiar figure to the public; but he soon attracted affection, for he radiated friendliness and courtesy. This affection was most clearly shown during the winter of 1928-29, when he became seriously ill. Bulletins were issued three or four times a day, and the whole nation was deeply affected. A Council of Regency was appointed, consisting of the Queen, the Prince of Wales, the Primate and the Prime Minister; the Prince of Wales, who was in Africa, raced home across France.

The King appeared to be happiest when sailing his famous cutter *Britannia*. On the second day of the Cowes Regatta, in 1924, in the handicap race for big yachts, the *Britannia* won easily, with Mr. H. Blundell-Weld's *Lulworth* second. The other competitors were Sir C. C. Allom's *White Heather* and Sir Thomas Lipton's famous *Shamrock*. The King himself took the wheel and raced his yacht to victory; but such pleasures were few and far between; most of his life was spent in hard, long, weary hours of service; there was always something to be done, some task to be performed. The King and Queen went everywhere, facing courageously the crises which imperilled the people and the throne, their quick sympathy and kindliness doing much to warm a chilly world. They showed personal interest in all that they saw.

Thus, when they visited Swindon in April 1924 they spent nearly two hours inspecting the railway works and seeing the men at work. In the iron foundry the words 'Welcome to the King and Queen' had been written in glowing letters of molten cast-iron lying in a mould of sand. In a few moments the letters and surrounding design had solidified into grey metal, and were permanent. Then the King climbed on to the footplate of the royal engine and, with Queen Mary beside him, drove it for about a mile.

Although the Army was now greatly reduced in size, the Royal Navy was still powerful, the greatest in the world. At the fleet review on July 26, 1924, the King saw 193 warships drawn up in his honour on a five-mile front. The old royal yacht, *Victoria and Albert*, led by the Trinity House yacht with the Duke of Connaught, Master of Trinity House, on board, left Portsmouth shortly before 2 o'clock with the King and the Prince of Wales on the bridge, followed by the Admiralty yacht *Enchantress*, bearing Mr. MacDonald, Mr. J. H. Thomas, Lord and Lady Chelmsford, Lord Beatty, Mr. Arthur Henderson and others. As the procession approached H.M.S. *Queen Elizabeth*, flying the flag of Admiral Sir John de Roebeck, the Commander-in-Chief, the guns of all the warships fired a royal salute. Every ship was dressed over all, seamen lining the forecastles and upper and quarter decks. As the royal yacht passed, bands played the National Anthem, and great bursts of cheering came from every ship. That night there was a brilliant searchlight display and illumination of the Fleet, the warships being outlined in golden fire reflected on the sea.

'Our Sailor King' he was called, but he was equally at home talking to miners, or laying a wreath at the foot of the Cenotaph in Whitehall. His subjects did not forget the photograph of him having an informal lunch in 1918, standing up against a railway wagon in a railway siding at Zeebrugge. They remembered him standing with his victorious generals when the Armistice came—Birdwood, Rawlinson, Plumer, Haig, Horne and Byng. And then, in 1920, he was shaking hands with players at the Hospital Cup Final at Richmond, when Guy's met Bart's. Their Majesties were always in the news, opening the Imperial War Museum, visiting the Isle of Man, going to Wales, unveiling the permanent stone

Cenotaph, entertaining the King and Queen of Denmark, the French President, the King of Italy, the Prince Regent of Abyssinia, attending the consecration of Liverpool Cathedral, opening the Wembley Exhibition, visiting Italy and France after an illness, on parade at the Trooping of the Colour ceremony, at the Royal Air Force display at Hendon, entertaining the Dominion Prime Ministers, opening the Belfast Parliament—there was always work to do.

Inspired by the love and support of Queen Mary, the King did not spare himself. And the other members of his family shared his duties whenever it was possible, so that the nation which had regarded Queen Victoria as a remote, almost unseen monarch and King Edward as a gay, pleasure-loving ruler, now felt nothing but affection and admiration for the royal family. The Prince of Wales, Prince Albert, Prince George, Prince Henry and Princess Mary, all were greatly loved. And when, only a few days before her eighty-first birthday, Queen Alexandra, the Queen Mother, died at Sandringham, the whole nation shared the King's grief.

On April 26, 1923, Prince Albert, the Duke of York, married Lady Elizabeth Bowes-Lyon, the daughter of the Earl and Countess of Strathmore and Kinghorne. On May 1, 1926, *Country Life* printed the following three-line caption: 'Our frontispiece this week is a portrait of H.R.H. the Duchess of York, the birth of whose baby daughter has been greeted with sincere rejoicing in all parts of the Empire.' At the time, the birth of a daughter to the Duke and Duchess was a happy, but hardly a momentous, occasion. Few imagined that the infant Princess would one day be Queen. On the night of April 20, 1926, the Home Secretary, Sir William Joynson-Hicks, had been dining out with his wife. They returned early, and Lady Joynson-Hicks was informed on the telephone by Sir Henry Simson, the obstetrician in attendance on the Duchess, that her husband might retire for the night. The event was a matter of official interest because the Home

Secretary was required to be in the house in which the birth took place.

After 'Jix' had been asleep for a short period, the telephone rang again and he was asked to go at once to Lord Strathmore's house in Bruton Street. Dressed in a tweed suit instead of his normal frock-coat, the Home Secretary hurried to Bruton Street, where the door was opened by the Duke himself. They talked together in the library for three hours, the Duke obviously very anxious, and 'Jix' very sleepy. Then they were asked to go upstairs.

'The Duke and I,' wrote 'Jix' later, 'went into a room adjoining that of the Duchess, and in a minute or two Sir Henry Simson brought the Princess to us. I congratulated His Royal Highness—but I cannot say that I made a very deep obeisance to the baby—and then went home to bed. In due course the announcement was issued from the Home Office, and the great bell of St. Paul's was rung. My duties in this connection were, of course, the reason for Her Majesty's kind suggestion that I should have a photograph of the baby on her first birthday. . . . It may well be that Princess Elizabeth may become Queen of England. It would be indeed interesting if once more we had a Queen Elizabeth on the throne of England. . . . '

But the lives of the royal brothers were rather overshadowed by the personal popularity of the heir to the throne, the Prince of Wales. The *Illustrated London News* summed up general opinion: 'Surely there has never been so travelled a Prince as ours, and there never has been such a successful ambassador.'

In spite of his natural shyness, the Prince was popular in the widest sense. No one except those around him appreciated the strain and fatigue of public ceremonial, yet he managed, while upholding the best traditions of the royal family, to appear to enjoy himself in his onerous task. When students at University College, Southampton, danced around him singing, 'Here we go round the Prince of Wales,' he stood in the centre, leaning on a walking-stick, his bowler hat tilted slightly to one side, smiling. He was just 30, and his day's work at Southampton had included four different ceremonies, all tiring. First he opened a new floating dock, the largest in the world; next he visited the Supermarine aviation works, and inspected one of the new giant flying-boats; then he placed a wreath on the City's Cenotaph, and went on to the University College. It was a typical long day in the life of Britain's 'Prince Charming,' the young man who was probably the most popular figure in the Empire.

Everything he did made headlines for the newspapers. When he went to the United States, first in 1919 and again in 1924, every word he said and every hour of each day were reported in the Press at home. When he fractured his collar-bone while riding, there was public concern in case he should be seriously hurt. He had no privacy, and his face was so well known that he could go nowhere without being recognized and photographed. During one of several informal visits to Wembley he took turns with Lord and Lady Louis Mountbatten to queue for the giant switchback. He was the only one of the party to go on the Whip, on which, seated in a little car with an official, he was 'whirled in wide jerky circles' and lost his cigarette. Even this was worth reporting, and put into headlines: PRINCE LOSES CIGARETTE.

Although the song *I've danced with a man who danced with the girl who danced with the Prince of Wales* was not a success in Britain, it was extremely popular in America, where the Prince was regarded as the most democratic young man in Britain, which perhaps he was. But with all this popularity, there appeared to be no conceit. As a junior officer in the Welsh Guards, often under shell fire in the trenches, he had said, 'My father has four sons, so why should I be fettered?' This remark gave the clue to his character.

Up to the time of his abdication from the throne in 1936 the Prince enjoyed a unique position in the thoughts of the people It was not only that he was good-looking and charming, but also because he represented the post-war generation. He was the product of the war, the leader of the ex-servicemen, and he made friends wherever he went. His personal and sincere interest in the British Legion kept alive the spirit of comradeship of the 1914–18 war. K. S. Ranjitsinghi, 'Ranji,' the Sussex and England cricketer, called him 'the lovable, the tactful, the experienced ambassador of fellow-feeling and friendship.'

In 1919 the Prince travelled more than 16,000 miles in four months, from one end of Canada to the other, from the Atlantic to the Pacific, across the frontier of the United States to visit Washington and New York, where he received the freedom of the city. It was the first of many Empire tours, made in H.M.S. *Renown*, and it was a tremendous success. Wherever he appeared he was given an overwhelming reception. An American newspaper paid tribute, and spoke for the nation:

> It's the smile of him, the unaffected modest bearing of him, the natural fun-loving spirit that twinkles in his blue eyes, and that surest of all poses, the recognition of duty to be done triumphing over a youngster's natural unease and embarrassment. That is what does it.

A leading American magazine ran a competition in which readers were invited to 'write a love-letter to the Prince of Wales.' And twenty bags of mail arrived in the editor's office.

Early in 1920 he set off again in the *Renown*, visiting the West Indies, San Diego, Honolulu, Fiji, New Zealand and Australia. In Barbados he dismissed the rumour that Britain might sell some of her colonies, saying, 'I need hardly say that the King's subjects are not for sale to other governments. Their destiny as free men is in their own hands.'

In Australia, the *Sydney Sun* reported:

> Before the Prince landed, the popular idea of princes was of something haughty and remote, but this smiling, appealing, youthful man, so pleased to meet with approval, has shown otherwise to the people of the democratic monarchy of the Empire.

At Canberra he laid the foundation stone of the new Parliament buildings. Near Bridgetown the royal railway carriage was derailed, but the Prince was unhurt. In New South Wales the Labour Prime Minister greeted him with the words, 'I am the head of the anarchist party.' Smiling, the Prince replied, 'Is that so, Mr. Story? Then I hope to meet a lot more anarchists.' When he sailed from Sydney he had visited every state and was known all over Australia as 'the Digger.' His right arm was sore and stiff with shaking hands.

In October 1921 he sailed in the *Renown* to India by way of Gibraltar, Malta and Aden. Arriving at Bombay in November, he was met by Lord Reading, the Viceroy, and received the ruling princes in an elaborate pavilion. Later he accepted an honorary degree from Calcutta University, shot his first tiger, and mixed with India's 'untouchables.' Burma, Mandalay, Delhi, Lahore and Karachi were all visited, and in April Tokyo was reached. When he returned home in June 1922 he was greeted by thousands of admirers.

In April 1923 he went to Belgium to unveil the British war memorial in Brussels, and then visited the battlefields and saw the graves of his comrades. Travelling as Lord Renfrew, he crossed the Atlantic in the *Empress of France*, landed at Quebec, made a short stay in Montreal, and went on for a holiday to his ranch in Calgary, Alberta. Returning home, he took up the position of President of the Wembley Exhibition, and a year later received the King at the opening ceremony.

During the summer of 1924 a second visit was made to the United States, in the liner *Berengaria*. And in 1925 another Empire tour began, in H.M.S. *Repulse*. This took him to West Africa, the Union, and then across the Atlantic to South America. His return in September was overshadowed by the death of his grandmother, the greatly-loved Queen Alexandra.

In Canada, where he went again in the autumn of 1927,

he attended the Diamond Jubilee celebrations of the Canadian Confederation. With him went Mr. Baldwin, the Prime Minister. In Toronto an amusing incident occurred when an ex-serviceman's hat blew off during a parade. Some forty thousand spectators saw the Prince chase it, catch it and return it to its owner, before continuing his inspection.

In 1928 he went on his fifth tour, to East Africa with the Duke of Gloucester, but this was cut short by the King's illness. The journey home, a distance of about 6,500 miles overland, took ten days. There followed an extensive tour of the 'distressed areas,' the industrial districts hard hit by the economic depression, during which the Prince mixed with large numbers of unemployed. What he saw in the slums led him to say:

> Some of the things I see in these gloomy, poverty-stricken areas make me almost ashamed to be an Englishman. . . Isn't it awful that I can do nothing for them but make them smile?

Later, he broadcast an appeal to the nation to help the unemployed.

2

The African tour was resumed when King George recovered from his illness, and that year the Prince unveiled the memorial in London to Marshal Foch. Then he went to Buenos Aires with Prince George, to open the British Empire Exhibition, where British goods worth over £4,000,000 were displayed. He returned in 1931, and in September volunteered a personal gift of £10,000 to the Exchequer to help the national crisis.

Trade followed the Prince. When he wore a white waistcoat with a dinner jacket, fashionable society copied him. When he wore a beret, so did tens of thousands of other people. Wearing straw hats when they were out of fashion, he brought them into favour again, to the great delight of the people of Luton. He was horseman, golfer, energetic dancer of the 'Charleston,' soldier, sailor, airman, statesman, and the hardest-working commercial traveller in the service of the Empire. Once, when buying a small article from a disabled ex-serviceman, he offered a pound note.

'Thank you, Sir,' said the man. 'I'll have it framed.'

'In that case I'll have it back,' said the Prince. 'I'll write you a cheque instead.'

When the King became seriously ill, many people thought that the Prince would soon be called to the throne. But his time had not yet come. When it did come, opinions were divided about his own personal choice of a wife. Too many people forgot the years of service which he had devoted to his country and his father's subjects. Yet he was the same man, and he might have been trusted to choose a partner who would suit him. Although the country was split by his decision, large sections of the public wished him only well, realizing that he had earned his happiness through his service. Today, almost in retirement, he might with some justification bitterly reflect that no further use has been made of the rare qualities of leadership and the devotion to duty which he showed in the post-war years. Few servants of modern Britain so well deserve happiness. Have we so many leaders? But how quickly English men and women forget.

By February 1929, King George's health having improved, His Majesty left London for a period of convalescence at Bognor, Sussex. On April 22nd, on his recovery, his message to the Empire included the words:

> Help has come from another source of strength; as month after month went by I heard of the widespread and loving solicitude with which the Queen and I were surrounded. I was able to picture to myself the crowds of friends waiting and watching at my gates, and to think of the still greater number of those who, in every part of the Empire, were remembering me with prayers and good wishes. The realization of this has been among the most vivid experiences of my life.

On July 7th, a great thanksgiving service was held in Westminster Abbey. Later the King expressed his surprise at the overwhelming reception of the enormous crowds. 'I am sure I cannot understand it,' he said, 'for, after all, I am only a very ordinary sort of fellow.' Throughout the day he was in great pain, but he was genuinely moved by the vast cheering multitudes of people.

When the Prince of Wales had visited Aden, some years before, he had been greeted with a large banner bearing the words *Tell Daddy we are happy under British rule*. Here, and in the tremendous number of people lining the route to Westminster Abbey, was proof, if any were needed, that the King and his family were regarded with sincere affection by their subjects. Yet it had not always been so. Many kings of England had been hated, and in other countries crowns were falling, and would continue to fall. In a changing world, and in difficult times, the British monarchy and the King's family kept abreast of the times, setting an example which the nation was pleased to follow.

Felix the cat, Pat Sullivan's famous character appearing in EVE'S FILM REVIEW *in 1925.*

CHAPTER SEVENTEEN

Speed and Sport

I

DURING THE twenties sport became of increasing interest to Britons, mainly because the development of mechanism in industry and shorter working hours gave the workers more leisure time. Newspapers, the wireless, film newsreels, all were now required to give more space to cricket, football, lawn tennis, golf, athletics, horse and motor-racing, billiards and even chess. It was an era of records and record-breaking. Year by year the crowds of spectators at sporting events multiplied. Racing and football were most popular; Ascot and Goodwood remained the fashion centres, the Derby at Epsom and the Grand National at Aintree were the two great 'classic' horse races. For every man who attended a race meeting, many more placed bets ranging from shillings to pounds on races they never saw.

At Wembley the Cup Final could draw 100,000 people and call for special police to line the route from London. Soccer was the sport of the masses, while rugger remained the pastime of public schools, the services and amateur clubs.

Suzanne Lenglen was 20 when she first came to London from France in 1919, but she attracted a crowd of over ten thousand to Wimbledon to watch her, in the presence of the King and Queen, defeat Mrs. Lambert Chambers in the ladies' singles. Her victory was more fully reported than any previous sporting event. Mrs. Chambers had been undefeated for eleven years, and the appearance of Mlle Lenglen created a minor sensation. She was immediately the best-known figure in the sporting world, creating an enormous interest in tennis, especially among women.

'I was a pale, thin person,' she said later, 'and father and mother were afraid I should always be an invalid. But tennis transformed me magically into a nut-brown maid, sparkling with health.' Her robust, almost acrobatic movements and her masterly accomplishment of the game prompted thousands of young English girls to take up not only tennis but also rowing, running, cycling and swimming. In moderation the pre-war young lady had enjoyed all these recreations, but only gently, and very discreetly and modestly clothed. Now Mlle Lenglen actually wore *short skirts*, and with the development of popular picture papers she could be seen in the *Daily Sketch*, *Daily Mirror and Daily Graphic*, leaping in the air, free and unrestricted, hitting out at the ball—an elegant, modern girl, heralding the approach of a new deal for women.

In February 1924 the match between Mlle Lenglen and Miss Helen Wills at Cannes aroused more interest than a boxing match for the world's title. 'There is no doubt,' observed the *Sunday Times*, 'that the prospect of the encounter has drawn even more visitors than usual to the Riviera this year, and it has proved a godsend to hotel-keepers, who would otherwise probably have to deplore losses resulting from a particularly rainy season.'

Sports news now shared the headlines with politics. When Joe Beckett was knocked out in the first twenty minutes by Georges Carpentier, the coal-miner from Lens, the London evening headlines read CARPENTIER WINS. In 1926, when 'Bobby' Jones, an amateur golfer, won the Open Championship, a crowd of twelve thousand people gathered around him. Soon he was earning £40,000 from the game. Enormous crowds went to see Jack Petersen, who won the heavyweight Lonsdale Belt outright, having beaten Reggie Meen, Jack Pettifer and Jack Doyle in succession. And when Gene Tunney beat Jack Dempsey, the 'Manassa Mauler,' in 1926 in a ten-round fight in Philadelphia, the news was flashed round the world. In 1923, in New York, Dempsey had knocked the giant Firpo clean out of the ring. He was swarthy, blue-chinned, but not a big man, and he was quiet and almost gentle—except when fighting.

Although Rugby football was not the most popular of games, the standard of play was very high. Few can forget the thirteen stone of bone and muscle that made up the dash of W. W. Wakefield, or the outstanding half-backs W. J. A. Davies and C. A. Kershaw, an almost perfect example of team-work and understanding.

In golf there were other great favourites, headed by C. J. H. Tolley, who won the amateur championship, and with Roger Wethered won the Walker Cup at St. Andrews in the face of keen American competition, only to lose it in 1926 to the brilliant 'Bobby' Jones, perhaps the greatest golfer of all time.

In the world of international tennis there were the American W. T. (Bill) Tilden, and the outstanding French team of Borotra, Lacoste, Cochet and Brugnon. Among the women players Suzanne Lenglen reigned supreme until Helen Wills arrived from America.

All sporting events drew large crowds, but in April 1923 the authorities were unprepared for the 160,000 people who wanted to see the Cup Final at Wembley. The new stadium had been built to hold 125,000, and the extra 35,000 people overflowed on to the football pitch and held up the game. Nearly three thousand policemen found themselves unable to deal with the situation, for this was before the time of wireless loudspeakers. When the King arrived in his car the pitch was completely covered by people, and many thousands more were pushing and fighting to get into the stadium. Eventually, a policeman mounted on a grey horse persuaded people to stand back along the touch-lines, and the game started nearly an hour late. A thousand people were injured in the stampede, and hundreds were knocked down.

Every year the question 'Who will win the Cup?' occupied the thoughts of hundreds of thousands of working-class men:

1920 Aston Villa beat Huddersfield Town (1–0)
1921 Tottenham Hotspur beat Wolverhampton (1–0)
1922 Huddersfield Town beat Preston North End (1–0)
1923 Bolton Wanderers beat West Ham United (2–0)
1924 Newcastle United beat Aston Villa (2–0)
1925 Sheffield United beat Cardiff City (1–0)
1926 Bolton Wanderers beat Manchester City (1–0)
1927 Cardiff City beat Arsenal (1–0)
1928 Blackburn Rovers beat Huddersfield Town (3–1)
1929 Bolton Wanderers beat Portsmouth (2–0)
1930 Arsenal beat Huddersfield Town (2–0)

The Boat Race continued to attract large crowds each year, but in 1925 the unfortunate effect of a wet day was the waterlogging of the Oxford boat. Having lost the toss, Oxford had to start on the rough Middlesex side of the river, and soon began to ship water. The boat did not actually sink—as both boats had done in the first race, in 1912—because there were 72 football bladders under the seats, but it could move only slowly. Just beyond Hammersmith Bridge the Oxford coach obtained the umpire's permission to stop the crew, but he had to tell them five times before they agreed. They then boarded a motor launch. Meanwhile the Cambridge crew was out of sight, far ahead. Oxford was using a new 'streamline' type of boat, specially designed for the occasion.

Cricket, said Sir James Barrie, was not so much a game as a way of life. In the test matches most of the chief successes were won by the old masters. The M.C.C. team which J. W. H. T. Douglas took to Australia in 1920 was defeated in all five matches, a disaster for English cricket. With the exception of Jack Hobbs, who made three centuries, the batsmen failed to realize expectations. In the spring of 1921 an Australian team, led by Warwick Armstrong, also proved superior. Hobbs was kept out of the first two test matches by illness, and had appendicitis at the beginning of the third match, and Hearne played only once. The English batting could not compete with the fast bowling of Macdonald and Gregory, who had claimed the majority of the wickets the year before.

Dudley Carew, in his book *England Over*, has summed up the ferocity of Gregory, 'his run up to the wicket, his last leap into the air, the expression of diabolical determination on his face, and the pace, shattering to us who had forgotten what fast bowling was like, of the ball off the wicket.'

Against South Africa, however, England did better. After a hard fight, the English team won the first two test matches, but when they went to South Africa they had to fight hard to win. The African bowling, led by Hall, Nupen and Blanckenberg, was excellent, although in England the unfamiliar soft turf made their task difficult. By the time the English team went to Australia again in 1924–25, a decisive success over South Africa had removed the feeling of inferiority. But apart from the bowling of Maurice Tate the English attack was not outstanding. Few batsmen could stand up to the Australian 'googly' bowling. The result was an Australian win, 4–1, but it was generally considered that English cricket had recovered, and was no longer in disgrace. Hobbs, Sutcliffe and Tate were now recognized as the world's three outstanding cricketers. No new batsman had ever enjoyed quite the success of Hobbs in Australia. His four centuries, a double century at Melbourne, established records which the Australians admired. And by the end of the tour Maurice Tate was considered the greatest bowler in the world. He had carried the whole attack, and had claimed 38 wickets in five matches.

In 1925 everyone in Britain interested in sport—which meant nearly everyone—was asking 'Will Jack Hobbs do it?' He had made 226 runs at Scarborough, 215 at Birmingham, and altogether 125 centuries in first-class cricket. Now enthusiasts were wondering if he would beat the record of 126 centuries held by W. G. Grace. When he eventually did so, at Taunton, he received the congratulations of the King and the whole country. By the end of 1933 he had raised his total to 196 centuries.

Altogether, Hobbs played in 41 test matches against Australia, the first being in 1907, at Melbourne. His highest score was 316 not out, against Middlesex at Lord's in 1926. As a fieldsman at cover point he was unsurpassed; at the wicket his footwork was so quick that it was not always possible to follow its movement in detail. He seemed to have some instinct of what manner of ball was on the way.

Hobbs's career had started when he was nineteen, as cricket coach at Bedford Grammar School. When he offered his services to the Essex County team they were declined. But Surrey accepted him, and in 1903 he became a member of the ground staff at the Oval. His first county championship match was in 1905, when he made 155 against Essex, who had refused him.

In 1926 the tide turned in England's favour, and Australia lost to England, 1–0. The first test match at Nottingham was abandoned owing to rain, after Hobbs and Sutcliffe had scored 32 for no wicket on the first day. Ten thousand people went to Lord's to watch the second test, to see Bardsley score 193 not out for the visitors. Hobbs scored 119 in five hours, Macartney 133 not out, and A. P. F. Chapman made his debut.

It was at The Oval, in the last match of the series, that Australia at last met defeat—for the first time for fourteen years. Hobbs and Sutcliffe, batting in rain on a wet wicket, were the heroes of the hour. England had at last won the Ashes.

The M.C.C. team which sailed for Australia under Chapman in 1928 was the strongest that England had produced for many years. It consisted of Chapman, D. R. Jardine, Hobbs, J. C. White, E. Tyldesley, Leyland, Staples, Hammond, F. E. Toone, Sutcliffe, Larwood, Freeman, Duckworth, Ames, Tate, Hendren and Geary. The success of the tour was Walter Hammond, who scored century after century, 905 runs altogether, and an average of 113. An almost unknown young Australian cricketer named Bradman made his debut, but was soon dropped. England won the first four matches. At Brisbane, Hendren scored 169, and the Australians suffered disaster after disaster. Gregory, their star bowler, suffered an injured knee, which ended his career; then Larwood played havoc with the Australian batting. Australia were all out for 66 runs.

In 1930 Australia won back the Ashes 2–1, when they visited England. All through the twenties matches had been won by pace, and by fast googly bowling, which were features of Australian cricket.

2

The war had greatly advanced aircraft development, and the first years of peace were the great years of pioneer long-distance flying. The Atlantic was crossed non-stop, and first direct flights were made to India, Australia and the Cape. Australia was circumnavigated. Other nations made similar flights to their distant colonies, France to Senegal and Madagascar via the Sahara; Holland to the Dutch East Indies. Trans-continental flights were made in America, and the routes of the world's air lines were planned. Soon there was not a continent or ocean which remained uncrossed. Between 1922 and 1932 more than fifty long-distance flights were made over Africa alone, by Sir Alan Cobham, Lady Bailey, and by British, French, Belgian and other pioneers and Air Force units.

Three outstanding flights took place in 1919. On the night of June 14–15 a Vickers-Vimy aeroplane, piloted by Captain John Alcock, D.S.C., and Lieutenant A. Whitten Brown, was flown across the Atlantic from St. John's, Newfoundland, to Clifden on the Irish coast in 15 hours and 57 minutes. The pilots shared £8,000 of the *Daily Mail* prize of £10,000 and gave £2,000 to the engineers and mechanics who had helped them. The two heroes were given a tremendous welcome in London, and were knighted by the King at Windsor. But Sir John Alcock's triumph was cut short when he was killed later that year in France.

The second important flight was made by the airship R 34, which crossed and recrossed the Atlantic, leaving England on July 2 and returning on July 13. During the 6,000-mile journey the naval airship was in constant wireless communication with the Air Ministry in London. On the first day over the Atlantic a stowaway was discovered, a man who had been ordered to stay behind but was upset at not going. He had concealed himself on the girders between the gas bags. When discovered, he was given a job on the airship.

The third flight was made in November by Captain Ross Smith, M.C., D.F.C., and his brother Lieutenant Keith Smith and two sergeant mechanics, flying in a Vickers-Vimy aeroplane from Hounslow to Port Darwin, Australia, in twenty-seven days. Both the Smith brothers were later knighted.

Many well-known pilots later flew over this route to the other side of the world, notably Sir Alan Cobham, Amy Johnson, Jim Mollison, and Squadron-Leader Bert Hinkler, who flew alone to Australia in sixteen days.

In 1920 *The Times* financed an expedition to the Cape, Captain F. C. Broome and Captain S. Cockerell piloting a Vickers-Vimy twin-engine 'plane *Silver Queen II* as far as Bulawayo, where the machine was wrecked. After an enforced rest of eleven days the journey to Cape Town was resumed in a small two-seater. Once again, the King knighted the airmen.

It was Alan Cobham who mapped the route for the giant air liners which later flew regularly to the Cape. In November 1925 he set off from Croydon with an engineer and a photographer, in a De Havilland type 50 'plane, flying in bad weather to Cairo, Wadi Halfa, Khartoum, Malakal and

Mongalla. Over the Victoria Falls Cobham brought his machine low to obtain photographs, but the spray entered the air intake, the engine spluttered and stopped, and the aeroplane lost height and threatened to dive into the water. But the engine picked up again, and the flight continued to Livingstone, Bulawayo, Victoria and Johannesburg, over land where no one had ever flown before. When Cape Town was reached on February 17, the crowd of waiting people was so enthusiastic that police protection was needed. On the return journey Cobham managed, by a few hours, to beat the liner *Windsor Castle*.

In 1926, Cobham flew to Australia and back in 230 flying hours, his flying-boat descending on the Thames opposite the Houses of Parliament. A year later, accompanied by his wife, he flew again to the Cape, travelling over 20,000 miles in his flying-boat. Also 1926 saw one of the most notable mass pioneer flights, organized by the R.A.F., when Wing-Commander Pulford and five officers flew from Cairo to the Cape in four Fairey III D biplanes and returned to Britain via Cairo. In the same year, at the Hendon Air Pageant, a tailless Hill Pterodactyle with a 35 h.p. Bristol engine was demonstrated.

The formation of Imperial Airways linked Britain at first with Europe, then with Africa, the Far East and Australia. In November 1924 the company advertised that it was the only British air line to and from the Continent which offered passengers cushioned arm-chairs, speed and height indicators, a lavatory, luncheons with or without spirits, and wireless in every machine. Imperial Airways were already travelling 135,000 miles a month. But they were already facing fierce competition from their rivals. The Dutch K.L.M. service had been started in April 1921 and had established a reputation for reliability and accurate navigation. The Deutsche Lufthansa service was founded in April 1926. Imperial Airways started their regular service from Croydon to India in the same year.

The flight which captured the attention of the whole world was made in 1927, when the 25-year-old American pilot Charles Lindbergh flew the Atlantic in order to win a prize of £5,000. The rules of the contest were severe; the machine was allowed only one engine, which must be air-cooled; and there was to be no radio. But on Friday, May 20, 1927, the little *Spirit of St. Louis* rose from the aerodrome at New York and turned eastwards towards the old world. Flying conditions were so bad that Lindbergh attempted to climb above the fog belt, but he found that ice was forming on the 'plane at eight thousand feet, so he flew down, just above sea-level, searching for shipping. For several hours nothing was visible except the sky and the broad Atlantic. But when at last he sighted the coast of Ireland, the news of his success was carried round the world by wireless.

At Le Bourget aerodrome outside Paris several thousand people stood waiting to greet him. When the little aeroplane touched down the crowd rushed towards it, lifting Lindbergh out of the cockpit and carrying him shoulder-high. The journey of 3,300 miles had been made in just over thirty-three hours. Young Lindbergh was now the hero of the world, receiving many decorations, including the Order of the Legion of Honour and the Order of St. Leopold. Later, when he flew to England, an enormous crowd met him at Croydon, and at Buckingham Palace the King awarded him the Air Force Cross.

It was not only in aeroplanes that records were being broken and new worlds discovered. As early as 1896 a Swedish scientist named Salomon August Andree had tried to reach the North Pole by balloon. In 1930 his body, with those of two companions, was discovered lying in their last camp. Photographs taken by the men thirty-three years earlier were developed. In 1924 the Oxford University Expedition to Spitzbergen took place, led by Professor George Binney, with the co-operation of the Air Ministry. Although Binney's seaplane was twice disabled and finally wrecked and abandoned, he made several flights over Spitzbergen. Two years later the American, Commander Byrd, flew from Spitzbergen to the North Pole and back. In 1928 George Hubert Wilkins, later to be knighted, flew across the Polar Sea from Point Barrow to Deadman's Island, Spitzbergen, in twenty-and-a-half hours, with Carl Ben Eileson, the famous Alaskan pilot.

On the ground, as well as in the air, the race for speed records claimed the attention of brave men, enthusiasts who captured the imagination of their fellow-countrymen. Thousands of people went at week-ends to watch motor-racing at Brooklands, near Weybridge, Surrey. In October 1924 the *Autocar* stated that racing cars were too fast for the existing roads and tracks. Steps should be taken to limit the race for speed; 12- or 14-horse-power cars with super-charged engines were now capable of speeds 'in excess of 120 miles an hour.' 'At such speeds,' said the *Illustrated London News*, 'these small cars are—not to exaggerate at all—infernally dangerous.' It was considered safer to drive Captain Malcolm Campbell's twelve-cylinder Sunbeam than one of the little two-litre racers, which travelled almost as fast.

During the late twenties people all over Britain were hoping that the 'triple crown' of the speed records would be won. In 1926 the land speed record was gained by Parry Thomas on the Pendine Sands, Carmarthenshire, at 178 m.p.h. On March 3rd of the following year he was killed in his Thomas Special when the driving chain broke and he was decapitated. In the same year Henry Segrave and Malcolm Campbell were competitors in the race to reach a speed of 200 m.p.h., and in 1929, on the same day that the death of Marshal Foch was announced, Segrave broke the world's record at Daytona, travelling at 231 m.p.h. with a burst radiator. Next day his rival, Lee Bible, was killed while trying to reclaim the record for America. Segrave's 1,000 horse-power *Golden Arrow* was then the fastest car in the world. And a few days later he won the speedboat record from the American, Gar Wood. In June 1930 he was killed while breaking the water speed record again, in his boat *Miss England II*, having devoted his life to British mechanical superiority.

Between 1927 and 1931 Britain won the international Schneider Trophy air race three times, retaining it on the

third occasion. And across the Atlantic the giant liners competed for the 'blue riband.' On August 26, 1924, the original *Mauretania* of the Cunard line, built in 1908, created four records, eclipsing all previous performances by any ship, by covering 3,157 miles in 5 days, 3 hours and 20 minutes. When the new German liner *Bremen* beat the record by nine hours, the Cunarder recaptured the trophy, but finally the *Bremen* and *Europa*, more modern in design and performance, regained it.

CHAPTER EIGHTEEN

Entertainment

I

THE MOST POPULAR form of entertainment was the motion picture. The end of the war found the United States the greatest film-producing centre in the world; the period 1920–29 has been called 'the golden age of Hollywood.'

During this time the personalities of American film actors and actresses became, in most cases, even more important than the productions in which they appeared. Film 'stars,' as they were now called (instead of 'picture players'), became household names. They gained wealth and prestige on a scale denied to most other people. Few but the Japanese knew the name of the Prime Minister of Japan, one of the leading nations of the world, but millions of people in every country knew the names of Mary Pickford, Douglas Fairbanks, Charles Chaplin, Rudolph Valentino, Ronald Colman, Greta Garbo, John Gilbert, Harold Lloyd and Clive Brook.

With the war had come abnormal values in everything, and salaries and the cost of making films rose. But when the war ended, and American industries returned to normal, many people in the United States who had invested money in liquor industries decided, with the coming of prohibition, to finance films. Soon Hollywood possessed the pick of the world's film players, the most experienced technicians, and the enterprise and industry to give the public what it wanted—entertainment.

Until 1928 the language of the cinema was silent, and was therefore international. Influenced by what they saw on the silver screen, people began to buy clothes and manufactured goods which they had seen in Hollywood films. Rudolph Valentino, wearing long 'sideboards,' set a fashion for large numbers of young men. To be a film 'star' was the housemaid's dream, and millions read about the daily and nightly activities of even minor players, as reported in detail in newspapers and magazines.

In Britain the habit of 'going to the pictures' had been, before the war, a pastime mainly for servant girls and the very young. But now the motion picture industry was growing up, and the quality as well as the entertainment value of the better films could not be denied. Such pictures as *The Kid* (1920), *The Three Musketeers* (1921), *The Four Horsemen of the Apocalypse* (1921), *Orphans of the Storm* (1922), and *The Big Parade* (1925), to mention only five out of many thousands, attracted people to the cinema who had rarely been before. And they found that the new Electric Palaces and Picturedromes, with their orchestras and palm-fringed upstairs cafés, were more comfortable, cleaner and safer than they had expected.

Most of the films which Britain saw in these new picture houses were American; until the year 1926 there were remarkably few British films; the industry had suffered so much during the war that in 1920 it practically collapsed. During one month early in 1925 there was not one feature film being made in England.

America, however, was exporting enormous quantities of film—nearly 112,000,000 feet in the first nine months of 1921. And who could resist going to see the wonderful Lillian Gish in D. W. Griffith's *Way Down East*, the melodramatic story of a girl turned out of her home into the snow because she had an illegitimate child? At the Cinema Royal down the road one paid 6d.—or perhaps 1s.—to see Miss Gish, and one judged her to be well worth it, even without the Topical Budget, followed by one of Mack Sennett's screamingly funny Keystone comedies featuring Mabel

XII. *London suburban houses in the nineteen-twenties.*

A table gramophone with a pleated diaphragm instead of a sound-box or horn cost £22 10s., in 1924.

ENCHANTING LINGERIE: AT DEBENHAM AND FREEBODY'S, WIGMORE STREET, W.

In 1924 this electro-plate oval nut basket with crackers cost £2, or £7 5s. in silver, with plated crackers.

XIII. *Passengers board the* never-stop railway *at Wembley exhibition, 1924. What would they think of next?*

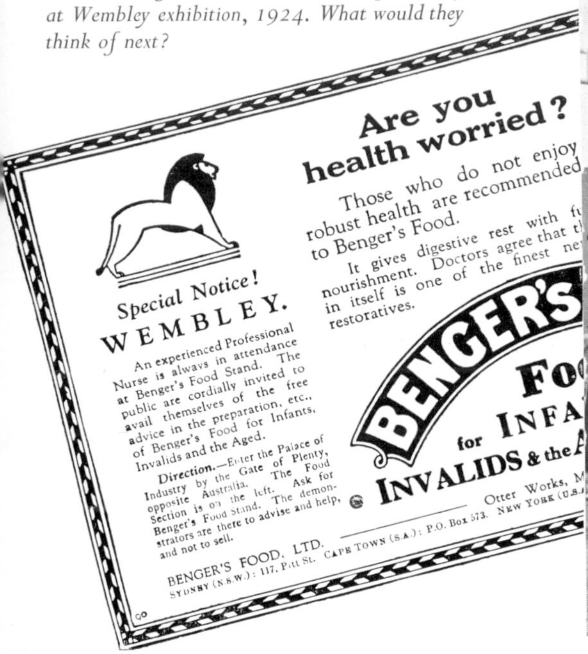

Queen Mary with the Queen of Italy at Wembley, May 1924.

Are you health worried?

Those who do not enjoy robust health are recommended to Benger's Food.

It gives digestive rest with fu nourishment. Doctors agree that th in itself is one of the finest ne restoratives.

BENGER'S Foo for INFA INVALIDS & the A

Special Notice!
WEMBLEY.

An experienced Professional Nurse is always in attendance at Benger's Food Stand. The public are cordially invited to avail themselves of the free advice in the preparation, etc., of Benger's Food for Infants, Invalids and the Aged.

Direction.—Enter the Palace of Industry by the Gate of Plenty, opposite Australia. The Food Section is on the left. Ask for Benger's Food Stand. The demonstrators are there to advise and help, and not to sell.

BENGER'S FOOD, LTD. Otter Works, M
SYDNEY (N.S.W.): 117, Pitt St. CAPE TOWN (S.A.): P.O. Box 573. NEW YORK (U.S.A

The Cup Final at Wembley, 1923, showing the crowd on the pitch being cleared by a policeman on a white horse.

Normand and Fatty Arbuckle. A comfortable plush seat, a fine accompaniment from the upright piano, a *free* printed programme, and the evening was filled with delight. When the stern father ordered Miss Gish out into the cold night, people in the audience cried, although they knew that sooner or later handsome Richard Barthelmess would rescue her.

That was in 1920, the year that saw Douglas Fairbanks in *The Mark of Zorro*, and Pearl White in *The Perils of Pauline*. The serial story had come to stay, and occupied an increasing part in the public's affection. Pearl White was the Queen of the Serials, and her thrilling escapes from death—every week—set audiences bouncing on their tip-up seats with excitement.

Between 1922 and 1926 the motion picture created another craze—the Valentino tradition. Apart from Douglas Fairbanks, no male film star enjoyed such popularity as this olive-skinned Italian. Because he had few rivals, his position on the screen was unique. Born Rudolph Alphonso Guglielmi di Valentino d'Antonguelia, he had settled in America in 1913, but was at first unable to obtain employment. Becoming a stage dancer, he appeared in London as partner to Gaby Deslys. In 1918 he reached Hollywood, where he got a chance to play extra parts, and eventually minor roles. When he was invited by Rex Ingram to appear as Julio in the film version of *The Four Horsemen*, his good looks, grace, virility and charm made him the idol of countless women. His later films included *The Sheik*, *Blood and Sand*, *The Young Rajah* and *Monsieur Beaucaire* (1924), which most people considered his best. In 1925 he visited England to attend the premiere of *The Eagle*, and was given an hysterical ovation. When he died, at the height of his success, in August 1926, thousands of people attended his funeral and women wept at his graveside.

The quality of American productions was generally much higher than could be found in English studios. And while Britain was busily importing reels of Lillian Gish, Pola Negri,

Gloria Swanson, Barbara La Marr, Richard Dix and Mae Murray, America spurned the more modest pictures made at little studios at Twickenham, Walthamstow, Ealing Green, Shoreham, Bushey and Shepherds Bush. Few English films crossed the Atlantic, and in 1922 only six were accepted for showing in the United States. Many British actors discovered that they could do better in Hollywood than at home, and so began the great exodus to Hollywood headed by Clive Brook, Ronald Colman, George Arliss, Lupino Lane, Ivor Novello, Victor McLaglen and Percy Marmont. A half-million dollar company was formed in New York to handle British films, but the quality of the product could not compete with the ambitiously conceived American *Robin Hood*, *The Covered Wagon*, *Scaramouche* and *If Winter Comes*.

Indeed, few Americans realized that Britain possessed film studios. But an effort to help the home industry was made with the formation of the British National Film League, which was inaugurated at a luncheon at which the Prince of Wales, Sir Arthur Conan Doyle, Sir Edward Marshall Hall and Mr. Ramsay MacDonald spoke. Cinema exhibitors were persuaded to present British Film Weeks, but the quality of the pictures was the biggest drawback. The effort ended in disaster, and in 1925 the government decided to fix a quota, requiring every cinema in Britain to show a proportion of one British film in ten. The quota was to rise annually, until by June 1929—it was hoped—one in every four films shown would be English. Thus quantity, if not quality, was assured.

In 1925 only thirty-four feature films were made in England, the most popular British stars being Ivor Novello, Betty Balfour, Chrissie White, Henry Edwards, Alma Taylor and Stewart Rome. The partnership of Henry Edwards and Chrissie White, which continued well into the 'talkie' era, was most affectionately regarded by the public. Many of the pictures which these stars made were of the highest quality. But the work of a few accomplished players and technicians could not raise the general standard, and it was clear that until the coming of the Quota Act the cinema industry was more interested in importing Miss Swanson in tins than in finding a rival for her in Britain. Home pictures could not compete in the open market with the ambitious and enormously expensive *Abraham Lincoln*, or *The Arab*, or *The Iron Horse*. Too many English producers lacked imagination—and cash.

The quota, however, was during the late twenties and thirties to be the means of training the technicians who, during the forties, became the senior producers and directors of an increasing number of well-made and distinctive English films which were able to compete in the markets of the world.

By 1923 America's supremacy in the production of films was being challenged by the German industry, where 150 producing companies were at work. In 1921 Germany had succeeded in placing 50 films in the United States at prices with which, owing to her low rate of exchange, the American industry could not compete. In 1920 Britain had produced nearly 250 films, more than ten times the number made in 1918, but most of them could not be shown to the public for at least a year after completion because in 1919 British cinemas had booked American films in advance in blocks of 26, 52 and 104, without seeing them or knowing what they would be like. In the face of this competition many British studios closed down. It was hardly surprising that some of the best English actors went to Hollywood, where there was work, and where some of the most highly-paid people in the world were the American entertainers, players and performers. In 1927, Chaliapin's fee for two operatic performances in Vienna was £1,200; and Charles B. Cochran paid him £2,500 for two opera appearances in the Albert Hall, that is £2,500 for forty minutes' singing. But in America the film stars were regularly paid enormous salaries. In 1926, Hollywood's payroll was headed by the following names:

	Per year £	*Per week* £	
Harold Lloyd	208,000	4,000	
Tom Mix	208,000	4,000	
Charles Chaplin	156,000	3,000	plus a percentage of profits
Douglas Fairbanks	156,000	3,000	do.
John Barrymore	104,000	2,000	
Buster Keaton	83,000	1,600	
Adolphe Menjou	52,000	1,000	
Reginald Denny	36,000	700	
Mary Pickford	104,000	2,000	plus a percentage of profits
Lillian Gish	78,000	1,500	
Gloria Swanson	72,000	1,380	
Norma Talmadge	72,000	1 380	
Colleen Moore	72,000	1,380	

Two thousand lesser-known film stars earned a total of £2,000,000 annually; when Miss Mae Murray was asked to appear in British films in 1927 she demanded £2,000 a week.

2

In his sermon at St. Paul's Cathedral on Easter Sunday 1922 the Bishop of London referred to 'the beautiful film called *From the Manger to the Cross*, produced with such reverent care by Christian men and women on the actual site of the Holy Land.' The film, which had been produced in 1912 and had been shown in London until late in 1913, was again being presented at the Queen's Hall. It had been made by an American company, and the part of Christ was played by an English actor, R. Henderson Bland.

On March 12, 1924, films were shown for the first time in a moving train. The Flying Scotsman from London to the north contained a carriage fitted out as a cinema, with seats for an audience of about twenty. During the run to York an American film, *Ashes of Vengeance*, was shown. In the same year came a notable British picture, Captain Noel's beautiful documentary film *The Epic of Everest*, depicting the gallant attempt of Mallory and Irvine to reach the peak of Chomolungma, the 'Goddess Mother of the World.'

When the synchronized film *Don Juan*, starring John Barrymore, reached London in 1926, the American Warner Brothers were already looking for a subject with which to exploit their new sound system. On October 6, 1926, they provided the answer, a melodramatic film called *The Jazz Singer*, in which the stage singer Al Jolson sang the song 'Mammy.' It was a unique novelty, and it killed silent pictures. For the almost bankrupt Warner Brothers it netted a profit of over £1,000,000. With *The Singing Fool* they made even more money. By 1927, when they produced *What Price Glory?* the new synchronized pictures, or 'talkies' as they were called in England, had more than doubled cinema attendances.

At first people were content to hear the noises, to listen to the incidental scratchy effects on the sound track or the disc. But soon they wanted to see what their favourites, the established stars, would make of the new medium. Would Chaplin talk? What did Greta Garbo sound like? They flocked to hear Ruth Chatterton in *Madame X*, Norma Shearer in *The Last of Mrs. Cheyney*, and the first English talking film revue, *Elstree Calling*.

Actually there was nothing new about sound films, which had been introduced in England before the 1914 war. In 1924 Dr. Lee de Forest's company, De Forest Phonofilms, had produced synchronized talking pictures made on the same principle as modern pictures. The 'talkies,' however, needed a big American company to exploit the novelty. In May 1927 the Fox company launched the Movietone newsreel, using sound. The film industry, turned topsy-turvy by the revolution, consigned the silent picture to the scrap heap, but many of the big stars resisted the intruder. Greta Garbo appeared with Lars Hanson in the silent picture *The Divine Woman* (1928), and Lillian Gish made *The Wind*; Norma Talmadge remained silent in *The Dove*, but *Lilac Time*, which had been started as a silent, with Colleen Moore and Gary Cooper, emerged with 'synchronized sound effects,' as did *Abie's Irish Rose*, with Nancy Carroll and Buddy Rogers.

Only the great Chaplin remained silent, and his 1928 picture, *The Circus*, remains a classic of the screen.

By 1929 most of Britain's cinemas were wired for sound. Mary Pickford was appearing in her first speaking part, *Coquette*, and then with Douglas Fairbanks in *The Taming of the Shrew*, which was advertised as being 'by William Shakespeare, with additional dialogue by Sam Taylor.' Norma Shearer and Basil Rathbone starred in *The Last of Mrs. Cheyney*, Joan Crawford talked in *Untamed*, and Gloria Swanson made a great personal success of her first sound film, *The Trespasser*.

There were also George Arliss in *Disraeli*, and a delightful French newcomer named Maurice Chevalier playing and singing opposite Jeanette MacDonald in *The Innocents of Paris*.

With the coming of the big musical picture, *Rio Rita*, followed by *Hallelujah*, *The Broadway Melody* and *Sunny Side Up*, only Garbo was left making silent pictures, although Chaplin stayed silent in *City Lights*.

The coming of the 'talkies' had brought with them the American wise-crack, the sharp retort, the—at first—extraordinary new language which now invaded homes by way of the cinema. 'You're telling me,' 'I guess . . . ', 'That's O.K. by me' and other strange expressions, usually delivered in a nasal voice, became part of English life. By mid-1929, when sound films had spread across Britain, there was hardly a town or village without some child who was saying 'O.K.' when previously he would have said 'Yes.'

In contrast to the 'vamps' of earlier films, headed by Theda Bara and Gloria Swanson, sex was epitomized in 1929 by a dazzling redhead named Clara Bow, who had been christened the 'It' girl by the popular romantic novelist Elinor Glyn. Miss Glyn, author of immensely successful passion stories, including *Three Weeks*, had taken Hollywood by storm; her creation, the exotic quality of 'It,' added mystery to the expression 'sex-appeal.' Women looked in their looking-glasses and wondered if they too had 'It'?

3

Since the war there had been a great extension of the means and opportunity for entertainment and sport. The old-time shows, fairs, circuses and music-halls still existed, but there was now an enormous increase in the number of spectators at football and cricket matches and boxing contests.

Theatres, however, still appealed to the same restricted public, and the number in London in the twenties was about the same as in 1913. The 'record run' in pre-war days was held by *Charley's Aunt* (1,466 consecutive performances); *Chu Chin Chow*, which was produced at His Majesty's on August 31, 1916, reached its 1,467th performance on October 17, 1919, and was eventually withdrawn after its 2,238th performance on July 22, 1921, having brought in over £700,000. Other long runs included *The Beggar's Opera* (1,463), *The Maid of the Mountains* (1,352), *A Little Bit of Fluff* (1,241), *A Chinese Honeymoon* (1,075) and *Romance* (1,046).

One of the most popular features of post-war London was the revue, which consisted of short sketches, some dance and chorus numbers and many topical allusions.

If he did not actually invent intimate revue, it was André Charlot who perfected it. His shows, *Charlot's Revue*, *Buzz Buzz*, *A to Z*, *Bran Pie*, *Wonder Bar* and *London Calling* brought quiet, graceful charm and topical humour to the stage.

'An awkward, lanky youth of 18 came to my room in the Comedy Theatre in 1918,' he once said. 'He said his name was Noël Coward, and he offered me a song, "The Story of

Peter Pan".' Charlot put the song into his revue *Tails Up*, and thus started Coward on his musical career. Later he asked him to write *London Calling* with Ronald Jeans. In another show he presented Beatrice Lillie for the first time, and paid her £15 a week; Jack Buchanan, replacing Jack Hulbert, was paid £25 a week; Gertrude Lawrence earned £3 10s. From the chorus he selected Jessie Matthews; and started June, later Lady Inverclyde, on her stage career with a weekly salary of £4.

In 1928, the B.B.C.'s programmes *Charlot's Hour* set a high standard in wireless entertainment, but by 1931 Charlot was bankrupt. In his twenty-five years in the London theatre something like £2,000,000 had passed through his hands: as his relatively unknown players found fame, so his fortunes rose and fell, so that at the end of one year he had a profit of £25,000, but at the end of another a loss of £40,000. But whatever the state of his bank account, London theatregoers knew that the sign 'André Charlot presents. . . . ' meant excellent entertainment. There was never anything cheap or second-rate in a Charlot show; songs, dances and sketches were always of the highest quality.

Charlot's rival, Charles B. Cochran, was better known to the public, a showman who presented not only revues, musical comedies and elaborate spectacles, but also great boxers like Carpentier, Bombardier Billy Wells, Micky Walker, Joe Beckett, wrestlers like Hackenschmidt, Zbyskio and Madrali, music-hall stars like George Robey, the clown Grock, the tennis champion Suzanne Lenglen, and a wild west rodeo at the Wembley Exhibition.

He gave Noël Coward his first major opportunities, introduced Alice Delysia to London, and presented such brilliant stage performers as Peggy Wood, Evelyn Laye, Jessie Matthews, Ivy St. Helier, Douglas Byng, Gertrude Lawrence, Nelson Keys, Sonnie Hale, Sacha Guitry, George Metaxa, and Diana Duff-Cooper. 'Mr. Cochran's Young Ladies' were world-famous, and many became stars;

Chaliapin was paid £1,250 a night for two nights' singing, the takings on the first night being £3,737 and the second night £3,881.

Like Charlot, Cochran made and lost vast sums of money, but he gave good value. Thus, the music for his revue *One Dam' Thing after Another*, at the London Pavilion in 1927, was by Richard Rodgers and Lorenz Hart, and included the song-hit, 'My Heart Stood Still'; the cast included Edythe Baker, Jessie Matthews, Sonnie Hale, Morris Harvey, Richard Dolman, Mimi Crawford, Max Wall, Greta Fayne, Douglas Byng, Joan Clarkson and Art Fowler. It was a great success.

The rodeo which Cochran presented at Wembley put Barnum and Bailey's circus in the shade; four hundred head of cattle, four hundred horses, and a posse of Canadian cowboys provided the entertainment. On their arrival at Tilbury the cowboys were met by seventy-five reporters and photographers; Cochran believed in publicity and gambled to win through with the aid of the Press.

The rodeo was to last for a fortnight, but it continued for three weeks, raising the average daily attendance at the Exhibition from 60,000 to 200,000. The stampedes, round-ups, steer-roping and broncho-busting were novelties which few Londoners had seen; £25 was offered to anyone who could succeed in keeping his seat for a minute, while riding a kicking steer. Only one out of hundreds of volunteers succeeded, a young gunner officer from Woolwich, the son of General Uniacke. There were casualties every day among the cowboys, anything from one to six men being seriously injured.

The rodeo was fiercely opposed by animal-lovers. At a meeting at the Caxton Hall, with John Galsworthy in the chair, H. W. Nevinson protested against it, and a petition was sent to the Prince of Wales urging him not to attend the show. When a black steer fell in a roping exhibition and broke a leg, the R.S.P.C.A. immediately sent a telegram to the Prime Minister asking him to stop the show. At the same time summonses were issued against the cowboys and the timekeeper who had caused the injury to the steer, and also against C. B. Cochran. The showman was charged with unlawfully keeping a place for fighting steers and causing animals to be cruelly ill-treated; he and several of the cowboys found themselves, to their surprise, in the dock at Wealdstone police court, defended by Sir Edward Marshall Hall, K.C. and facing a full bench of about twenty stern-faced magistrates, with the prospect of being heavily fined or even sent to prison.

When one of the cowboys was asked if he carried a revolver he replied 'sure,' produced one, and opened it in court, emptying the live cartridges over the floor.

Although the defendents were acquitted, the suspicion of cruelty remained. Few people believed that the R.S.P.C.A. would have taken action unless there was cruelty, or the danger of cruelty. The show was forced by public opinion to close, but the truth was that there had been many empty seats at every performance. Cochran wisely abandoned rodeo in favour of revue, substituting Coward for cowboys.

Revue sketches were usually built up to a 'tag line' or surprise ending which was followed immediately by a blacking out of the stage lights. In the revue *The Punch-Bowl* at the Duke of York's Theatre (1924–25) one of the attractions was a ballet entitled 'Punch and Judy Up-to-date,' set to the music of Norman O'Neill. A sketch called 'Old William' showed the commandant of a meat depot in the war being shot in a restaurant by the waiter (Alfred Lester) who cannot stand the noise his customer makes while drinking soup. This was followed by 'Until To-morrow,' a sentimental ballad sung by Colin Ashdown and Norah Blaney, dressed as eighteenth-century Venetian romantics. A sketch, 'A Night Club Episode,' introduced the versatile Mr. Lester in a moustache which put Harry Tate's to shame, partnered by Enid Stamp-Taylor. Then came a fake Negro spiritual by Greatrex Newman and Melville Gideon, sung by Mr. Ashdown.

After Miss Blaney had delivered a topical monologue entitled 'Eros and Me,' lamenting the fact that the famous statue had been removed, and Marjorie Spiers had danced with Hugh Dempster, Sonnie Hale had danced with Annie Kashmir, and Norah Blaney and Gwen Farrar had sung together at the piano, the audience went home, happy.

Most of the revues were topical and entertaining. The Cochran-Noël Coward production *This Year of Grace* (1928) exceeded even the success of the earlier *The League of Notions*. *Punch* said that it should earn Mr. Cochran a peerage. Of twenty-four items, Noël Coward was personally responsible for twenty. The programme was as follows:

1. *A Tube Station* showing the sheep-like attitude of the British public.
2. Jessie Matthews singing *Mary Make Believe*, with the chorus of Mr. Cochran's Young Ladies.
3. The three current plays *The Wrecker*, *The Silver Cord* and *Young Woodley* potted into a few lines, with the author laughing at himself in *Any Noël Coward Play*.
4. *Mad About You*, sung by Sheila Graham and William Cavanagh.
5. *The Bus Rush*, with Maisie Gay.
6. *Lorelei*, with Lauri Devine on a moonlit rock, designed by Oliver Messel, luring mariners to their doom.
7. *Snowball*, a tiny expert and a banjo.
8. *Ignorance is Bliss*, showing the startling difference in honeymoon techniques in 1890 and 1928 (a sketch whose theme was widely copied in later revues).
9. Tilly Losch, dancing.
10. *A Room with a View*, sung and danced by Jessie Matthews and Sonnie Hale.
11. *It Doesn't Matter How Old You Are*. Maisie Gay as a drunken, blowzy charwoman.
12. *Teach Me to Dance like Grandma*, sung and danced by Jessie Matthews and the chorus, with Tilly Losch and Jean Barry.
13. *The Lido Beach*. Satirical attacks on the rich and vulgar and aristocratic, with a quartet singing:

   We may be little women
   But we're not good wives . . .

14. Maisie Gay as a channel swimmer.
15. *Ballet—The Legend of the Lily of the Valley*. A burlesque, with Sonnie Hale.
16. *Rules of Three*. The eternal triangle theme as it would be treated by James Barrie, Frederick Lonsdale and Edgar Wallace.
17. *Dance Little Lady*. Coward's satirical song, with masks by Oliver Messel.
18. *Chauve-Souris*, with Lance Lister.
19. *Gothic*. Tilly Losch and Lauri Devine in a duet.
20. *Try to Learn to Love*, sung and danced by Jessie Matthews.
21. *A Sketch About Policewomen*.
22. *A Spanish Dance* by Jean Barry and Jack Holland.
23. Castleton and Mack, dancers.
24. *Finale*.

Many of the plays of the period reflected the freedom of conduct, frankness of speech, and the neuroses of the time. Miles Malleson's *The Fanatics* (1927) included a girl who wanted a trial marriage, with birth control. Mordaunt Shairp's *The Green Bay Tree* was the story of an attractive youth kept by a rich bachelor. The youth fell in love with a charming girl, and the plot centred on his struggles between normal love and homosexual security. The latter triumphed. *Prisoners of War* treated the same subject from a more psychological point of view.

The favourite and most brilliant playwright and actor of the twenties was Noël Coward, of whose *Fallen Angels* (1925) with Edna Best and Tallulah Bankhead, *Punch* said, 'an unpleasant subject, you may say? Well, not edifying or elevating, certainly, but Mr. Coward has written it so gaily and wittily and they play it so lightly and briskly that it is relieved of all offensiveness . . . we ought to rid our minds of cant in these matters.'

Coward's first play was put on by Lady Wyndham at the New Theatre. It was not the first he had written, but the first to be produced. He claimed to have written it in four days.

'I like the plot,' said Lady Wyndham, 'but what is it called?'

'I'll leave it to you!' replied Coward, thus naming it.

The young actor-playwright was not yet 21, and although *I'll Leave it to You* did not reveal the pattern of what was to follow, it was well received. Coward himself played a part. The plot concerned an uncle who returns to England when the fortunes of his sister's large family are low, and promises to give each of the five children a fortune. The personalities were, as in many later Coward plays, those of people going through life without doing any real work, playing at living and contributing little.

Coward's next success was *The Young Idea*, which Robert Courtneidge produced at the Savoy Theatre on February 1, 1923. It appealed particularly to the intelligentsia and to Bohemians, and was a hard-hitting comedy with lines which people claimed were witty, if slightly extravagant. It concerned the problem of a man, George Brent, married to a second wife, who entertains the children of his first wife. Coward played one of the children. After the initial success of these two plays he went into the André Charlot revue *London Calling* at the Duke of York's Theatre in the autumn of 1923; in addition to contributing a number of sketches to the show, including a parody of the Sitwells, he appeared in support of Gertrude Lawrence, Tubby Edlin and Maisie Gay.

His next play, *The Vortex*, was a sensation because of its theme, that of a young man who took drugs. At first it was difficult to find anyone to put it on, but Michael Arlen, then a rising but not yet successful writer, backed it with £500, and it opened on November 25, 1924, at the little Everyman Theatre in Hampstead. It immediately took the town by storm, and was transferred to the Duke of York's, where it both delighted and shocked London theatre-goers.

'It is an unwholesome, immoral and degenerate piece,' said one critic. But James Agate, in the *Sunday Times*, considered that there was the imprint of truth upon it, that the craftsmanship was beyond reproach and that the dialogue was taut and spare. 'It shimmers with wit,' he said.

So many people thought it wicked that Coward decided to

satisfy them. 'I would like the reporters to know that I have a dreadfully *depraved* mind,' he announced, adopting the pose of the wicked, cynical, devastating Mr. Coward who was out to shock—and delight—the public. If his object was to achieve rapid fame and success, this seemed an admirable way of doing it. People flocked to the theatre to see and talk about this play, full of depraved characters, written by a young man who posed—in a gay silk dressing-gown—as being decadent, but whose dialogue was shockingly entertaining. Were people really like Mr. Coward's characters? Were these nervy, excitable, neurotic young people typical of the post-war generation, and what was this *clever* Mr. Coward trying to say? Was he laughing at them and their society, or did he agree with them? Many theatre-goers could not make up their minds. It was, perhaps, a little too early to decide about Mr. Coward, who was reported to say, as well as to write, such astonishing things.

The Vortex ended with Nicky Lancaster, played by Coward, and his equally unpleasant mother shouting at each other. She had confessed to adultery, and he to taking drugs. But it finished on a highly moral note, with some hope for the future.

On the evening of February 4, 1925, Arnold Bennett wrote in his diary:

> This play has made a great stir. First act played 43 minutes, and the first half-hour, and more, was spent in merely creating an atmosphere. Talk whose direction you couldn't follow. No fair hint of a plot till nearly the end—and hardly ever then. Five unforeseen entrances of important characters. One might have been excused. In 2nd act, some tiny glimpses of dramatic talent and ingenuities. The end of this act, where the son plays the piano louder and louder while his mother makes love to a young man, is rather effective, original and harrowing. The atmosphere of a country house week-end party is fairly well got. Technique marred by important characters coming in unperceived and over-hearing remarks. The 3rd act contains the whole play, and is in effect a duologue between mother and son. Coward plays the son well, and Lillian Braithwaite gets through the mother as a sort of *tour de force*, but she never gives a convincing picture of an abandoned woman. The

end is certainly harrowing to a high degree. But not much effect of beauty. Some smartness in the play, and certainly the germs of an effective dramatic skill; but really I saw nothing that was *true* except in minor details. I dozed off once in the last act and Evelyn had to waken me.

Large sections of the public thought the play disgusting, and they were not surprised when Coward produced, in 1925, a comedy called *Fallen Angels*, in which two bored wives got drunk while their husbands were away playing golf.

This was even more sensational than *The Vortex*, and queues formed outside the Globe Theatre to see Edna Best and Tallulah Bankhead carrying on as no ladies—surely—would ever behave.

Coward claimed attention, and could not be ignored. 'He knocked at the door with impatient knuckles,' says Somerset Maugham, 'and then he rattled the handle, and then he burst in.' *Fallen Angels* was the rattling, and the situation was summed up by one of the women characters:

> . . . I never realized there were two of me until this moment so clearly defined. I want terribly badly to be a true, faithful wife and look after Fred and live in peace, and I want terribly to have violent and illicit love made to me and be frenziedly happy and supremely miserable.

By June 1926, when he produced *Easy Virtue*, Coward was the most promising of the new playwrights, and had proved that he was no mere sensation. The characters in *Easy Virtue*, not being drunken women or dope-addicts but the kind of people to be found in any English village, were more easily recognized and more acceptable. *The Queen was in the Parlour*, which followed, revealed an even less decadent Mr. Coward, who had written a charming, sad and distinctly virtuous romantic play in which duty was more obviously displayed as the goal. Now Mr. Coward touched the hearts of the audience, and sent people home remembering not only the witty lines but also the beauty of the play.

His next work, *Home Chat*, was a failure, and in November 1927 the production of *Sirocco*, with Ivor Novello and Frances Doble, drew hisses on the first night. The auditorium suddenly became alive with booing, disappointed, disapproving theatre-goers. Miss Doble wept, and fighting broke out between those who liked the play, or supported it, and the larger number who did not. Noël Coward met this disaster by calmly walking on to the stage and bowing graciously to the shouting audience.

This reversal was followed by triumph. When Cochran's revue *This Year of Grace* opened in Manchester, Coward had written the lyrics, the music and most of the sketches, had personally chosen the dresses, and had assisted in the production at every stage. It was a tremendous success, society flocking to the London Pavilion on the first night to greet the revue with enthusiasm. But the author did not respond to the cheering cries for his appearance when the curtain fell. He was up in the dress circle, wearing a grey flannel suit.

This Year of Grace made so much money that Cochran took it to New York, with Coward and Beatrice Lillie playing in it. By 1929, when *Bitter Sweet* was presented, its author was world-famous and rich, and had proved that he was no mere writer of decadent plays about immoral people. The beauty of the production of *Bitter Sweet* and the captivating music set the seal on the career of this extraordinary young man of the theatre. Sentimental and emotional, it took London by storm. Soon the words of the song which ends the play were being sung all over Britain and America; and would continue to be sung in the thirties and forties, reminding men in the 1939 war and wives at home of that unforgettable production at His Majesty's:

Though my world has gone awry,
Though the end is drawing nigh,
I shall love you till I die,
Good-bye!

THE VALENTINO VOGUE.

Young Woman. "YOU DON'T TANGO? THEN YOUR WHISKERS ARE A SHEER WASTE."

4

In 1925 came Frederick Lonsdale's play *The Last of Mrs. Cheyney*, with Gladys Cooper, Gerald du Maurier and Ronald Squire. Mrs. Cheyney was a shop girl discovered by a gentleman crook, who persuaded her also to become a crook. Lonsdale specialized in 'high society' drawing-room comedies, and most of them had record runs. *Mrs. Cheyney* ran for 514 performances, and his earlier musical show *The Maid of the Mountains* ran for 1,352.

At the Palace Theatre, in the same year, long queues formed to see *No, No, Nanette*, with Binnie Hale as Nanette, George Grossmith as Billy Early, Seymour Beard as Tom Trainor, Joseph Coyne as Jimmy Smith, Vera Pearce as Flora of Nice, Florence Bayfield as Winnie of Harrogate, and Joan Barry as Betty from Bath. In one scene the chorus, led by Binnie Hale, wore bathing costumes. When Queen Mary went to a matinée at the Palace she turned her head away from the stage, and would not look at the scanty clothes.

Nineteen hundred and twenty-five saw the production in America of John van Druten's *Young Woodley*, which was banned in London by the Lord Chamberlain, but was a great success in New York. Two years later, when the ban was lifted, it was presented with even greater success in London. *Punch* found that it 'contained no word that would have caused a blush to mantle the cheek of Councillor Clark of mixed-bathing fame, or of Mr. Brown, the borough librarian of Northampton.'

Nineteen hundred and twenty-five was indeed a vintage year for London's theatre-goers. This was their choice in mid-April:

Aldwych	Tom Walls, Arthur Finn, Ralph Lynn in *It Pays to Advertise*
Apollo	Jack Hulbert in revue *By the Way*
Comedy	Lilian Braithwaite and Noël Coward in *The Vortex*

DRURY LANE	*Rose Marie* with Billy Merson, Edith Day, and Derek Oldham
DUKE OF YORK'S	*The Punch Bowl* with Robert Hale, Norah Blaney, Gwen Farrar
EMPIRE	Jack Buchanan with June in *Boodle*
GAIETY	*Katja the Dancer* with Lillian Davies, Ivy Tresmand and Gene Gerrard
HAYMARKET	John Barrymore in *Hamlet*
HIPPODROME	*Better Days* with Maisie Gay, Norman Griffin, Madge Elliott, George Baker, and the Savoy Orpheans
NEW	Matheson Lang and Isobel Elsom in *The Tyrant*
NEW OXFORD	*Kismet*
PALACE	*No, No, Nanette*
PALLADIUM	Revue *Sky High* with George Robey and Lorna Pounds
PLAYHOUSE	*White Cargo*
PRINCE OF WALES	*Charlot's Revue* with Beatrice Lillie and Gertrude Lawrence
QUEEN'S	*Dancing Mothers* with Godfrey Tearle and Gertrude Elliott
REGENT	*Saint Joan* by G. B. Shaw, with Sybil Thorndike
SAVOY	*The Sport of Kings* by Ian Hay
ST. MARTIN'S	*Spring Cleaning*
SHAFTESBURY	*Summer Lightnin'* with Horace Hodges
STRAND	*The Sea Urchin* with Peggy O'Neill
THE OLD VIC	*A Winter's Tale*
VAUDEVILLE	Nora Swinburne, Francis Lister in *Tarnish*
WINTER GARDEN	*Primrose* with Heather Thatcher and Leslie Henson
WYNDHAM'S	Irene Bordon in *Little Miss Bluebeard*
Variety Theatres	
ALHAMBRA	Layton and Johnstone, Jack Hylton and his band, Lily Morris
COLISEUM	Joe Johnson, Lydia Lopokova, Mr. and Mrs. Graham Moffat, John Birmingham and his band
Cinema Theatres	
CAPITOL	Nazimova in *The Redeeming Sin* and Jack Pickford in *Waking up the Town*
LONDON PAVILION	D. W. Griffith's *Isn't Life Wonderful*

Philharmonic Hall	*I.N.R.I.*—a film of humanity
Polytechnic	Captain C. W. R. Knight's *Aristocrats of the Air*
Stoll	Harold Lloyd in *Hot Water*
	Priscilla Dean and Stuart Holmes in *The Siren of Seville*
Tivoli	Syd Chaplin in *Charley's Aunt*

Shaw's *St. Joan*, after a long and immensely successful run at the New Theatre, was attracting all London to the Regent, where a Shaw repertory season had been held. Other Shaw seasons were held at the Chelsea Palace and at the Court, Sloane Square, where Barry Jackson presented the Birmingham Repertory production of *Back to Methuselah*. The cast of *St. Joan* at the Regent included Sybil Thorndike as the Maid of Orleans, Raymond Massey, Robert Cunningham, Ernest Thesiger, Beatrice Smith, Milton Rosmer and Bruce Winston. At the Old Vic, Miss Lilian Baylis and Robert Atkins remained faithful to Shakespeare.

John Barrymore's production of *Hamlet* at the Haymarket had been eagerly awaited for months. The cast included Fay Compton as Ophelia, Constance Collier as Gertrude, Herbert Waring as Polonius and Malcolm Keen as the King. Mr. Malcolm Watson of the *Daily Telegraph*, who went to interview Barrymore, wrote: 'I found him in a charming little house, down Chelsea way. Somehow I had pictured him as a tall, burly, imposing figure; as a matter of fact he is slim and of medium height, his general appearance reminding me forcibly of William Hilton's portrait of the poet Keats. We discussed yachting—one of Mr. Barrymore's chief delights—deep-sea fishing, and a pleasure trip to the South Sea Islands.'

White Cargo at the Playhouse was playing to packed houses, although it had been criticized as 'melodrama rather than drama,' and 'too highly coloured to be an accurate picture of a white man's life in the tropics.' One critic protested:

Our friends come home on leave every nine or twelve months; some of them have white wives to ease their lot; their talk when they look us up is full of the tennis they play, of the dances they attend, of bridge parties and social evenings.

But what was Mr. Leon Gordon's play at the Playhouse about? The one relaxation of his characters appeared to be in drinking; whisky bottles loaded the tables and sideboards. One man had been without home leave for seven years, staying on in spite of illness. A doctor had been at the station even longer. Periodically a young man came to the outpost and fell in love with a beautiful half-caste woman, Tondeleyo. With everyone consistently irritable and quarrelsome, their nerves on edge, their talk rich in insults and violence, it was hardly surprising that *White Cargo* had full seats for months ahead.

Arnold Bennett found the audience at the Playhouse on October 11, 1924, 'terrible':

> In the 3rd act, at perhaps the most tragic moment of the play, a character has to say of another, 'Poor bloody fool.' Roars of laughter. Why? The censor has only just begun to allow the word 'bloody' on the stage.

It Pays to Advertise, at the Aldwych, was one of the highly successful farces, most of them written by Ben Travers, with which the names of Tom Walls, Leslie Henson, Ralph Lynn, Robertson Hare, Mary Brough and Winifred Shotter became associated. The series had been started when Walls and Henson produced *Tons of Money*, which had run for two years. In *Rookery Nook*, *Thark*, *Plunder* and many other hilarious comedies of bedroom manners, locked doors, and obvious misunderstandings and vanishing trousers, Ralph Lynn played the 'silly ass' to perfection, Tom Walls was the exasperated business partner, colonel or uncle, and Robertson Hare was the mild, inoffensive, nervous little man who lost his trousers while dashing from one bedroom door to another.

There was a vogue for opening and shutting doors in the comedies and dramas of the twenties. Thus, in *The Man Who Changed His Name* there was a door (right) used for silent entrances by the butler, a garden entrance (centre) for the arrival of late visitors, corpses etc., and a door (left) which opened noiselessly so that conversations could be readily overheard. It all helped the plot.

One of the most popular of stage stars at this time was Melville Gideon, who was according to Leslie Henson a crooner before the introduction of the microphone. He wrote many songs and achieved fame in the highly successful *Co-optimist* shows with Henson, Stanley Holloway, Phyllis Monkman, Davy Burnaby, Gilbert Childs and Laddie Cliff. Blending sentiment and charm, he captivated audiences. His songs, according to Gale Pedrick, the radio scriptwriter and journalist, reflected the gay, rather unsettled times in which he lived. He died when he was only 49, and even with the development of the wireless there was no one to replace him adequately. His songs, *I'm in Love with a Girl in a Crinoline Gown*, *I'm Tickled to Death I'm Single* and *Ghost of a Chance* were among the most melodious tunes of the twenties.

Not all the music was melodious, and most of it came from America, to provide the background for the fox-trot, the one-step, the charleston, black-bottom, waltz and tango. The dancing craze, introduced by the gramophone, was made widely popular by the wireless, when listeners were invited to 'roll back the carpet . . . and take a few steps.'

'You shuffled round the room,' said C. E. M. Joad later, 'in what a contemporary wit called "a form of country walking slightly impeded by a member of the opposite sex," and you called it a fox-trot. You slid round a little faster and called it a one-step . . . eventually the fox-trot and the one-step merged into a uniform shuffle which presented no difficulty to anybody.' But millions took their ballroom dancing seriously; Santos Casani demonstrated the steps of the Charleston on the roof of a taxi moving down Regent Street, and later Jack Payne wrote dancing articles in the London *Evening News*. His band, like the Savoy bands, created enormous interest not only in dancing but also in the quickly-changing melodies of the moment. These were some of the songs which people sang in the post-war years:

1920 Dreamland Lover
By the Silver Sea
Sometimes in my Dreams
1921 12th Street Rag
Look for the Silver Lining
Dancing Time
1922 The Sheik of Araby
Ma, She's Making Eyes at Me
Ain't We Got Fun
The World is Waiting for the Sunrise
April Showers
1923 Yes, We Have No Bananas
Coal Black Mammy
I'm Just Wild about Harry
Marcheta
Kiss in the Dark
1924 Horsey, Keep Your Tail Up
California, Here I Come
What do you do Sunday, Mary?
1925 Tea for Two
I Want to be Happy
Indian Love Call
Jealousy
Rose Marie
Tie a String around Your Finger
1926 Valencia
Barcelona
Babette
Deep in my Heart (*The Student Prince*)
Dinah
Paddlin' Madelin' Home
Let me Call You Sweetheart
Five Foot Two, Eyes of Blue
Fascinating Rhythm
I Never See Maggie Alone
Who?
Sleepy Time Gal
Two Little Bluebirds
Trees

My Cutey's Due at Two-to-Two Today
Bird Songs at Eventide

1927 The Riff Song
My Heart Stood Still
Chinatown
Blue Room
Shepherd of the Hills
Ain't She Sweet?
Do, Do, Do
Side by Side
Mary Lou
Blue Skies
Halleluja
Only a Rose
Birth of the Blues
The Vagabond King
The Man I Love
Sometimes I'm Happy

1928 Fancy Our Meeting
Ah, Sweet Mystery of Life
When Day is Done
Miss Annabelle Lee
A Room with a View
My Blue Heaven
Dance Little Lady
That's My Weakness Now
Ol' Man River
All by Yourself in the Moonlight
Roll Away Clouds
Sonny Boy
Chloe
Spread a Little Happiness
My Melancholy Baby
I Can't Give You Anything But Love, Baby
C–o–n–s–t–a–n–t–i–n–o–p–l–e
Ballin' the Jack

1929 What is this Thing Called Love?
Ain't Misbehaving?
Let's Do it Again
Broadway Melody
Lover Come Back to Me

Is Izzy Azzy Wozz?
Blue Moon
Softly, as in a Morning Sunrise
Mean to Me
I'll See You Again
Glad Rag Doll
You're the Cream in my Coffee
I Kiss Your Little Hand, Madame
Piccolo Pete
Back in your Old Back Yard
Button Up Your Overcoat
Singing in the Rain

In 1926 the *Melody Maker* was founded, a paper for jazz musicians. For people who wanted better music there were concerts, but not often of a high standard, at the Albert Hall and the Queen's Hall. 'Since the commencement of the war,' wrote Ernest Newman in 1929, 'the London public has not known, until quite recently, what good orchestral playing is; the older people who used to go to concerts in the pre-war days had forgotten what a first-rate orchestra is, while the younger people, whose interest in music was a post-war growth, had never heard one. The standards of all of us had been insidiously, imperceptibly lowered by what we have had to listen to in Queen's Hall since 1928.'

When, in June 1922, the Leeds Choral Society gave a superb performance of Sir Edward Elgar's *The Apostles* at the Queen's Hall, according to George Bernard Shaw there were only Princess Mary, Viscount Lascelles and about four other people in the stalls.

'The occasion,' said G. B. S., 'was infinitely more important than the Derby, Goodwood, the Cup Finals, the Carpentier fights or any of the occasions on which the official leaders of society are photographed and cinematographed laboriously shaking hands with persons on whom Molière's patron, Louis XIV, and Bach's patron, Frederick the Great, would not have condescended to wipe their boots.'

Orchestral concerts at well-known seaside resorts were

sparsely attended, but dance-halls and cinemas were thronged. Theatres did well if the play was good; Nigel Playfair's memorable revival of *The Beggar's Opera* at the Lyric Theatre, Hammersmith, opened in 1920 and ran for three and a half years. The public flocked to see the serious plays of Shaw. Before the war an evening at a West End theatre had been a social event; patrons in the stalls and dress circles wore evening dress, and no smoking was permitted. Now fewer people wore evening dress, most theatres allowed smoking, and 'going to a matinée' was, somehow, not quite the same as in pre-war days. But there were HOUSE FULL boards up outside if the play was worth while, and there was no sign, even with the competition of the cinema and the wireless, that the living stage had lost its old magic.

Theatregoers queued to see *Mr. Pim Passes by*, with Irene Vanbrugh and Dion Boucicault, which ran for 246 performances in 1920, and *Ambrose Applejohn's Adventure* in 1921. *Bulldog Drummond* attracted them in 1921, and in 1923 Karel Capek's *R.U.R.* set London talking. In 1925 came R. C. Sheriff's *Journey's End*, which perfectly fitted the post-war feeling of pacifism, and—like most of the audience—looked back rather than forward.

But only Mr. Coward seemed to be able to present the new generation with an accurate picture of itself. And, as we have seen, many people at first found this unacceptable.

In spite of the excellence of the theatres, the night-life of London was far from bright. A French woman summed it up in 1922: 'Most of the people in the streets look as if they were going to a funeral. Watch and see how many smiling faces you will see during a walk—scarcely one. As to a laugh, I fancy that is absolutely forbidden by one of your many laws.'

But there was always the music-hall, although J. B. Priestley considers that in the twenties it had already passed its peak:

'But some of the ripe old turns were still with us. You could look in at the Coliseum, as I often did on a winter afternoon, and see Little

Tich and Harry Tate, and there were still some glorious drolls at the Holborn Empire (a sad loss; it had a fine thick atmosphere of its own), the Victoria Palace and the rest. There were no microphones and nobody needed them. There were no stars who had arrived by way of amusing farmers' wives and invalids on the radio. There were no reputations that had been created by American gramophone records for teenagers. The men and women who topped the bills had spent years getting there, learning how to perfect their acts and to handle their audiences. Of course there was plenty of vulgar rubbish, but all but the very worst of it had at least some zest and vitality. And the audiences, which laughed at jokes and did not solemnly applaud them as B.B.C. audiences do now, were an essential part of the show; they too had vitality, and were still close to the Cockneys who helped to create, a generation earlier, the English music-hall of the period, the folk art out of which, among other things, came the slapstick of the silent films, especially those of Chaplin.'

The established home of Shakespeare in London, the centre of an exceptionally high standard of production and acting, was the Old Vic, founded in 1880 by Miss Emma Cons and carried on by her niece Miss Lilian Baylis. The producers for the 1919–20 season included Russell Thorndike, Charles Warburton, Betty Potter and Ernest Milton. Under Robert Atkins, from 1920 to 1925, every play in Shakespeare's First Folio was presented. In 1925 Andrew Leigh took over, and in 1929 Harcourt Williams became producer.

In 1922 the theatre announced that it needed £30,000 to carry on; the money was found, and that year saw the first public performance in England of Ibsen's *Peer Gynt*, with Russell Thorndike. In November 1923, a performance of *Troilus and Cressida* was given in the presence of Princess Mary, in honour of Shakespeare's tercentenary. According to Sybil Thorndike, John Gielgud and Harcourt Williams put the Old Vic on the map of the world. But the personality behind the success of the theatre, constantly battling against difficulties, competition, lack of funds, overcoming disaster after disaster, was Miss Baylis, who frankly said she had lost so much money that in despair she had turned to Shakespeare.

Theatrical folk delighted in the countless stories about this remarkably capable and outspoken woman, who was said to conclude her evening prayers with the words—'Please God, send me some good actors—cheap.' Her prayers were answered, the Old Vic discovering and nursing a wealth of talent, to the benefit of the English theatre. From 1919 to 1929 the Old Vic companies included—among others—such distinguished names as:

Richard Ainley	John Gielgud
Elizabeth Allan	Balliol Holloway
Heather Angel	Martita Hunt
Robert Atkins	Gyles Isham
Wilfred Babbage	Stephen Jack
Eric Bloom	John Laurie
Lewis Casson	Esmond Knight
Esme Church	Ernest Milton
George Colouris	Ion Swinley
Edward Cooper	Florence Saunders
Nora Desmond	Russell Thorndike
Adele Dixon	Sybil Thorndike
Edith Evans	Austin Trevor
Barbara Everest	Genevieve Ward
Leslie French	Donald Wolfitt
Jean Forbes-Robertson	John Wyse

Miss Baylis once explained to Queen Mary why the portrait of King George in the theatre vestibule was not quite as large as that of 'Aunt Emma,' Miss Cons, the founder, who had died in 1912. The explanation given to the Queen was 'because your dear husband has not done so much for the Old Vic.'

While Miss Baylis was at the Old Vic, and there were young actors like Gielgud on the stage, the future of the London theatre was assured.

CHAPTER NINETEEN

Crime

I

THE RISING CIRCULATIONS of popular newspapers were due not only to an increase in literacy, stunts, the presentation of free gifts, mass insurance and benefit schemes, but also to the more candid reporting methods now employed. The morals and manners and habits of the time were more fully presented. Events which before the war would have been reported in a more restrained or dignified manner were now given headlines. Especially murder.

Few of the crimes of the twenties attracted such attention as the Thompson and Bywaters case, which started tragically on the evening of October 4, 1922, and soon aroused the interest of the entire country.

Mr. and Mrs. Thompson were employed in the City of London and together they earned between £10 and £12 a week. On the evening of the tragedy they were walking home from Ilford station after visiting a theatre. It was then that a young man named Frederick Bywaters came up to them, stabbed Thompson in the neck and ran off. Mrs. Thompson immediately called for help, but she did not tell the police that she knew Bywaters. In fact, Bywaters, a good-looking and likeable young ship's steward, knew the Thompsons well and had stayed in their house until a quarrel led Thompson to ask him to leave. By then he was Mrs. Thompson's lover, and her subsequent passionate letters to him became important items in the case for the prosecution.

Both Bywaters and Mrs. Thompson were charged with

murder, once the facts were known, but Bywaters insisted that he alone had stabbed Thompson. He had attacked him, he said, because he would not consent to a divorce; but the blow had been struck in self-defence in a moment of panic when he thought Thompson was going to shoot him. This was a very weak defence, and there was little doubt that Bywaters would hang. He was, however, only 20, and it was clear that he had been strongly influenced by Mrs. Thompson, who was a woman with a strongly romantic nature. Her love letters, when read out in court, aroused considerable indignation because it was felt that she had been largely responsible for ruining young Bywaters. Little thought was given to the dead and greatly wronged husband. The evidence against Mrs. Thompson included her own letter describing her attempts to poison her husband, press-cuttings which she had sent Bywaters referring to poisoning and death pacts, and suggestions that she would like her husband removed from the triangle.

When Edith Thompson was condemned to death she became, instead of someone who had plotted and encouraged the murder of her husband, almost a public heroine. This was mainly because she was the first woman to be hanged for fifteen years. Large sections of the public expressed their dismay at the sentence; the newspapers were full of letters of protest. It would be a crime, said public opinion, to hang this woman. Nevertheless she was hanged. And afterwards there were rumours, later substantiated, of the horrifying nature of the execution. A few weeks later these were revived by the attempted suicide of Ellis, the executioner, who later succeeded in killing himself.

Another case which aroused enormous interest in 1922 was the Ronald True murder. True was a lunatic who murdered a girl named Olive Young in a Fulham flat. Despite strong evidence that he was insane, the jury remained unconvinced and after a five-day trial he was sentenced to death. A commission of three medical experts then examined him and confirmed that he was a lunatic. The Home Secretary at once ordered his removal to Broadmoor, but this action caused an uproar in the popular press, partly because a youth of eighteen named Henry Jacoby had recently been sent to the scaffold in spite of the jury's strong recommendation to mercy, and partly because of the revolting nature of the murder that True had committed. When it was clear that True was to live although Jacoby had died, the correspondence columns were filled with angry protests. Rumours spread that True was really the illegitimate son of an influential person who had intervened and saved him. What was the point in a jury finding that a man was sane if the Home Secretary could then offer him the comfort and security of Broadmoor?

Replying to these criticisms, the Home Secretary, the Rt. Hon. Edward Shortt, M.P., said, 'I had no option to act otherwise than as I did in ordering an inquiry into True's mental condition. I am bound by the law, which says that no insane person shall be hung. . . . ' [*sic*]. On the same day, at Devon Assizes, Mr. Justice Avory publicly deprecated leaving the penalties of the law to 'the discretion of experts in Harley Street.' The only real deterrent to crime, he said, was the certainty that the appropriate penalty would follow. His Lordship did not say that whether True were mad or not he should still have been hanged, but the general public considered that a monster had outwitted the law and escaped the gallows.

In 1922 the Armstrong case excited great interest. Herbert Rowse Armstrong was a poisoner who had killed his wife and whose clumsy attempts to destroy a rival solicitor led to his downfall. It was on New Year's Day, 1922, that the inhabitants of the small Welsh town of Hay in Brecon learned that Major Armstrong, a respected solicitor, had been arrested for the attempted murder of Mr. Oswald Martin, another solicitor in the town. The body of Armstrong's wife, who had died a year before, was then exhumed. Poisoned chocolates, arsenical tea parties, and a local doctor who suspected Armstrong of being a poisoner and had gone to the Home Office with his suspicions, figured in the case. After Armstrong's arrest a packet of arsenic was found in a bureau in his house. In spite of a severe summing-up by the judge, Lord Darling, many people expected Armstrong to be acquitted. It was proved, however, that he had poisoned his wife, and he was found guilty.

A particularly gruesome murder, which became of national interest, took place in the spring of 1924. Patrick Mahon was an adventurer of 34 who had enjoyed considerable success with women. At the age of 21 he had been bound over for forging a cheque for £123, having taken a girl to the Isle of Wight on the proceeds. Later he had served two years' imprisonment for embezzling money from a dairy firm in Wiltshire. At Sunningdale in 1916 he had beaten a girl unconscious with a hammer, for which he received five years' penal servitude. Although he was married and had a daughter he seemed incapable of living without constantly indulging in love affairs, and he held a peculiar fascination for weak-minded women.

Early in 1923 Mahon met Emily Kaye, a typist of 37, one of whose attractions was a small savings account. A violent love affair developed, and Miss Kaye paid £300 to Mahon, who then began to show signs of tiring of her. The girl tried to persuade Mahon to go away with her, and in April 1924, under an assumed name, he rented a small furnished bungalow at the Crumbles, between Eastbourne and Pevensey Bay. On Saturday, April 12th, he bought a cook's knife and a saw in London, and went by train to Eastbourne, where he met Miss Kaye. They spent the week-end together, and on Tuesday they went up to London for the day. On their return to the bungalow, a violent quarrel developed, as a result of which the girl was killed. At his trial Mahon said that they were sitting together when Miss Kaye became hysterical; he went towards the bedroom but she picked up an axe which had

XIV. *Binnie Hale and the chorus of* No, No, Nanette, *1925.*

Ivor Novello and Mae Marsh in the British film The Rat, *1925. He has bought himself a new suit, which he proudly displays.*

The dance that remains typical of the gin and aspirin age—the sensational, high-kicking Charleston, which swept first America and then Europe.

XV. *Bywaters murder case, December 1922. The crowd outside the Old Bailey awaiting the result.*

A different kind of crowd, queuing for the dole outside Walworth Labour Exchange, London, 1929.

been used for breaking coal, and threw it at him; she then leapt at him, clutching at his face. They fell together to the floor, her head striking the coal-scuttle, so that she died; he dragged the body into the bedroom and covered it with a coat; then he went out for a walk. In the morning he went to Eastbourne, where he had an appointment with another girl, whom he invited to the bungalow for the following week-end. The rest of the day he spent cutting up the body. The new girl arrived for the week-end and went away on Monday, but failed to notice anything wrong. Mahon continued his cutting up, packing parts of the body into a suitcase; he put the head on the fire, smashed up the bones, and scattered them in the garden. Travelling up to London by train, he threw parts of the body out of the carriage window. The bag, containing blood-stained rags, was left in the station cloak-room.

On May 2nd, when Mahon went to collect the bag, he was arrested. At the Old Bailey on July 18th he was cross-examined by Sir Henry Curtis-Bennett, prosecuting for the Crown:

Sir H. C.-B.: Do you still say you burned the head?
Mahon: I not only say I burned the head, but I did burn the head.
Sir H. C.-B.: In which room did you burn the head?
Mahon: In the sitting-room.
Sir H. C.-B.: The front sitting-room?
Mahon: (indicating the plan) This sitting-room here.
Sir H. C.-B.: How long do you say it took?
Mahon: I cannot say. Six hours, probably.
Sir H. C.-B.: Are you not clear upon the matter at all?
Mahon: I am clear that I burned the head.
Sir H. C.-B.: Are you not clear about the time? This was a terrible thing you were doing. Did you not realize how long it took?
Mahon: If you knew the circumstances in which the head was burned—I can only say burned—I could not even stay in the room while it was burning.
Sir H. C.-B.: I want to test this story of yours a little. You say it took six hours?
Mahon: About six hours.

Sir H. C.-B.: Did you say to Sergeant Frew: 'I burned the head in an ordinary fire. It was finished in three hours. The poker went through the head when I poked it.' Do you remember saying that?

Mahon: No, I do not remember saying that.

When Sir Bernard Spilsbury proved that death could not have been caused by Miss Kaye hitting her head on the coal-scuttle, and stated that she had been pregnant, there was no hope, if there had ever been any, for Patrick Mahon. There was no sympathy for the murderer, but crowds flocked to the Crumbles to look at the bungalow. On one day nearly a thousand people paid a shilling to walk inside and see the sitting-room, the fireplace and the coal-scuttle. Part of the takings went to charity; motor-coaches brought sightseers from Eastbourne, Pevensey and Brighton. Teas were served at the entrance to the bungalow, and a stick of peppermint rock, marked *Crumbles Bungalow Rock* through the centre, could be bought for sixpence.

2

When asked if he had anything to say after being found guilty of murdering a woman at Swindon in January 1925, William Bignell replied, 'It is not a very good verdict.' He was then sentenced to death. His victim had been found in a field with her throat cut. It was stated on Bignell's behalf that he was not responsible for his actions, and that his brain was sapped by a disease which he had contracted from the woman. His mother had attempted suicide, he had tried to drown himself, and his brother had died in an asylum. But the prison doctor certified that his mental condition was totally normal.

There was no doubt about the sanity of John Thorne, who was tried two months later at Lewes for the murder of his fiancée, Elsie Cameron, but there was a difference of opinion in the medical evidence which left some doubt as to whether Thorne had actually committed the crime for which he was later hanged. The case was known as the 'Crowborough murder,' and it involved a man of 24 who had been motherless from the age of 9, a Sunday-school teacher and a Band of Hope leader at 15, a scoutmaster at 17, an aircraftman at 18 and a poultry farmer charged with murder at 24.

The disappearance of Miss Cameron had led to a nationwide search. Thorne gave the police every assistance, and wrote to her parents inquiring after her. But he had dismembered her body, wrapping it in sacking and burying it in his chicken-run. Her head lay nearby in a tin box; her suitcase was in a potato patch near the gate. When the police received reports from people who had seen Miss Cameron approach Thorne's hut but had not seen her return, they searched the chicken-run and found the dismembered body. Thorne was immediately arrested and charged with her murder.

The *Daily News* reported that Wesley Farm, the scene of the tragedy, was now the haunt of morbid sightseers. Hundreds of people, most of them women, visited the place, many of them taking children in perambulators. In addition to gazing over the gate, they climbed through gaps in the hedge and invaded the chicken-run where the body had been found. But for the police officer in charge of Thorne's hut the place would have been overrun by souvenir hunters.

Thorne's defence was that Miss Cameron had hanged herself, and that he had concealed the body. He had been too nervous, he said, to go for help when he found her hanging in the hut. For the prosecution, Sir Henry Curtis-Bennett said, 'Within one hour the man who had not the nerve to go out for help had the nerve to do what I imagine no one of us could ever do—to cut up and dismember the body of the girl he loved.'

Sir Bernard Spilsbury testified that the marks on the dead girl's neck had been naturally caused, not by a rope. Microscopic pieces of skin taken from her neck and face and mounted on glass slides played an important part in the trial. But three other doctors disagreed with Sir Bernard, and declared that the marks were caused by the pressure of a cord.

'Do you expect,' asked Counsel for the Defence, 'when you hear the great Sir Bernard give evidence that no opinion could be set against his? What a travesty of justice it would be if this life had to depend on the accuracy and infallibility of one individual.'

But the jury accepted Sir Bernard Spilsbury's opinion, and found Thorne guilty. The prisoner, with his lips tightly pressed together, stood rigid in the dock, but said nothing while sentence of death was passed. When asked if he had anything to say he shook his head. Outside the court hundreds of people waited to hear the verdict. When Miss Caldecott, whom Thorne in court had said he loved, emerged into the street, she was greeted with hissing from a number of women and girls. Crowds followed her to Lewes railway station, hissing and booing.

In April, extraordinary last-minute efforts to save Thorne failed. Sir Arthur Conan-Doyle and the *Law Journal* had cast doubts upon the verdict of the jury and the decision of the Court of Appeal. Thorne had to be forcibly removed from the court while his appeal was being heard. He loudly protested his innocence, and continued to do so up to the time that he was executed.

Another crime, which aroused wide public interest in the spring of 1927, was the Trunk Murder, for which John Robinson was hanged. A fresh-complexioned, honest-looking young ex-barman, Robinson had been unsuccessfully trading as Edwards & Company, Estate Agents, in two rooms in Victoria Street, London. Returning to his office after lunch on May 4th, he was accosted by a prostitute whom he took up to the two rooms were he worked. A dispute about money led to a fight, during which Robinson knocked the woman down and silenced her by placing a cushion over her mouth.

Finding himself with a dead woman on his hands, he decided to cut her up and put her in a trunk, which he planned to leave in a railway cloakroom.

Robinson bought a knife at a nearby ironmonger's shop, and spent the night cutting up the corpse. Next morning he bought an old second-hand trunk, informing the man from whom he bought it that he needed it for packing some of his belongings which were to be sent abroad. Taking the trunk to his office, he wrapped the dismembered body in the woman's clothes, put them into the trunk and dragged it into the corridor. He then washed away all traces of blood from the floor, a considerable task which he did so thoroughly that the police were later unable to find any bloodstains. He now took the trunk in a taxi to Charing Cross Station and deposited it in the cloakroom, announcing that he would call for it later.

On May 10th Scotland Yard was informed that a trunk containing human remains had been discovered in the cloakroom. The only apparent clue was the name *Holt* on some of the clothing wrapped around the severed limbs. When inquiries were made for news of a missing woman of that name a woman named Holt came forward and recognized the body as being that of Mrs. Roles, who had worked for her as a cook. She had given her some clothes, which she also recognized.

The search now continued, and a man named Roles was discovered who admitted that he had been living with the woman as man and wife when she was actually married to an Italian waiter named Bonati. The waiter, however, had not seen her for several years, and Roles was able to prove that he had not seen her since she became a prostitute. It was clear that neither Roles nor Bonati knew anything of the crime.

Just as the police were beginning their search for fresh clues a shoeblack walked into Scotland Yard with a cloakroom ticket which he had picked up on the platform at

Charing Cross. This was, surprisingly, the receipt for the trunk, which the murderer had dropped or thrown away. The date and time when the body had been deposited could now be established.

The police immediately took photographs of the trunk and asked the press to print them. A day later a man who kept a shop in Brixton announced that he recognized the trunk as one he had sold on May 5th, although he could not describe the customer. Further inquiries produced a taxi driver who recalled driving a passenger with a heavy trunk to Charing Cross station on May 6th. He identified the trunk as the one he had carried, and although he was unable to describe his passenger he was sure that he had picked him up with the trunk outside a block of offices in Victoria Street. When he had jokingly asked if the heavy trunk was full of money, his passenger had replied, 'No, books.'

The offices were immediately searched, and as a result of inquiries a clerk volunteered the statement that he had seen a black trunk two weeks before standing outside the rooms then occupied, but since vacated, by Edwards, Estate Agents. The landlord of the building then gave the police a cheque, signed by John Robinson, which he had received for the rent of the rooms. From the bank detectives obtained the address of their customer, an apartment house in Camberwell. But Mr. Robinson had already flown, saying he was going to Lancashire.

There was a telegram in the house, sent by Robinson to a friend, asking him to come to Camberwell to see him. By mistake, the post office had failed to deliver this, and had returned it marked 'Not known.' It was decided to watch the house because it was considered that Robinson might return. And two days later the front door bell rang, a policeman opened the door, and there stood John Robinson. But he remained calm, even when he heard that his office had been searched. There was, he said, no connection at all between him and the trunk murder, and he had never heard of Mrs. Bonati. Even when asked if he would meet the shopkeeper and the taxi man he did not hesitate. Why not? And as by chance both of them were ill at home, he agreed to go with the police for interviews.

When the shopkeeper saw Robinson he failed to recognize him. Robinson calmly pointed out that this was hardly surprising, because the police were making a mistake. He was quite certain, he said, that the taxi driver would not know him either. And he was right, because although the man looked at him long and intently he did not recognize him, and said so.

There was now no official reason to connect Robinson with the murder, and he was allowed to go home, although he was watched. Meanwhile detectives had been active in the Victoria Street offices, and it was here that a bloodstained matchstick was found in a waste paper basket. A bloodstained duster from the trunk was now washed and examined and was seen to bear the name *Greyhound*. As Robinson had been a barman, it seemed likely that this was the name of a public-house, and his previous connection with a house of that name was quickly established. The duster had belonged to a girl working in a bar with Robinson, and she had taken it home to the house where she lived with Robinson, who had bigamously married her. A typist who had worked with Edwards & Company now stated that she recognized the duster, which she had used every day in Robinson's office.

The police went to the house in Camberwell, awoke Robinson at eight o'clock in the morning and arrested him. At Scotland Yard he made a statement, which at first seemed plausible. He agreed that he had taken the prostitute to the office, where they had quarrelled because he refused to give her the pound she demanded. She had, he said, shouted and sworn at him, and in a temper he had pushed her. She fell, striking her head against the grate. Finding that she was insensible, he moved her on to the chair and left her to recover. But when he returned next day he saw her still there, dead. In a panic he then decided to cut her up.

When at the Old Bailey he described this operation in detail, he did so with such frank innocence that many listeners believed his story was true. But the experts did not agree. They proved that Mrs. Bonati died not from a fall but from suffocation. Found guilty and sentenced to death, John Robinson turned and walked down the stairs towards the cells, still calm and collected.

3

A feature of the twenties was the number of monetary scandals involving well-known people. When Farrow's Bank closed its doors in 1920 about a hundred thousand people, mostly small traders, lost their life savings or their capital. The bank had been hopelessly insolvent for several years, and in June 1920 there was a deficit of £2,800,000. Two years later another financial scandal shook the country, involving an even greater number of small investors.

The people who were ruined were those who had invested money in Horatio Bottomley's Victory Bond Club scheme which, Mr. Bottomley claimed, gave each investor the chance of winning £20,000 for a pound. *The British Empire is your security. You cannot possibly lose your money*, announced Bottomley, modestly.

Bottomley, former editor of *John Bull* and public exposer of countless petty frauds, champion of the poor and under-privileged, was the biggest swindler of the post-war years. This was first publicly proclaimed in a pamphlet written and distributed by Reuben Bigland, a bookmaker from Birmingham who had worked for Bottomley and knew many of his secrets. The pamphlet was entitled *The Downfall of Horatio Bottomley, M.P. His latest and greatest swindle. How he gulled poor subscribers to invest £1 notes in his great Victory Bond Club.*

Copies followed Bottomley everywhere; they were distributed outside hotels where he stayed, they arrived with his letters on his breakfast table, and they were given to other Members of Parliament. Bottomley begged Bigland to desist, without success; he therefore had no course but to do the one thing which Bigland wanted, and issued a writ for libel.

When Mr. Justice Darling acquitted Bigland the Director of Public Prosecutions served a writ on Bottomley, charging him with converting £5,000, the property of the shareholders of the Victory Bond Club, to his own use. At Bow Street he was also charged with having stolen a £100,000 Allotment letter, the evidence against him being provided by the Midland Bank and the Crédit Lyonnais.

Sixty-three years old, Bottomley looked younger than his years when he appeared in court. Tubby, broad-shouldered, cheerful, nodding to friends and acquaintances, he was confident that his considerable ability as a public speaker would see him through. He conducted his own defence, and at once began to take charge of the case, making it plain to everyone in court that he would soon dispose of these ridiculous charges. The magistrate, however, committed him for trial at the Old Bailey, bail being allowed when Bottomley guaranteed £5,000 and two friends added sureties of £2,500 each. Just before the proceedings ended Bottomley made a speech, full of emotion, in which he said that the whole of his life had been devoted to his country and that the dear boys who were asleep in France knew that he had never betrayed them.

With a magnificent gesture he said, 'Scour the country and you will never find a jury to say that Horatio Bottomley could be guilty of so cruel a crime against God and man!' This sounded fine, but neither the judge nor the jury at the Old Bailey lived up to his expectations. Wearing a black morning-coat, striped trousers, and carrying a top hat, every inch the successful financier and politician, he pleaded *Most decidedly*, *Not Guilty* in a loud voice, and then asked if he might conduct his own defence from the solicitors' table.

His opening speech, delivered in the quietly confidential traditions of legal delivery ended with an appeal to the jury which brought tears to his eyes:

> Gentlemen, a terrible load of responsibility rests on you. This is a wicked prosecution, a panic prosecution, a callous prosecution.

Four days before the finish of the trial, Bottomley went to the Crystal Palace to watch Bombardier Billy Wells fight Goddard. People who saw him there observed that he was not unduly worried. But next day he gave a poor speech in court, and there was no doubt that his long run was ending. Before he entered the dock on the following Monday he was searched. It was recalled that another financier, Whittaker Wright, had committed suicide rather than go to prison.

The judge's summing up was against him. For lunch Bottomley drank his usual bottle of champagne, and returned to hear the jury bring in a verdict of guilty. When Bottomley attempted to speak the judge stopped him, saying that in this kind of case the convicted man had no right to say anything before being sentenced.

'Oh, really,' sneered Bottomley, 'so much the better for you, because I should have had something offensive to say about your summing up.'

Passing sentence, Mr. Justice Salter said:

> Horatio Bottomley, you have been rightly convicted by the jury of this long series of heartless frauds. These poor people trusted you, and you have robbed them of £150,000 in a few months. The crime is aggravated by your high position, by the number and poverty of your victims, and by the trust which they reposed in you. It is aggravated by the magnitude of your frauds and by the callous effrontery with which your frauds were committed. I can see no mitigation whatsoever. The sentence of the Court upon you is that you be kept in penal servitude for seven years.

Warders placed their hands on Bottomley's shoulders and he turned slowly and shuffled to the back of the dock and went down the stairs that led to the cells. On the wall above the judge hung the Sword of Justice which Bottomley had told the jury, in his final speech, 'will drop from its scabbard if you give a verdict of Guilty.'

A week or two later, Mr. Austen Chamberlain, the leader of the House of Commons, moved that Bottomley should come to the House from Wormwood Scrubs, but he did not appear, and a writ was issued for a by-election at South Hackney.

When he came out of prison in 1927 Bottomley started a paper called *John Blunt*. This was intended to rival Odham's *John Bull*, which had made him an outright payment of £25,000 some years before his trial to end their association, and had now risen to a position of stability and respectability. Although *John Blunt* was widely advertised, the magic of Bottomley's name had ceased to work, and the life of the paper was short.

During his prosperous years Bottomley had spent at least £1,000 a week, kept a neglected wife in the country and several mistresses in London, drunk unlimited champagne and moved among shady companions. He called himself 'an oratorical courtesan.' In his own way he was something of a genius, and for a time wielded enormous power as the champion of the common man in his struggle against injustice. As a country squire he was respected by the villagers, even after serving his sentence. As a patron of the arts he backed Sir Johnston Forbes Robertson in *Hamlet*. For a while he was one of the most important men in the country; the Government sent for him when troops mutinied in 1919. Ramsay MacDonald called him 'one of the greatest scoundrels this country has ever known,' yet for thirty-six years before his downfall he was a prominent public figure. Although thrice made bankrupt and constantly involved in legal cases, he was twice returned to Parliament. 'Today,' says H. R. Trevor-Roper, the historian, 'the working-man, whether he votes Labour or Conservative, does not need an irresponsible swindling demagogue as his "friend." The age of Bottomley is over. . . . '

Had Bottomley been honest he might have made a brilliant success of his life. He had few equals in the art of swaying a crowd or capturing applause. In the words of Sir Seymour Hicks he was a 'genial back-slapper, Corona-giver, champagne-opener, and apparently happy-go-lucky tip-giver, who endeavoured above all to create an atmosphere of brotherly love for everyone, so that not only his guests but the footmen waiting on him and the taxi-men who drove him learned to sing "For He's a Jolly Good Fellow." '

4

Apart from the major crimes which occupied the headlines, there were murders considered less important taking place every week, almost every day. On November 4, 1922, Lindsay Linsey, a cashier employed at a Pall Mall bank, shot dead another clerk named Gray, and then committed suicide in the bank, as a result of jealousy over a woman. Five days later Sir William Harwood, the Commissioner of Police, was suddenly taken ill at Scotland Yard after eating chocolates which had been sent to him by post. They contained poison. It took three months to find the man who had sent the chocolates, Walter Frank Tatam, who was charged with administering poison with intent to murder. At his trial he was found guilty but insane, and was ordered to be detained.

On the night of May 9, 1923, a London taxi-cab driver named Jacob Dickey was shot dead in a Brixton road after a struggle with the passenger in his cab. A walking stick found in the cab led to the arrest of Alexander Campbell Mason, who had borrowed the stick from its owner. At the Central Criminal Court on July 14th, Mason was found guilty and sentenced to death but the sentence was later commuted to penal servitude for life.

Two months later guests at the Savoy Hotel in the Strand were awakened by the sound of revolver shots. Porters ran to the suite from where the noises came and found a rich young Egyptian, Ali Kamel Fahmy Bey, lying dead on the floor. His French wife, Marie Marguerite Fahmy, was arrested. At her trial she gave graphic details of the dead man's cruelty and threats, and declared that she had had no intention of killing him and had thought the pistol was not dangerous. After a trial lasting six days she was acquitted.

On September 12, 1923, the body of 29-year-old George Eric Tombe, who had been missing since April 1922, was found in a disused cesspool at a racing establishment near Kenley, Surrey. A coroner's jury found that he had been murdered in April 1922 by Ernest Dyer, the owner of the premises, who had shot himself in November during a struggle with detectives who were inquiring into another matter.

On January 10, 1925, a young Bradford pianist named Herbert Musgrave was fatally stabbed in the street by a married woman, Catherine Thorpe, who was found guilty and sentenced to death, the sentence being later commuted. Eight days later, at Wolverhampton, a police constable was shot dead while observing three youths who had escaped from a probation home at Harpenden. At Stafford, on February 27th, two of the boys, aged 19 and 17, were sentenced to death, the sentences being subsequently commuted.

Some people blamed the war for the crime wave. On January 4, 1922, the *Daily News* reported a 'wave of startling crime and grim mystery.' There were four crimes claiming attention, the Armstrong poison case, the chance discovery at Derby of the body of a woman in an allotment and the arrest of her husband, the discovery of the body of Miss Irene Wilkins at Bournemouth, and the murder in Paris of Mrs. Draycott, who had been battered to death with a hammer.

On March 20, 1922, Henry Jacoby, an 18-year-old pantry

boy at the Spencer Hotel, Portman Street, London, was charged with the murder of Lady Alice White. The boy told the police that he heard the sound of voices in the hotel basement late at night. 'While I was walking down the stone passage,' he said, 'I heard someone whispering. It seemed to be the sound of two men's voices talking in low tones.' Jacoby, however, was found guilty of the murder and was hanged.

But of all the crimes of the period few created such interest as the Browne and Gutteridge murder case, which started early on the morning of Tuesday, September 27, 1927, when the body of an Essex policeman named Gutteridge was discovered lying in the road between Ongar and Romford. He had been shot four times, once in each eye and twice through the cheek; his notebook lay by his side and his pencil was clutched in his hand. There were tyre marks nearby, and two bullets were found in the roadway. A third was found in the constable's brain.

Later that morning an abandoned car was found at Brixton. It had been stolen at 2.30 that morning from a doctor's house at Billericay, and there were bloodstains on the running board and an empty cartridge case inside.

It was not until the following year, on January 20, 1928, that the police arrested a garage owner at Battersea. His name was Browne and he had first been convicted in 1911 for stealing a bicycle. There was no connection with the Gutteridge murder, and he was now wanted for car stealing. But in his pocket the police found a pair of artery forceps identical with those which had disappeared from the doctor's stolen car in 1927. And in another pocket were twelve cartridges. A further search revealed a Webley revolver, fully loaded, in the driver's seat of the stolen car.

Browne's accomplice in the Gutteridge murder, Kennedy, was arrested in Liverpool. When approached by Detective-Sergeant Mattison of the Liverpool police, he drew a pistol from his pocket and, thrusting it at the sergeant's chest, pulled the trigger. There was a click, but the pistol misfired, the policeman grasped the weapon, and arrested Kennedy.

Browne did not involve Kennedy. He said that a man had worked for him, but he refused to give his name. The revolver, he said, came from a sailor at Tilbury and had been bought in April. He carried it because he had once been held up and robbed at night. The surgical instruments were used in his garage work.

'I have no connection with the murder of P.C. Gutteridge,' he said. 'Personally I am not interested in it because it does not concern me.' Kennedy, however, made a statement which took three hours to write down. It was dictated with great care, and told how Browne had taken him to Billericay to steal a car. Browne drove it away, and Kennedy sat in front next to him. They had not gone far when they saw a lamp flashing, but they ignored it. Then a whistle sounded, and a policeman forced them to stop. When the policeman asked for the number of the car, Browne replied, 'You'll see it in front.'

'I know the number, but do you?' asked P.C. Gutteridge.

Then Kennedy gave the number, TW 6120.

'All right,' said Gutteridge, 'I'll take particulars,' and produced his notebook. Then Kennedy saw Browne standing over Gutteridge, who was lying in the road, and he heard him say, 'What are you looking at me like that for?' Browne then shot the policeman through both eyes.

This was Kennedy's statement. Browne, however, said that the fatal shots had been fired by Kennedy, and that they later exchanged weapons. In the end, neither statement saved them, and they were both hanged. The public regarded with horror the fact that Gutteridge had been shot through the eyes after he was dead. It was presumed that this was due to the popular belief, quite erroneous, that the last scenes witnessed by a dying person remain on the retina of the eye, as a photograph.

The most sensational of all the crimes of the twenties

belonged not to Britain but to France, and involved a man who soon became known as the 'French Blue-beard.' The fantastic career of Henri Desiré Landru interested the whole world, for he was convicted of the murder of ten women and a boy and it was proved that he had been the lover of at least 283 women. Ten of his 'fiancées' had been hacked to pieces at his villa near Versailles and burned in his stove. No one could be sure that there were not many more victims. In Britain women shuddered, and read about him with horror. Such things, they assured themselves, could never happen in England.

It was by chance that in April 1919 the sister of a missing woman saw Landru in the Rue de Rivoli in Paris. She connected him with the mysterious disappearance of her sister and informed the police, who arrested Landru. On the way to the police station he attempted to throw away a small notebook but the police took possession of it, and from this moment the fate of the mass murderer was settled, for the book contained all the evidence which convicted him. To their surprise the police found that ten of the names written in the book belonged to women who had disappeared since 1915. And the others? No one knew, but the investigations into Landru's amorous activities lasted for two years, and were hampered because he had lived in eleven different parts of Paris, under several names, and sarcastically refused to give any information.

By means of advertisements offering marriage he had met hundreds of women, with whom he had enjoyed love affairs. The entries in his little book showed that he was successful with 283. Sometimes he courted as many as seven women at the same time. When his villa was searched a large number of love letters was discovered, prepared in advance and ready to be sent out. His wife and son lived in a separate house, and knew nothing of his crimes.

The Landru trial lasted for twenty-three days, starting in October 1921. All Paris stormed the Versailles courtroom.

Mistinguette, the idol of the Paris music-halls, was there, and Sir William Orpen sketched the prisoner.

'Except for his extraordinary eyes,' reported Webb Miller, of the United Press, 'he had no outward feature to account for his success with women . . . they were large and serpent-like in their fixity and brilliance.'

The love letters indicated that his methods were based on the broadest flattery. Writing to middle-aged widows, he said, 'Your hands are beautiful and delicate and full of expression.' He used the same phrases, *en masse*. Two hundred and forty-six fragments of human bones were found among the ashes in his stove; 147 of these were pieces of skulls. Neighbours gave evidence that dense, nauseating smoke had been seen rising from the villa. During the trial an attractive girl of 29, who had been courted by Landru at the time of the arrest, said, 'He was good, so gentle to me, and at the same time such a passionate lover.' She refused to testify against him. 'I loved him and would have married him,' she declared. 'He showed delicate attentions to my mother, and used to bring her flowers.' At the trial it was revealed that Landru had been simultaneously 'engaged' to another girl, from whom he had borrowed money.

Four hundred troops were drawn up outside the prison at Versailles where Landru was executed at dawn on February 25, 1922. Nearly a hundred officials and newspaper men gathered around the guillotine. Landru, whose long black beard had been cut off, had asked to be shaved.

'It will please the ladies,' he said.

CHAPTER TWENTY

Depression

I

IN 1929, ON THE tenth anniversary of the Treaty of Versailles, it seemed that the peace settlement which Clemenceau had so hotly contested had been, after all, successful; Germany was prosperous again, playing a leading part in a rebuilt Europe in which the general standard of living was higher than it had been before the war; America had enjoyed a wave of tremendous prosperity, having captured many of the world's markets. But actually the nations were on the verge of a great economic slump.

Since the war the mechanical and industrial progress of the United States had been stupendous. Labour-saving devices had reached a peak in development, and American workers had experienced unheard-of prosperity. Shop windows were full of goods which almost anyone could afford to buy; the dollar, representing the vast resources of the country, had become all-powerful. But in October 1929 came the sudden end of the boom, when the whole of the Wall Street stock market collapsed and hundreds of thousands of Americans were ruined and thrown out of work.

In Britain it was becoming increasingly difficult for the nation to maintain her position in the midst of keen competition without the superior organization, which was lacking. Mere tradition and the glories of the Victorian and Edwardian ages were not enough. The British working man was still anxious to cling to a wage level which was no longer compatible with the advancing depression. He worked no harder, but he kept on demanding rises in pay. What had really changed to the detriment of England was her economic position in the world; the widespread industrialization of other countries had produced new conditions, depriving England of her position as the factory on which other countries relied. Her exports, on which her wealth was based, were threatened by the factories of America, Germany, Italy, Japan—even the Dominions. Yet English manufacturing costs were still among the highest in the world, and Englishmen constantly demanded a higher standard of living. How hard were they prepared to work for a place in the sun? Soon the country would be working only from Monday morning until Friday night; there would be longer week-ends instead of longer working hours.

In five years of rule, Baldwin had found few solutions to the country's difficulties. His supporters, however, pointed out that much had been accomplished; there were nearly 600,000 more insured workers employed than in 1924; the cost of living had fallen; the housing problem had been eased by 930,000 new homes; income tax had been lowered; improvements had been made in the Old Age Pensions Act and in the National Health Insurance scheme. So far so good, but the people as a whole were not content with this record.

The most prosperous nation, even when hit by the depression, was the United States. Britain had lost the initiative. But when the time came for a general election, Mr. Baldwin chose as his slogan the uninspiring words, 'Safety First!'

The main issue in the 1929 election was the unemployment problem. On May 10th the House of Commons was dissolved, and the election date was fixed for May 30th. The Liberal Party, now only a shadow but well financed by Lloyd George, vainly expected to regain its old position, and issued a booklet entitled *We can Conquer Unemployment*, in which it proposed vast national works which would reduce unemployment without adding a penny to taxation. People who were already being well paid for doing nothing were now to work on national projects.

Ramsay MacDonald boldly stated that if Labour was returned to power he would nationalize coal, transport, the power industries and life insurance; he would move miners into other industries; he would develop electricity on a national scale; and he would increase taxes on the very rich. Wealthy families shuddered.

In comparison, the Conservative 'Safety First!' cry seemed out of date, and its leader tired. Recalling the 1926 strike, Mr. Baldwin reminded electors that his Government had saved the country from the dangers of Socialism. He did not point out that the crisis in which Britain now found herself could be gauged by her fall in exports. From 1913 to 1927 they had declined 21 per cent, although the world's exports as a whole had risen by 18 per cent.

The election created much more interest than that of 1924 because *all* women of 21 and over now had the right to vote. It had been felt that it was time that women should have the same powers as men. There was little agitation to secure this, although a young woman who tried to deliver a petition to the King was carried kicking from the gates of Buckingham Palace by a policeman. Women had proved their ability, and very few wished to deny them the vote. A Bill, the Representation of the People (Equal Franchise) Act, had therefore been introduced in the House, and passed its first reading. At the second reading Sir William Joynson-Hicks, the old enemy of night clubs, drinking and smoking, said that the Bill was the logical conclusion of a series of reforms dealing with the Act of 1832. The Act of 1918 had added thirteen millions to the voting strength. Under the new Bill the qualification would be the same for men and women, three months' residence in premises or occupation of business premises of not less than £10 annual value. He said he could not imagine anyone would suggest that women were intellectually unfit to vote, or that their judgment was not as sound as that of men. At the moment a woman could become a Member of Parliament at 21, but she could not vote. The new Act would create a feminine majority of two million voters. The Bill passed its second reading with only ten dissentients.

The Labour Party regarded it as a device to gain Conservative votes, and called it the 'Flappers' Bill.' The Duchess of Atholl proclaimed that it was unfair to call them 'Flappers'; if girls of 21 would only lower their short skirts an inch or two the insulting word would soon be forgotten.

At the third reading Mr. Baldwin had said that once the Bill became law the last inequality between the sexes would be gone forever. A Conservative Member gloomily suggested that once all women had the right to vote no Conservatives would be returned to Parliament because the Socialists would promise working-class girls such a heaven on earth that Labour would get all their votes. Lord Peel replied that, on the contrary, women would have a steadying influence on politics. The Bill was passed by a majority of 40 to 1.

Speaking at the Queen's Hall on March 9, 1928, Mr. Baldwin said, 'Sixty years ago John Stuart Mill moved a Franchise Bill in the House, and now in a few weeks you will have legal recognition of your equality with men.' The Bill was passed by the House of Lords, there were no speeches, and it became law.

'I thank God that women have the vote,' said Lady Astor. 'You may fool the men, but you cannot deceive the women, who know only too well that the evils of society come from the evils in the human heart.' When Mrs. Pankhurst, the great suffrage leader, died in June 1928, women from all parts of the country, many wearing the old sashes of purple, green and white which were the colours of the movement, attended her funeral. She had lived to see her hopes realized.

Disillusionment over the Conservative Government had begun early in 1927. Young Tories and their supporters considered Baldwin's leadership ineffective. By 1928 he was decidedly unpopular, and appeared to be marking time, hanging on until the 1929 election. His claim that the unemployment problem was 'greatly exaggerated,' shocked large sections of the public.

In the election the Labour Party relied on only one poster, a drawing of Ramsay MacDonald with the inscription underneath—*Make him Prime Minister Again!* Speaking on the eve of the poll at Middlesbrough he said:

> You have a great chance to-morrow. You can strike a blow that will resound not merely through England but through Europe. See to it here in Middlesbrough that when on the day after the declaration of the poll you go to work—those of you who have work to go to—you are able to beat out with your feet on the pavements the music of another great Labour victory.

The national electorate was the largest that had ever gone to the polls, over twenty-seven million strong, of whom five million were new electors. Labour, which had held only 160 seats in the previous Parliament, was returned with 289, and the Conservatives dropped from 396 to 259. But the Liberals, with 58 elected candidates, confused the issue until Stanley Baldwin resigned and made way, on June 5th, for Ramsay MacDonald.

The rise of the British Labour Party since the election of 1900 reflected the changing course of Britain:

1900	2 seats
1906	29
1910 (Jan.)	40
1910 (Dec.)	42
1918	57
1922	142
1923	191
1924	151
1929	289

The Conservatives considered that many of their supporters had not troubled to vote. 'We were in possession,' wrote Sir William Joynson-Hicks later. 'Our Party could afford the luxury of criticizing their leaders. They could enjoy the delightful feeling that it did not matter whether they went to the poll or not. In my division there were about 15,000 Conservatives who did not trouble to go to the poll.'

Many of Labour's new seats had been won because of the unpopularity of Baldwin, who had left 1,100,000 unemployed on leaving office. He had, in the words of A. G. Gardiner, 'thrown down a challenge to the nation to join him in a great adventure, to help him to fashion a world nearer the heart's desire, and for a moment he created the atmosphere in which it seemed that vision might be translated into reality. He called himself a revivalist . . . but revivalism is not a policy, and fine emotion is not an achievement.'

Later, in 1936, Baldwin could look back and say:

> If I have succeeded in accomplishing anything during these last fourteen or fifteen years I have tried so far as I can to lead this country into the way of evolutionary progress, but I have tried to warn it against revolutionary progress, and I have tried to bring about a unity of spirit in the nation.

He had done that, he said, not only because it was right in itself, but because Britain had become, year after year, more urbanized, more industrialized. The potential danger lay in the fact that the country's communications, the constant flow of food and raw materials, might be interrupted.

Much of his work and nearly all of his fame was swept away by subsequent events, but Baldwin's main object, the formation of a united family under the throne, was in fact achieved. At the beginning of the twenties Britons had been anything but united. Although his reputation was to suffer greatly during the 1939 war, it should be remembered that in the 1935 election he asked for authority to rearm the nation. But Britain, swayed by pacifist thought, refused. The mass of people, during the twenties and thirties, did not want to rearm, and were haunted by the fear of bombing and poison gas. By 1928, says Sir Robert Bruce Lockhart, 'the English had thrown away, together with their other war cares, even the rudimentary precautions of defence. Never interested for long in foreign affairs, the people were indifferent, and, in the words of a popular post-war song, nobody knew and nobody seemed to care.'

Ramsay MacDonald was now Prime Minister once more, leading a team which included Lord Hankey as Lord Chancellor, Philip Snowden as Chancellor of the Exchequer, Arthur Henderson as Foreign Secretary and George Lansbury as First Commissioner of Works. Margaret Bondfield was Minister of Labour, the first woman Cabinet Minister and Privy Councillor. She has described the Cabinet's journey to Windsor to take the oath of allegiance:

> The Lord President then called the names of the five new Members, who advanced together to within about two yards of the King, knelt on the right knee, and took the oath of allegiance by holding the brand-new red Testament (presented for permanent retention to each one) while Hankey read the declaration. Then, in turn, each went forward to kneel on King George's footstool, holding out the right arm. The King placed his hand upon it to be kissed. When my turn came, he broke the customary silence to say:
>
> 'I am pleased to be the one to whom has come the opportunity to receive the first woman Privy Councillor.' His smile as he spoke was cordial and sincere.

Sidney Webb went to the House of Lords as Lord Passfield, and became Secretary of State for the Colonies; Sir Oswald Mosley joined the Cabinet as Chancellor of the Duchy of Lancaster, but becoming dissatisfied with the unemployment policy of J. H. Thomas, the Lord Privy Seal, he resigned in 1930. Later he founded a party of his own, which became the British Union of Fascists.

Unfortunately, the new Labour Government was no better than its predecessor. It came to office shortly before a time of unprecedented financial crisis, and soon the full effect of the American slump was felt in Europe; but the fault lay mainly in MacDonald's leadership. Although Mr. Henderson could claim later that the Prime Minister would 'live in history, not only as the first Labour Prime Minister but as a statesman and servant of the people of the first order,' subsequent events hardly justified his loyalty. As the world crisis matured, so confidence in the Government dwindled. But, surprisingly, MacDonald weathered the storm. At least one man, Hilaire Belloc, openly declared that he had no faith in his leadership. To MacDonald he said, 'Take care, lest I make you immortal with an epigram.'

Mr. J. H. Thomas, specially created Minister for Unemployment, announced that by February 1930 the unemployment figures would be better. The month came, but the figures were much worse. Later he said, 'I broke all records in the number of unemployed.' By December 1930 over 2,300,000 people were out of work.

There was some hope, in 1929, that Labour's foreign policy would succeed. Arthur Henderson created a favourable impression in the Council of the League at Geneva, and returned home convinced that he had achieved a step towards world disarmament. But the Wall Street crash, echoing through Europe, created five million unemployed in Germany, whose youth was sent clamouring to join the party which appeared to offer a constructive national policy with hope for the future. And so at the German elections of 1930 Hitler polled six-and-a-half million votes and returned 107 National Socialist members to the Reichstag; his promise to amend the Treaty of Versailles appealed to all Germans, who were turning towards hysteria, revolution and the myth of the Aryan race.

England's attempt to create a 'land fit for heroes' had failed because the people had looked backward instead of forward. The people, and the House of Commons in particular, had accepted the opinions of their chosen leaders, because they *wanted* to accept them. The final nail in the coffin of the Versailles Treaty did not come until June 1935, when Sir Samuel Hoare signed the pact which, in violation of the existing treaties, gave Hitler a larger fleet than that of France or Italy; an achievement of which Mr. Baldwin was to boast.

Two years earlier, in 1933, the Nazis had come to power in Germany, and the stage was set for the Second World War.

Here, in the autumn of 1931, Ramsay MacDonald, repudiated by Labour, resigned as head of the Government and returned at once as Prime Minister of a National Coalition Government which ruled until 1935 with a predominantly Conservative policy. Then Baldwin replaced MacDonald as Prime Minister, winning the general election in the autumn, and continuing the National Government with a reduced majority. And in the same year, in Germany, General Ludendorff proudly boasted: '*At the moment we Germans are the people which has freed itself furthest from the teachings of Christianity*.'

It had all started with the Armistice in 1918, and it finished with the advent of 1930, when the era of apathy and having a good time ended, and the great industrial depression set in. Ahead lay more unemployment, appeasement, and finally another terrible war and the mushroom cloud.

Stanley Baldwin summed up the period when, in May 1937, he told the Empire Rally of Youth at the Albert Hall:

> You may attempt to explain these twenty years in terms of economics or in terms of politics; some see only the one, some see only the other. Some blame the treaty, some the bankers, some the statesmen, some the diplomats. . .

EGYPT ASKS FOR MORE.

John Bull. "AREN'T YOU OPENING YOUR MOUTH RATHER WIDE? YOU'VE ALREADY HAD AS MUCH AS IS GOOD FOR YOUR CONSTITUTION."

BIBLIOGRAPHY

F. L. Allen: *Only Yesterday.*

Gerald Barry: (Ed.) *The Week-end Calendar.*

Arnold Bennett: *The Journals of Arnold Bennett 1921–1928.*

F. L. Benns: *Europe Since 1914.*

Margaret Bondfield: *A Life's Work.*

P. V. Bradshaw: *Seen in Perspective.*

Patrick Braybrooke: *The Amazing Mr. Noël Coward.*

James Bridie: *Mr. Bridie's Alphabet.*

T. C. Bridges and H. Hessell Tiltman: *Kings of Commerce.*

Collin Brooks: *Devil's Decade.*

Ivor Brown: *The Way of My World.*

Sir Robert Bruce Lockhart: *Your England.*

John Buchan: *The King's Grace.*

Viscount Cecil: *A Great Experiment.*

Winston S. Churchill: *Great Contemporaries.*

Irene Clephane: *Ourselves, 1900–1930.*

John Collier and Iain Lang: *Just the Other Day.*

R. J. Cruickshank: *Roaring Century.*

R. C. Davidson: *The Unemployed, Old Policies and New.*

Blanche E. C. Dugdale: *Arthur James Balfour.*

W. H. Edwards: *This Pact Business.*

Hon. Mrs. C. W. Forester: *Success Through Dress.*

A. G. Gardiner: *Certain People of Importance.*

John Gloag: *Men and Buildings.*

John Gloag: *What about Enterprise?*

Douglas Goldring: *Nineteen Twenties.*

Charles Graves: *The Bad Old Days.*

Robert Graves and Alan Hodge: *The Long Week-end.*

Arthur Groom: *Edward the Eighth.*

J. Hampden Jackson: *Europe Since the War.*

Seymour Hicks: *Not Guilty M'Lord.*

Sir Travers Humphreys: *A Book of Trials.*

Allen Hutt: *The Post-War History of the British Working Classes.*

Aldous Huxley: *Antic Hay.*

C. E. M. Joad: *Under the Fifth Rib.*

Thomas Jones: *Lloyd George.*

W. E. Johns: *Some Milestones in Aviation.*

David Keir: *Newspapers.*

Elsie M. Lang: *British Women in the Twentieth Century.*

James Leasor: *Wheels to Fortune.*

Donald Lindsay & E. S. Washington: *A Portrait of Britain 1851–1951.*
Roy Lewis & Angus Maude: *The English Middle Classes.*
B. H. Liddell Hart: *Foch: Man of Orleans.*
A. M. Low: *Wonderful Wembley.*
A. G. MacDonell: *England, Their England.*
H. F. Maltby: *Ring Up the Curtain.*
Viscount Milner: *Questions of the Hour.*
R. J. Minney: *Viscount Southwood.*
Charles Loch Mowat: *Britain Between the Wars.*
Ralph Nevill: *Yesterday and To-day.*
Beverley Nichols: *Crazy Pavements.*
Beverley Nichols: *Twenty-One.*
Harold Nicholson: *King George the Fifth: His Life and Reign.*
Vivian Ogilvie: *Our Times, 1912–1952.*
George Orwell: *The Road to Wigan Pier.*
Frank Owen: *Tempestuous Journey: Lloyd George, His Life and Times.*
J. B. Priestley: *Angel Pavement.*
J. B. Priestley: *Coming to London (Encounter Magazine, February 1956).*
C. H. B. & M. Quennell: *The Good New Days.*
Lord Reith: *Into the Wind.*
Lord Riddell: *Intimate Diary of the Peace Conference.*
A. P. Ryan: *Lord Northcliffe.*
A. Siegfried: *England's Crisis.*
D. C. Somervell: *The Reign of King George the Fifth.*
H. A. Taylor: *Jix—Viscount Brentford.*
Malcolm Thompson: *The Life and Times of Winston Churchill.*
Alec Waugh: *Kept.*
Alec Waugh: *Myself When Young.*
Evelyn Waugh: *Decline and Fall.*
Evelyn Waugh: *Vile Bodies.*
Harold F. B. Wheeler: *The Twentieth Century.*
Angus Wilson: *For Whom the Cloche Tolls.*
Sandy Wilson: *The Boy Friend.*
G. M. Young: *Stanley Baldwin.*
G. Zilliacus: *The Mirror of the Past.*

INDEX

GEORGE ALLEN & UNWIN LTD

Head Office
40 Museum Street, London W.C.1
Telephone: 01-405 8577
Sales, Distribution and Accounts Departments
Park Lane, Hemel Hempsted, Herts.
Telephone: 0442 3244

Athens: 7 Stadiou Street
Auckland: P.O. Box 36013 Northcote Central N.4
Barbados: P.O. Box 222, Bridgetown
Beirut: Deeb Building, Jeanne d'Arc Street
Bombay: 103/5 Fort Street, Bombay 1
Calcutta: 285J Bepin Behari Ganguli Street, Calcutta 12
Cape Town: 68 Shortmarket Street
Delhi: 1/18B Asaf-Ali, New Delhi 1
Hong Kong: 105 Wing On Mansions, 26 Hancow Road, Kowloon
Ibadan: P.O. Box 62
Karachi: Karachi Chambers, McLeod Road
Madras: 2/18 Mount Road, Madras
Mexico: Villalongin 32, Mexico 5, D.F.
Nairobi: P.O. Box 30583
Philippines: P.O. Box 157, Quezon City D-502
Rio de Janeiro: Caixa Postal 2537-Zc-00
Singapore: 36c Prinsep Street, Singapore 7
Sydney N.S.W.: Bradbury House, 55 York Street
Tokyo: C.P.O. Box 1728, Tokyo 100-91
Toronto: 81 Curlew Drive, Don Mills